THE TRAVELER'S KEY TO
MEDIEVAL FRANCE

THE TRAVELER'S KEY TO

MEDIEVAL FRANCE

A GUIDE TO THE SACRED ARCHITECTURE OF MEDIEVAL FRANCE

JOHN JAMES

In collaboration with François Bucher,
Jeanine Stage, and Hilary James

Alfred A. Knopf New York 1986

THIS IS A BORZOI BOOK
PUBLISHED BY ALFRED A. KNOPF, INC.

Copyright © 1986 by John James
All rights reserved under International and Pan-American
Copyright Conventions. Published in the United States by
Alfred A. Knopf, Inc., New York, and simultaneously in
Canada by Random House of Canada Limited, Toronto. Dis-
tributed by Random House, Inc., New York.

Library of Congress Cataloging-in-Publication Data

James, John
The traveler's key to medieval France.

Bibliography: p.
Includes index.
1. Church architecture—France—Guide-books.
2. Architecture, Medieval—France—Guide-books.
3. Churches—France—Guide-books.   4. Christian
art and symbolism—Medieval, 500–1500—France—
Guide-books.   I. Title.   II. Title: Medieval France.
NA5543.J35   1986   914.4′04838   86-45394
ISBN 0-394-55531-7

Manufactured in the United States of America

First Edition

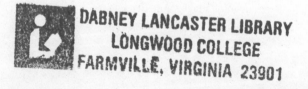

CONTENTS

ACKNOWLEDGMENTS

Many have helped me along the historical and spiritual journey that has made this book possible. Berenson and Spengler and Jung, Ram Dass and Bhagwan and Marx, Robert Branner and John Harvey and Jean Bony have all been my mentors. From John Michell came my sense of numbers, while thirteen years spent among some of the most practical and commonsensical people on earth—Aussie builders—gave me the eyes to observe mortar and stonework with precision. Henry and Dorothy Kraus showed me that reality is knowable, if only we can find where to look, and Peter Kollar and Adrian Snodgrass gave me a feeling for the integratedness of all things everywhere.

From my father—painter, advertiser, and enquirer—I learned that though questions may produce answers, they are essentially the springboard for an endless process of more questions. From Rudolf Schwenck and, later, breath therapy, came an intimate acknowledgment that history, like life, is a boundless continuum onto which we impose categories and definitions for our own safety.

Jeanine Stage helped with the research, Val Clack and Pauline McKelvey read and proofed the text, and John Ward, a true medievalist, checked the historical data with much care; though none of them should be blamed for anything in this book, for that responsibility is mine alone. Hilary James printed all the photographs impeccably and studied every site during one busy memorable summer, again and again lifting me to unexpected levels of perception. François Bucher has been my kindred spirit in this venture, and through his love of the Middle Ages he has tutored me in the balance needed to understand a complex period. In the end, this series of *Traveler's Keys* is the gift of my editor, Toinette Lippe, who knew it was needed, and has supported all of us with her care and fortitude.

INTRODUCTION

The Middle Ages is wondrously silent, and it is our pleasure to make it talk.

Dorothy Kostuch

Enthusiasm for the Middle Ages has never before been so great. The Middle Ages is one of the most fascinating periods in history. From it grew the modern world, both capitalist and socialist. Out of it came the technology and thirst for energy which have made our times possible. The complex and contradictory beliefs and attitudes of medieval men have shaped our lives, from democracy and the independence of scholarship to infinite series and factory production.

This traveler's guide to the sacred architecture of medieval France is a key to understanding medieval churches and abbeys and the ideas they embody. It is remarkable that sacred architecture expressed the vision of its time so well, and with such finesse, that it is still relevant today.

We have pitifully few statements from contemporaries telling us why they built as they did. There is nothing describing the rib vault until almost two centuries after its first use; virtually no one tells us the function of the labyrinth or the crypt, in spite of their size, and there is no explanation of what galleries were used for. Even on many nonarchitectural subjects our understanding is pretty meager. For example, there are not enough documents to enable us to understand the liturgy properly, and we have no statistical basis for analyzing the trade fairs in the Champagne, although they are considered to have been Europe's major exchange centers during the twelfth century. We have almost nothing to indicate what people wanted from life. They did not write letters to the editor, the Church carried out no market surveys, and the first census in France came two centuries after the first Gothic building. Occasionally an educated contemporary drops hints about the meaning of what they were building, but these comments are sadly rare.

Nevertheless the meanings are there and must at times have been discussed, if only to justify the cost and effort of erecting two towering spires when only one was necessary, or altering a choir just a few years after it had been completed. Of course, as in all artistic endeavor, many decisions would have been made unconsciously. It is our purpose to lay bare the common themes underlying medieval religious architecture, and as we lack documents that might explain it, we have worked backward from the best evidence we have, the architecture itself. This analysis is inevitably subjective. We will be interpreting how we *feel* about a building and then attempting the tricky task of putting these feelings into a medieval context. However, many of the ideas offered here are found in other studies of these things, such as the relationship between the crypt and ancient worship in caves, and that between vertical movement and the masculine principle. Much is based on Jung's studies in the collective unconscious, that unmeasurable substratum of imagery and associations that seems to affect us all, whether we are aware of it or not.

THE MIRACLE OF 1130

Since art reflects the times, we should be able to garner something of the intentions and hopes of medieval men from their art. Whether they discussed the problems or not, their buildings and sculpture show that something remarkable happened in the area around Paris after 1130, and the revolutionary Gothic style was the result.

To alter architecture radically in a traditional society requires a great deal of energy. The argument presented here is that this energy arose when a deep contradiction in community beliefs was resolved through the cult of the Virgin which suddenly blossomed into an overwhelmingly popular penitential ritual. Though we have chosen 1130 as the most appropriate date, the numbers of stories about the Virgin's miracles had been growing for the previous thirty years, and her fully independent role as intercessor would not be completely established for another thirty. This date marks the cusp between two great waves of emotion.

Around 1100 people's mortal fear of damnation seems to have been intensifying just as living conditions were improving fast enough to give confidence in the future. This contradiction between present hope and future uncertainty seems to have created a profound conflict in society that was expressed in the sculpture and architecture of Vézelay and Charlieu.

Devotion to Mary was the relief valve. It liberated people's pent-up hopes for salvation, and the architectural changes suggest that this deliverance released the energy that transformed medieval culture. Architecture benefited particularly because it was believed that God Himself descended at the consecration to inhabit the very stones of the church. To build was therefore to bring heaven down to earth. This was the miracle of 1130.

Most of the time we look for rational explanations for medieval architecture, but in a more spiritual age symbolic reasons were probably more potent. These need not have

The nave of Saint-Hilaire-le-Grand, Poitiers.

been analyzed consciously; probably the strength of symbols often resides in their not being understood.

For example, the middle story or gallery was a very expensive part of the buildings. Was it intended to hold additional altars, for crowds of pilgrims, or for the singers? The staircases to the gallery are generally too small for public use, the main altar is only rarely visible from it, and as a corridor for meditation, too few continue all round the building. No practical explanation has yet been offered that would justify the enormous expense of construction. However, their symbolic role does offer a viable reason, which will become clear when we visit Conques and Nevers.

Similarly costly features included crypts—which have few practical functions that could not have been exercised in the main church—the multiplicity of spires, and the elevated and almost inaccessible western chapels. Many of the most important costs in construction, for which a great deal of extra effort was needed, were to satisfy spiritual, not functional needs.

THE MIDDLE AGES AND THE PRESENT DAY

The popularity of the Middle Ages sank as the Renaissance gathered momentum, for the two cultures were at opposite sides of the esthetic universe. Where the Classical form is orderly and controlled, the medieval appears free, complex, and mysterious. Renaissance scholars divided history into three stages, or rather saw a continuum with the unfortunate interlude of the "barbarous Goths." The name "Gothic" was bestowed on the architecture of the Middle Ages in memory of those fierce invaders from the Crimea who had sacked ancient Rome. Gothic architecture was likened to a dark flood that obliterated the rational style of the Classical period.

However, in many ways medieval culture was more modern than the Classical, and its architecture was closer to ours than any that had gone before. We also have many of the same dreams, for both communists and capitalists share the archetypal hope for a Golden Age where everything will be provided in abundance.

Earlier societies saw in all aspects of life meanings which transcended daily cares. The first two centuries of the Middle Ages continued in this spiritual awareness and in some aspects took it to new heights. The last two centuries, while still professing faith, had lost a substantial part of it; not in lore or learning but in attitude. This is clearly seen in church architecture: the earlier buildings are so deeply sacred that we still respond to their message, while the later are clearly clever but, in the real sense of the word, uninspired.

It was during the Middle Ages that one of the deepest urges felt in all earlier societies was abandoned. Today spiritual matters have almost no relevance to the tone of daily life. Most of us know nothing of the piety or rituals that used to affect an individual's every act and every waking moment. We do not see God in each living thing. Sacred ideas have become so diluted that we usually focus on them only on such special occasions as Easter and death.

One of the purposes of this book is to take you through this great historic drama so that you may witness in the stones of these magnificent buildings one of the most profound social transformations ever experienced by man.

HOW TO USE THIS GUIDE

Our theme could not be closer to the most intimate purpose of the cathedrals. It is to display the innermost significance of these works of art and to explore the spiritual and symbolic meanings built into them.

Religion, like every aspect of human activity, changes with time. Though deep belief will often represent those concepts which are common to all people in all places and climes, the way they are expressed is usually relevant to a particular moment. The needs people had in the tenth century, while living under the threat of pillage and war, were different from those of the twelfth century, when conditions were good, the crops ample, and one felt alive in the prosperity of one's fellow men.

This book has five parts. The first deals with the general

issues of geography and population, history and agriculture, the universities and the towns. It covers those things that are given in the situation. This is background reading; it would best be absorbed before you reach France.

The second part concerns faith—on the principle that architecture is based on belief, both spiritual and psychological. Therefore there are sections on relics, on the changing perceptions of Christ, and, most significantly, on the role of the Virgin Mary in the great transformation around the year 1130.

The third and most important part offers a historical interpretation of the symbolism of architecture. Some aspects of the period are more germane to our subject than others. The role of the Cistercians was far more important than that of the Franciscans or the inquisitorial Dominicans, and so the monks of the Virgin receive a considerable amount of space. The cathedral of Chartres expresses more clearly than any other building the innermost sacral concepts of the times, and therefore it is discussed in great detail. It is the key building in this study; the reader is advised to visit the cathedral early in his journey and to return at the end of it.

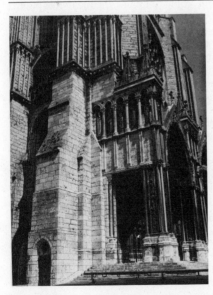

Chartres cathedral south porch.

Overall, the earlier centuries, and in particular the creative years between the choir of Saint-Denis and the Sainte-Chapelle, have received a great deal of attention. The endlessly awful years of the Hundred Years War, the Black Death, and the general decline of France do not merit much study here, for that period lacked the wherewithal to construct more than a few remarkable buildings. Finally, the end of the period, for all of the sensuous delightfulness of Saint-Maclou, possesses little of the profundity of Laon or Conques, for by then the spiritual meanings had been lost in meretricious cleverness.

The fourth part of this book describes the working methods of the masters, and it is followed by a fifth long section that considers the symbolic significance of sixty key buildings. Although this number is only a tiny proportion of the more than 60,000 medieval churches erected in France, these buildings clearly illustrate our themes and are among the most beautiful.

Where a concept is best comprehended in one building (such as the lantern at Laon or the rose window at Chartres), a full discussion of it will be found in that section. But where an element may be better studied in many places, it will be analyzed in Section Four. Some of the churches are in the north, some in the south, so no matter where you enter France, you can begin your spiritual journey immediately. The maps have been arranged by period to help you to plan your own itinerary.

The headings and the table of contents will generally lead you to any argument you may wish to pursue. You will soon grasp how to use this guide to unlock the meanings of any medieval church, for the issues are universal. You may find it useful to purchase some encyclopedic guide as a companion to this one, for the range of medieval architecture is so great that no book that aims at presenting the fundamental issues in any depth could do justice to them all.

This is a guide not to all medieval architecture but to the essential issues which inspired it. It is the story of the community of believers who expressed their faith in some of the most magical buildings on earth and for a short time lived with a mystic sense of God's presence. The ultimate decay of these ideals and the annihilation of the society that produced them in pestilence, war, and religious chaos was a sad, if almost inevitable conclusion. Perhaps the message is that, like Icarus, we may approach the highest only for a brief moment and should not be surprised if the sequel appears as another expulsion.

THE TRAVELER'S KEY TO MEDIEVAL FRANCE

1
THE
SITUATION

THE BACKGROUND

GEOGRAPHY AND LANGUAGE

Medieval France was smaller than modern France, and before the eleventh century the king's influence was in practice restricted to the area of the Royal Domain. This was less than three percent of the country; it consisted of Paris, the Île-de-France, a corner of Burgundy, and isolated enclaves in the north and center. The English kings ruled the entire Atlantic coast, the Germans along the Rhône from the Rhine to Provence. Reims, Lyon, and Avignon were therefore frontier towns.

The Massif Central was sparsely populated, with few rivers or roads, and effectively divided the country in half, the north being part of the culture which stretched from Ireland to the Baltic, the south being more Italian. The principal route from Paris to the Mediterranean was then,

Foliage carved on the north porch of Chartres cathedral.

as now, down the Rhône and Saône rivers, and the wealth from it flowed to the German emperors, not to the French kings. Poor communications and aristocratic independence left each region to develop its own cultural and political identity. A Burgundian considered a Poitevin a foreigner, a man from Provence probably had less in common with a Parisian than a German. Besides innumerable dialects, the north and south each had their own languages, the *langue d'oïl* in the north and the *langue d'oc* in the south, meaning those who say yes as "oïl" or "oc." The former became the "oui" of modern French, while the *langue d'oc* was considered by many to be as fine as Italian or English.

The Viking raids had forced the north to reorganize society around defense, while the south had been less troubled by prolonged invasions. In the north, land was often held in fief in return for regular military service and dues, so the great principalities of Normandy, Anjou, and Champagne were more centralized and authoritarian states than were Toulouse or Aquitaine.

Before the Albigensian Crusade the south was rich in luxury and refinement, whereas northerners were more spartan and monklike, and hunting was their major amusement. Southern travelers found the northern courts bleak and the women withdrawn; northerners complained that the south was frivolous and lacking in faith.

Southern land was usually free from feudal obligations, hence southerners could not raise a feudal army and relied more on mercenaries. This structural weakness lay at the root of their brutal conquest by the northern kings during the Albigensian Crusade early in the thirteenth century.

POPULATION

In the fifth century the population of this smaller France and the Low Countries was about five million. That number was almost halved during the next one hundred fifty years, mainly because of the colder climate, plague, and the lawlessness that followed the decay of the Roman Empire.

During later centuries the population began to increase once more as the weather improved and the growing season lengthened, and by the year 1000 the population had reached six million. The numbers continued to increase, especially during the one hundred fifty years after 1150, when the population had reached the staggering figure of nineteen million. In some areas the numbers in the countryside were as great as they would be at the end of the eighteenth century.

By the mid-thirteenth century most of the better lands were thickly settled, with much overcrowding and overcropping. Technological advance had slowed; between 1100 and 1350 the average yield of cereals only doubled while the population quadrupled. The plagues after 1348 eliminated perhaps half the people, so there were only eleven million or so in 1450.

As in most preindustrial societies, one person in three was under fourteen, and their support and training imposed a considerable burden on the rest of the community. An artist or a mason who finished his education by the age of twenty-one could expect to have a working life of a further twenty-one years. However, many lived longer; Bernard de Soissons was master mason of Reims cathedral for thirty-five years and must have been in his sixties when last heard of.

The heavy work in the fields brought susceptibility to malaria and tuberculosis, and the death rate among children of less than a year was enormous. Because many women died from childbirth before the age of forty, there would have been six or seven men to every five women in the countryside, though in the cities the numbers were almost even. If a man lived to maturity, an average life span would be about fifty-five years while five percent still lived into their eighties. To put these statistics into perspective: the ancient Roman average was about twenty-five years, and English life expectancy a century ago was barely above forty years. Medieval people lived as full and healthy a life as Europeans had ever lived until recently.

AGRICULTURE

Agriculture was the basis of medieval society. By the tenth century a number of key inventions had transformed farming so totally that the center of economic power had shifted from the Mediterranean to the great northern plains, where it has remained ever since.

Delicately undercut capital from Bourges cathedral north porch.

The most important inventions were the rigid collar, the horseshoe, and the wheeled plow. However, the plow required the use of up to eight oxen and a great deal of iron at a time when iron was expensive, and the bit in the horse's mouth once cost more than the horse.

To suit the new plow, land was laid out in long strips. As the strips were hard to guard individually against animals, all the arable land of a village was combined and fenced in one block, which was then split into three large fields, one for autumn planting, one for spring, and one to be left fallow—the famous three-field system, which was more prevalent in the north than in the south.

The social changes this wrought were enormous. Not only had ancient property rights to be altered, but the control of planting times, the sharing of oxen, and other matters all had to be regulated by a village council. Such cooperation had not been known before. After the eleventh century the peasants carried this habit of communal autonomy into the city, from which naturally evolved the municipal councils that played such an important part in our history. By 1200 these changes had produced a prosperous peasantry across the whole of northern France. Yet the sixfold population increase more than undid the advantages, and even with the halving of the population after the Black Death, the peasants of the fifteenth century were worse off than those of the twelfth had been.

SOCIETY AND LIFE STYLE

A thousand years ago people experienced life more intensely than we do, with the free and spontaneous gaiety of those who live in the present moment because the next is uncertain. They enjoyed the good times with gusto and vigor, and they endured the rest because they had no choice. Such natural calamities as floods and drought were seen as a punishment from God. Hospitals had none of the cleanliness that we know, nor were doctors averse to causing as much pain or suffering as they may have been attempting to cure. Barbers were also dentists, and eyeglasses were available only to the rich. Few painkillers were known, none of them effective: rich and poor alike suffered equally from disease and the pain of childbirth. Privacy was rare, and even in the greatest castle life was lived in a perpetual crowd. Earls and their wives, their daughters, and governesses often slept all in the same room. In the towns the overcrowding was so great that a dozen could be found asleep on the same floor. Beds were a luxury. Cold and darkness were real adversities, houses were drafty and the bedding often damp, and few houses had running water.

In famous churches with powerful relics, the gusto and noisy jollity and the close heat from thousands of candles and the many bodies could be overpowering. Tears and laughter mingled with the moans of the sick and the joyous singing of the newly healed. Wine was safer than water, and tipsiness was found as often inside the church as outside it.

Smells were ever-present—some exquisite, others abominable—while butterflies were as common as flies. Sanitation was crude but water abundant in the street fountains, and the narrow lanes were used as much for drainage as for access. Food was fresh in the summer, bread baked anew each day, and the fragrance of spring traveled unsullied in the unpolluted air. Public baths with hot water, to be found in many cities, were very popular.

In the early years of the period communities were small and travelers rare. That villagers could be held collectively responsible for the crimes of strangers bred a general suspicion of foreigners. Life was monotonously regular and traditional; even as towns expanded and the size of Paris grew beyond a hundred thousand, agriculture continued to be the main source of wealth and power for the overwhelming majority. As late as the mid-nineteenth century, with the Industrial Revolution well on its way, only England had extracted half its population from the land.

Ten bushels to the acre was an exceptional yield, and a normal harvest would feed little more than the locality. Grain was expensive to store, rats consumed a fifth of it, and cartage by road was difficult. Before 1130 a traveler might pass in a single day from an area of plenty to one where fodder was unobtainable and people were starving by the side of the road.

Even in good times the winter diet of both rich and poor was far from healthy. Bread was the chief source of vitamin B and almost the only source of carbohydrates. People depended mainly on milk, eggs, and fish for other vitamins, and the shortage of green vegetables and fresh fruit encouraged scurvy in the winter. Thus arose the most common medieval maladies: stones in the bladder and urinary tract and failing eyesight. Combined with the cold and ever-present damp and the ineradicable tuberculosis, life was often debilitating.

The phenomenon of ergot, or Holy Fire, came from moldy rye. The symptoms included a psychedelic component, so the less afflicted might see visions of the Virgin coming down from the altar or the body of Jesus flowing with blood. Because the climate was wetter in the first half of the twelfth century, ergot added greatly to the list of miracles in circulation. The debilitating effect of fasting on bread and water during Lent immediately after the rigors of winter, and the outpouring of religious sentiment at Easter, set the stage for powerful religious feelings. So medieval mysticism may owe more to damp rye bread than we might suspect.

CONTROL AND JUSTICE

The extent of a man's community was defined by his parish. In his church, and only there, would he be baptized and married, attend mass, pay his tithes, and in the end be buried. In some places laws forbade a man to attend mass or to confess in any church but his own, for the local priest "should be able to see the face of every member of his flock." The reason was, ultimately, control. Confession was not private, and priests were instructed to investigate sin by cross-examination.

The political and judicial world of medieval times was nothing like that which we know today. Every geographic unit, each town, and at times even a street owed allegiance to its own lord, temporal or ecclesiastic. Justice was not maintained by the state but was a property that produced income for the owners. In Paris alone there were a couple of dozen *seigneurs*, most of them churchmen, with their own courts of justice. At times the justice inside the house was different from the justice on the street, and even that could be changed on market days or festivals when lord or king held the rights for the occasion. Nevertheless it worked, and even large towns were as orderly and peaceful as Paris is today. The revenue from justice was enormous. Sentences were far harsher than modern ones, complete confiscation was not uncommon, and assessors were thorough. Jews were particularly heavily penalized, and *seigneurs* would vie for the justice over them. Punishment was public

View from the choir clerestory, Chartres cathedral.

and was carried out at once. Executions and flogging were as visible as the stocks and were enjoyed as an entertainment. It is reported that the good people of Mons paid for a highwayman so they could watch him being quartered, "at which they rejoiced more than if the body of some holy saint had risen from the dead."

Nevertheless one would have felt immensely alive then; events were experienced with the immediacy and directness of childhood. People's moods and emotions swung between the terror of damnation and the most naive joy, between awful cruelty and an intense attachment to the delights of life.

A SHORT HISTORY
OF MEDIEVAL FRANCE, 1000–1500

Following are approximate dates for the trends in the history of the period, to help provide a matrix on which to hang the details in the rest of the book.

9th to 10th centuries	A time of invasion and terror that reduced Western Europe to penury and forced the authorities to reorganize the entire social structure. Feudalism was the result.
10th to mid-13th centuries	The end of the invasions, the expanding population, and a warmer climate encouraged a period of great prosperity and enlightenment.
13th to mid-15th centuries	A period of decline associated with a series of disasters: the Crusades failed, there was civil war against the south, and over-population and a sudden shift in temperature reduced food production. At about the same time a dynastic dispute began a war which, to everyone's horror, went on for the next hundred years. A little later the whole of Europe was attacked by plague, which reduced the population by half. It was one of the worst periods in France's history.
later 15th century	Conditions improved once more until the Protestant wars again reduced France to misery.

THE INVASIONS AFTER 800

The Dark Ages is the name given the chaotic period between the collapse of the Roman Empire in the fifth cen-

Exterior of the choir gallery, Notre-Dame, Paris.

tury and the flowering of medieval culture. It was a time of survival; there was little effective government or law, pagans were more numerous than Christians, roads and bridges went unrepaired, and there was no money for building in stone.

From the beginning of the ninth century the Vikings laid waste to the entire northern and western seaboard. The fertile river valleys of France, with their rich towns and abbeys, were easy prey. The Norse *drakkars* rowed or sailed up every river, and beyond France even as far as Constantinople and Newfoundland, in search of plunder.

On land the Vikings proved to be good horsemen and masters of guerrilla warfare. They massacred any who opposed them. The monks fled in terror with their relics, and the peasants abandoned their fields to group around any castle that might defend them. No king could stop the raids which devastated the same countryside again and again, and few towns or monasteries escaped attack.

As if this were not enough, the Arabs harassed and in places occupied the southern provinces of France, and the Hungarians repeatedly invaded the east. No centralized government could cope with the rapidity and unexpectedness of the raids, for the king seldom heard about an attack before the invaders had done their worst and left.

Society had to be restructured if any semblance of order

was to reemerge. As only the locals could defend their territory, people transferred their allegiance to the nearest baron, providing food and services in exchange for protection. From this elementary relationship came what we call the feudal system, in which everyone owed allegiance to some lord, each lord to another above him, until all were vassals of the king.

In the tenth century the king was able to neutralize the Vikings by giving one group a large territory around the Seine west of Paris, which is to this day known as Normandy.

THE AGE OF THE MONASTERIES

With the end of the Viking invasions optimism returned. As the Burgundian monk Ralph Glaber noted:

> every nation of Christendom rivaled with the other, to see which should worship in the finest buildings. The world shook herself everywhere in a white garment of churches. (*Miracles de Saint-Benoît*)

As eleventh-century society was overwhelmingly rural, the monasteries were the first to benefit from improved living conditions. Organized and stable, they were the major civilizing force in the countryside; like brokers for salvation, the monks dedicated their lives to bringing the City of God closer and converting the rest of the world to Christianity. The most vital monastic order was controlled by the Benedictine house at Cluny.

The monks taught that the world was a huge and treacherous ocean and that the ever-present threat of shipwreck

The allegory of music on a capital from Cluny.

could be avoided only through close association with a monastery. In one Cluniac charter we read:

> Just as a man who enters onto the deeps of the sea avoids ship-wreck by reaching the shelter of a harbor, so we, who are placed upon the seas of the world, desire to avoid the shoals of this life by reaching the haven where none may suffer shipwreck. No one can come to it unless he prepares the way by giving generously to those who are laboring in Christ's vineyard, so that by the virtue of their prayers, he may enter together with them into eternal joy.

The punch line was the last: it made Cluny the most power-ful religious and financial institution in France. The sump-tuous rituals and the eye-catching churches Paray-le-Monial and Charlieu bear witness to their efforts. By 1100 some fourteen hundred monasteries were dependent on Cluny, many of the most important being situated along the pilgrimage routes to Spain. To prevent the pilgrims from wandering off the track and visiting other shrines, the monks are known to have bought off or raided the posses-sors of competing relics.

But as the twelfth century advanced people became less and less sympathetic to elaborate rituals. A new spirit was inhabiting the country, and the decline of the Cluniac order after 1130 reflected this. People turned to a less osten-tatious approach to God, as represented by the Cistercians.

THE CISTERCIANS

In 1098, just as Cluny was approaching the zenith of its power and prosperity, the Cistercian order was formed to revive the original Benedictine simplicity. Its growth is at-tributed to Saint Bernard, who entered the order with four of his brothers and personally founded seventy-two of the 340 Cistercian houses existing at the time of his death. The historian Steven Runciman wrote of Bernard:

> It is difficult to appreciate the tremendous impact of his personal-ity on all who knew him. He was the dominant influence in the religious and political life of Western Europe. The fervour and sincerity of his preaching combined with his courage, his vigour and the blamelessness of his life to bring victory to any cause he supported. *(A History of the Crusades)*

Consequently, Cistercian rules bluntly prohibited anything that distracted from the total contemplation of God. During the summer the monks ate two meatless meals a day in si-lence while the scriptures were read, and during the winter they ate one. In the only heated room in the entire monas-tery the monks dried parchments and prepared inks, oiled their shoes, and received their monthly haircut and sea-sonal bloodlettings. However, the order was so popular and successful that by the end of the Middle Ages there were more than 1500 dependent houses, of which about half were for women.

*Interior of the
Cistercian abbey
of Fontenay.*

The Cistercians' dream of self-sufficiency and rejection of the world was, in a way, not unlike the back-to-the-land movement and the hippie communes of our own day. Both possessed the same pioneer spirit, the same disregard for comfort, and the same religious belief in simplicity and nature. The Cistercians became expert stockbreeders and foresters and were unsurpassed in their knowledge of fisheries; they were pioneers of mining and smelting. Their wealth could only increase, and by the thirteenth century Cistercian monasteries were very rich indeed, owning extensive estates, forests, mills, and mines from Russia to Ireland.

Strict decrees were issued about building works. They demanded extremely simple architecture with no decoration. The Cistercians had no intention of emulating the sumptuous Cluniac monasteries. Bernard wrote in his *Apologia*—that bitter, brilliant condemnation of ecclesiastical extravagance—that

> the church's walls are dazzling, but her poor are needy. Her stones are clothed in gold but her children are abandoned in their nudity. The eyes of the rich are regaled at the cost of the poor. The curious find pleasure, but the needy do not find the means of sustenance.

He argued that monks were like the advance guard of the faith and that the luxury of the Cluniac order separated the

Church from the people. Above all, the Cistercians exemplified the strong wish that people then had for self-denial, for putting themselves into the harshest situations in the hope that this would be good for their souls. The Crusades, which began at about the same time as the Cistercian order was founded, were another aspect of this need.

THE CRUSADES

It is hard to appreciate the intense feelings generated by the home of Christ, where Christians had a better chance of achieving eternal bliss than anywhere else. Ever since the overland route had been opened in the tenth century, a ceaseless flow of pilgrims had visited Jerusalem each year. In one way the invasions mounted in the West to wrest the Holy Land from Islam were an armed extension of the pilgrimage. Never since has the western world shown anything like the energy and unity with which she flung herself on the East and for the moment made the East recoil.

The First Crusade—introduced by Pope Urban II—turned out to be the central event of medieval Christianity. How strange and miraculous it must have seemed at the outset! The chronicles catch the sense of wonder and exaltation, the credulity and emotion that had no parallel until the invasion of the New World four centuries later.

Though the First Crusade of 1096 succeeded, it was a mismanaged affair. Before the Crusade Christian, Jew, and Moslem had lived side by side with reasonable tolerance; but afterward the Crusaders treated the Moslems so badly that potential allies were turned into fanatical enemies. By 1187 Jerusalem itself had fallen to Saladin, and shortly afterward the kingdom had been reduced to a few towns on the Syrian coast.

There were other Crusades, the most lamentable being the Fourth of 1202. The Crusaders allowed themselves to be used by the Venetians to sack the Christian seaport of Zara, then were persuaded to storm and pillage Constantinople, which for five hundred years had been the bastion of Christendom against the onslaughts of Islam.

The general enthusiasm affected everyone, so there was even a Children's Crusade. The huge army was an embarrassment; it was directed to Marseilles and embarked on seven large ships. Two were lost in a storm, and the masters of the others sold the children into slavery, to live out their miserable lives working for the Infidel they thought they were going to conquer.

Even though the Crusades failed to turn the Holy Land into a Christian kingdom, they brought East and West into closer contact, stimulated trade, new methods of transport, and means of scientific and financial exchange, and happily occupied the attention of the warlike barons who would otherwise have been disturbing the peace at home.

THE FRENCH KINGS
AND THE INVESTITURE CONFLICT

During the invasions of the ninth century and the restructuring of Carolingian society, the French monarchy lost nearly all the power it had once held. Although the French kings had to work from a weak power base, a line of shrewd and long-lived monarchs divided their opponents and took advantage of every opportunity to extend their rights and their income. It was a relentless process in which the monarchy edged closer and closer to complete control. The gradual triumph of central power was the most salient process in the history of medieval France, but during the papal reforms of the eleventh century the French kings, unable to exert a strong policy, sought compromise.

The popes believed that as Saint Peter was the head of Christ's kingdom, so they ought to head all earthly kingdoms. However, the reality in the tenth and eleventh centuries was quite different: popes and bishops were appointed by the nobility, many monks and priests had wives, and posts were often sold to the highest bidder.

When the popes began to institute reforms they determined to stop rulers from selecting bishops, but because many bishops were lay lords, the right to appoint them was a crucial aspect of royal authority. What followed, called the Investiture Conflict, threatened the power of every ruler in Christendom and debilitated many communities in Italy and Germany until the issues were resolved in 1122.

In France, because the kings lacked the strength to do otherwise, the conflict did not occur. Instead a fruitful partnership evolved between Crown and Church, one that helped France enjoy a unique harmony that made her the leading power in Europe, politically, intellectually, and artistically, during the next two hundred years. The sculptures flanking the west doors at Chartres illustrate this unity.

One of the men responsible for the historic compromise was the king's minister, Abbot Suger of Saint-Denis. He was a practical man, both diplomat and politician; his writings have made him the Cellini of the twelfth century. If his books had been lost, we would have much less to say about the architecture he inspired, for his words are always relevant and fascinating. With little humility he demanded a place in heaven to reward his efforts:

> O Great Denis, throw open the gates of Paradise,
> And grant unto Suger thy holy protection.
> Mayest thou, for whom I have built thy new dwelling
>   place,
> Receive me into a dwelling place in Heaven,
> That I may eat to the full at the heavenly table.

Suger was born in 1081. His parents were farmers who offered him to the monastery of Saint-Denis, and there he found himself at school with his future patron, the young King Louis. At forty-one he became abbot of the abbey that schooled him, and later he became the king's chief minis-ter—an indication of the opportunities for advancement that were possible through the Church at that time.

Like a modern promoter, Suger advertised the impor-tance of his abbey by having ballads composed and sung in the street theatres. He modified the *Song of Roland* to sug-gest that Saint-Denis had once been the capital of France, and he changed another work to suggest that Charlemagne had promised the whole of France to Saint-Denis. Otto von Simson commented:

> Transparent as these claims may seem to us, they were taken very seriously then. The Christian religion is the only one to set such visible store by the written word. A direct legacy of Juda-ism, it is the only church that in its sculpture and paintings con-stantly shows the saints and martyrs holding scrolls and books as proofs of their messages. They believed that what was written was true, and that what was ancient was irrefutable. *(The Gothic Cathedral)*

The campaign succeeded. The king accepted the saint's banner as the royal battle flag, and for many generations the French monarchs were buried in the abbey.

TRADE AND THE GROWTH OF A MONEY ECONOMY

The tenth century was reliant more on barter and service than on money. But the growth of the population, the con-sequent increased circulation of money, and improvements in agriculture brought prosperity. The cash needed for pil-grimages, the Crusades, and building was raised by selling or borrowing on the most important asset: land. In the elev-enth century money came mainly from the monasteries,

The town wall of Carcassonne.

but from the twelfth century onward it came from the towns, which benefited most from the redistribution of wealth.

The north traded woolen cloth, furs, and amber, the south silks, leather, weapons, jewelry, and in particular spices, which were exotic but essential in an age without refrigerators, for by the end of winter spices alone made palatable the remaining supplies of meat butchered in the autumn. Most spices, and the precious carpets and cloth that came with them, were brought from India, Java, and even China.

Widespread trade brought wealth to those merchants who were free, though most townsmen were irked by lords or bishops who wanted their revenue without being the least interested in how it was earned. Thus traders made efforts to obtain the right to run their own affairs, and those characteristic inventions of the Middle Ages, civic pride and municipal government, were the result.

The kings came to realize the advantages of supporting the townsmen and the merchants, though royal friendliness was at times no more than an excuse for needling the local bishop or extracting a little more revenue.

The story of Laon is typical of the early twelfth century. During a controversy between the merchants and their lord bishop, the king was asked to arbitrate. The commune offered the king 400 livres for their freedom (an enormous sum at a time when the daily wage of a skilled artisan was only a few pennies), but the bishop outbid them by 300 livres, enabling King Louis to decree that things should be left as they were. The bishop then tried to raise this money by taxing those who had just failed to gain their freedom. This, not surprisingly, sparked off a savage insurrection in which the bishop, caught hiding in a barrel, was beheaded.

In the end royal encouragement of the independent cities was one of the most important factors in the growth of the monarchy, for the king needed the support of the townsmen against the local barons. On his death Louis IX advised his son to support "the strength and wealth of the great cities" so that the lords would "fear to undertake any action against you."

TOWN LIFE

On the whole, medieval towns were vital, noisy, dirty, stimulating, and overcrowded, although little of this mattered because the countryside was only a short walk away. Unlike today, no medieval town lost itself in extensive suburbs or factories but—like Carcassonne—was bounded by defensive walls to protect both the ruler and the merchants who sought shelter there.

The air was fresh, the birds and flowers never far off. Garbage was organic matter that dissolved easily into the earth. Even so, hygiene was little known and the streets were smelly, as were most men's bodies. Excrement dribbled out of pipes into castle moats or nearby rivers and even into the drains that ran down the centers of the streets. Lepers and beggars would display their deformities at every worthwhile place.

Slaughtering areas were treated like airports today—they were necessary, but no one wanted them nearby. The disposal of the offal was difficult and the smell from contaminated meat quite powerful. The punishment for selling bad meat was to be put in the stocks and suffer the putrid flesh being burnt under your nose.

The townsmen instigated a most important change in our perception of time. On any weekday in Chartres you will still hear the great bell tolling at seven in the morning and again at seven at night. Since around 1300 the tolling of the bell has determined the working period—an innovation that marked a fundamental change in work itself. Rather than let the seasons, the immutable round of religious services, and the heat and the cold determine the working span, it was now determined by an impersonal and unvarying mechanism.

This change profoundly affected men's view of the world. Classic and early Christian time had been without punctuation, rhythmic, and stretching to infinity. After the fourteenth century time became secularized, tied to earthly rather than heavenly events. Where the sun and the seasons had controlled men's rhythms, now the pendulum and the escapement did. The first comments we have about "wasting time" occur early in the fourteenth century, and it was rapidly raised to a major sin.

The process of regulating time probably began with Saint Benedict's first monastery in the sixth century, for he instigated the exceptional rule that monks pray at regular times throughout the day and night, irrespective of the seasons or the weather. Where the farmer rises with the sun and lives in the midst of birth and death, planting and reaping, the city man has come to understand less and less of the seasons and how the grain for his bread is grown or his egg conceived.

THE TWELFTH-CENTURY RENAISSANCE

Many people still think that the Italian Renaissance of the fifteenth century introduced classical literature and philosophy into Europe, yet nearly all the works of antiquity that were known to Dante were also known to Abbot Suger. Indeed, the evolution of the Renaissance was so imperceptible that historians cannot agree on when it began. The twelfth century saw the revival of Latin and Greek science and law and the origin of the first European universities. During the century that saw the invention of Gothic architecture, learning achieved more than it would in the next five hundred years.

The soaring height of Beauvais cathedral.

The experimental spirit, virtually unknown before in Europe, was evident everywhere by 1200, and with Albert Magnus around 1200 ("Experience is the best teacher in all things") we are on the threshold of modern times.

It was a period of unparalleled experimentation and inventiveness. Expanding commerce prompted new methods of finance, the increased use of metals stimulated the design of new types of kilns and bellows, the refinement of clothes led to the use of new dyes and chemicals, and the clamor for more food from a swiftly growing population stimulated new methods of cultivation.

Where the Romans had had no incentive to reduce their dependence on slave labor, after the tenth century Europe began adding to its sources of energy as the last traces of slavery were disappearing from the western world. Water- and windmills were erected in the thousands to grind grain, work cloth, and drive smithies' hammers and bellows. Ingenious cranes and ballistic devices and a host of other marvelous gadgets gave medieval people ten times the power of their Classical counterparts.

The invention of eyeglasses in the thirteenth century transformed people's lives, for up till then folk had seldom worked beyond middle age at jobs requiring close scrutiny. (One wonders what happened to the sculptor, the illuminator, or the cobbler who lost his sharp youthful vision.)

Probably the most innovative aspect of medieval science and technology lay in architecture. The Gothic achieve-

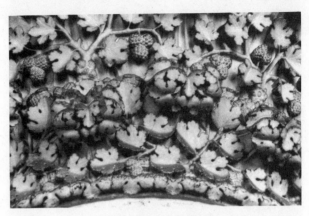

The stone has come alive: each leaf was observed directly from nature in this capital from Reims cathedral.

ments were based on ideas for which there were no ante-cedents in the ancient world. The geometric concepts used to solve the structural problems of the cathedrals were among the highest intellectual products of the period.

The philosophers and theologians were able to state their views in such clear terms that all architecture, sculpture, and science was affected. Practicing in the universities which were being established in the later 1100s, they en-couraged nimbleness of mind rather than learning by rote. For this the universities may have been the most important medieval contribution to civilization, and by 1240 these schools were the most independent organizations in France.

SCHOLASTICISM

The philosophy of the scholars deeply affected everyone, for it was not a body of knowledge but a revolutionary method of searching for the truth. It was based on the assumption that duality is innate to the universe and that through de-bate the truth on both sides could be found. The technique involved two concepts, *manifestatio* and *concordantio*: the first was to make the propositions clear by using a reasoned and formalized process of argument; the second was to see that kernel of truth which had to exist in both propositions.

It was assumed there would be truth on both sides be-cause every question worth arguing was founded to some extent on divine revelation. The Bible was the most impor-tant source of truth, and after it came the teachings of the Fathers such as Augustine and Gregory. As these writings were seldom consistent, yet had to be accepted as revealed truths, theologians needed to interpret them again and again until the common truth had been extracted. The establishment of the truth came not through the outright victory of one position over the other but through a reconciliation. Indeed, the strength of the method was that where opposing views appeared to be completely irreconcilable, some common agreement would still emerge, even where applied to such diverse topics as the fundamental "Is God single?" or the entertaining "Was the pig led to market by the rope or by the driver?" These questions excited such controversy that they were publicly debated for centuries.

In Scholasticism, as in architecture, there were three phases: during the Romanesque period the Platonic view was popular, during the creative years of Gothic it gradually gave way to Aristotelianism, and finally both were supplanted by Nominalism.

In the Platonic view popular around 1150, a plant was thought to exist as a copy of the idea of a plant, an idea in the mind of God of which the plant was only an imperfect reflection. By 1200 this view had been reversed and the plant was thought to exist in its own right; where God had once been assumed to be the basic condition of existence, by 1200 the perfection of the universe had itself become the proof of God. Thus people came to love the beauty of the world as the proof of divinity. Scientific observation and sculpture that was lifelike and humane were then possible.

The correspondence between philosophy and architecture was very close. Though it is unlikely that many master builders read the philosophers, they would have been exposed to their ideas in innumerable other ways. Their work brought them into contact with the priest-scholars who devised the iconography for the sculpture, and they listened to sermons and heard debates that were well-attended public events not unlike pop concerts. The geometric methods of the master builders were Scholastic, pitting one figure or number against another to reconcile such irreconcilables as square roots and whole numbers.

The third phase, Nominalism, took over from the middle of the fourteenth century, following the Black Death and the Hundred Years War. This philosophy tended to be agnostic, arguing that as only those things which could be perceived by the senses could exist, therefore God could be, amazingly, only a probability. Where Abelard believed he could use language to prove a point, the Nominalists argued that the words themselves were not real but only conventions.

The philosopher Peter Aureolus wrote that "man exists by virtue of himself and nothing else." In these words lies the change in man's status that anticipated the modern world—in which Copernicus proved that we were not the center of the universe and Galileo showed that mere mechanical forces were enough to move our planet round the sun.

ECONOMIC BOOM AND BUST

During the second half of the twelfth century northern France was more prosperous than at any time before the Revolution. It was a confident, deeply religious, and wealthy society that enjoyed the highest prestige in Europe. During this boom time prodigious sums of money were spent on architecture. An enormous proportion of the labor force must have been employed on construction, perhaps one in ten of all able-bodied men.

From this enthusiasm for building, the Gothic style was born in the small area known as the Paris Basin, that limestone massif which extends from Chartres to Reims and from Senlis to Sens. Yet it is strange that before the 1130s the Basin had not contributed anything original to the evolution of architecture.

Three factors explain why most of the buildings in the new style should have been built only in the Basin: materials, skills, and a cash surplus. The best materials came from around Senlis and Braine, and their export would have brought cash into the region. Some dozen of the larger builders came from these districts and probably traveled with their stone as far afield as Rouen and Bourges. They may have sent large sums home as do the itinerant Turks and Mexicans today.

Most of the cash surplus seems to have come from local wine production, much of it for export. Both the profits to be made and the quantity were enormous, for later documents indicate that just the export of wine through Paris was about twice as great per capita as that grown *and* exported in France today. Wine was produced for local consumption wherever it would grow, even in England where, according to the French chancellor at the court of Henry II, one had better gulp it down "with closed eyes and a tight jaw." The best vineyards lay in the area where Gothic was perfected, and the years of their prosperity coincided with the time in which the new style was being created. From Laon to Paris wine production brought enormous wealth to the owners of the vineyards. The areas that became famous after the thirteenth century, Bordeaux and Burgundy, were little known in the twelfth because the climate was different then.

TIME OF CRISIS

Temperatures fluctuate over long periods, increasing and decreasing in cycles that stretch for hundreds of years. From sometime in the ninth century the climate had been steadily improving until, around 1200, the summer may have been a month longer and conditions had become exceptionally favorable to wine production. Then a series of hot summers and droughts desiccated the fields and burnt out the vineyards. These hard years were followed, almost without pause, by a steady and disastrous decline in temperature. The economy went into a prolonged recession, and quality viticulture in the north was virtually extinguished by this mini ice age which lasted intermittently until the seventeenth century.

Three crucial events occurred just after 1200: the insane sack of Constantinople and the failure of the Crusades which followed, the war against the Cathars, and the increasingly political role of the papacy. This was also a pivotal time in medieval architecture: as if on the fulcrum of a swing, the deep calm and inner authority found at Chartres disappeared. It is clear when we compare Saint-Savin with Saint-Maclou that, for all the skillful workmanship in the later churches, something precious has been lost.

These events coincided with a long-term decline in the economy and a sixfold increase in population at a time when the area of land under cultivation had only doubled. Some districts supported as many inhabitants as they would at the beginning of the twentieth century. Because the inheritance of land was divided equally among all the children, one small parcel might be owned by fifteen or more people, each receiving a minuscule proportion of a harvest that was reduced by the rapid deterioration of the climate.

The result of all these elements coming together was a series of harvests so disastrous that in places nothing was left even for the next year's seed. It was as if the sun had taken the veil. Salt production came to a virtual stop because there was not enough heat to evaporate the seawater, so it became impossible to conserve what little meat there was. Starvation was rife, and in some cities up to ten percent of the population died for lack of food.

Simultaneously the rulers became increasingly isolated from the realities of daily life, as if leadership were just a game. At court even the most ordinary actions acquired the quasi-religious character of mysteries. Meals were attended by a complex array of breadmasters, carvers, cupbearers, cooks, and other servants, all of whom had to follow a prearranged ritual not unlike a high mass. It was a noble game which denigrated the religion it emulated while reality disappeared behind an empty formality.

The crisis was worsened by protracted wars and epidemics that recurred for almost three hundred years. War, plague, and climatic change had broken Roman society and may yet break our own; happily for the fifteenth century, the merchants of the towns were stable enough to partially rebuild the economy once the wars were over.

THE CATHARS AND THE ALBIGENSIAN CRUSADE

One of the early events leading to this crisis was the crusade against the heretics of southern France, called the Cathars ("the Perfect"), or the Albigensians after their stronghold at Albi. Like Christianity, the Cathars' beliefs were of eastern origin, and they attracted adherents in a swathe across central Europe. In the south of France they were allowed to preach without persecution, so by the end of the twelfth century they were strong enough to face the orthodox Church on almost equal terms.

Christians who believe in an infinitely powerful and loving God have found it hard to explain the existence of evil. In the Catholic view, God could control evil but prefers to leave man with free choice. The Cathars argued that evil and good were equal powers in the universe, that one had created the material world and the other the spiritual. Not having created the material world, God could not control it, and to that extent He was not omnipotent. But through detachment from mortal needs and aspirations people could bring the spirit into matter. So they abstained from meat and wine as well as marriage and procreation, which, they believed, only multiplied an evil species. Those who achieved this detachment, both men and women, were called "the Perfect."

The Cathars also rejected the Catholic view that God could be approached only through the Church, believing instead in the direct experience of God that made priests superfluous. Can we wonder that the curia in Rome felt threatened? Nothing in its long experience had prepared the western Church for such a crisis, and it was forced to retreat before this rival movement. But, as Saint Bernard wrote:

> Errors are refuted by argument. Nevertheless if, after repeated warnings, the heretics persist in their errors they must be excommunicated, and if it appears that even then they would prefer to die than to believe, then let them die.

Fortress architecture, the cathedral of Albi.

Recognizing the dangers, the pope appealed to the French king to destroy the Cathars. The invasion was called a crusade and was stimulated by the offer of indulgences to all who joined it. The horror and savagery of the war that ensued reflected both the Church's fears and the abhorrence felt by the Cathars for the religion they had abandoned.

The first town to be attacked was Béziers, where in 1208 the army demanded that the city fathers hand over the 222 Cathars known to be there. When the request was refused, the city was taken and every man, woman, and child was killed—20,000 people. Not even the priests were spared. At Castres no one could decide whether the penitent heretics who had returned to the Church should be burned along with the impenitent or released. The Cistercian Arnaud-Amalric ordered that both alike should die, for "God would recognize his own!"

The war lasted forty-five years, a tenacious and horrifying struggle without parallel in modern history, and its consequences went far beyond the original war aims. An independent Mediterranean principality was conquered by Frankish armies who imposed heavy taxes; this impoverished the south and brought enormous wealth to the monarchy. For the first time since Charlemagne, the authority of the French monarch stretched from the North Sea to the Mediterranean.

The other major consequence was the creation of the Inquisition, which was organized through the Dominican order founded by the Spanish monk Dominic Guzman in 1216. The Inquisition became the major ideological weapon of the curia and was given the role of weeding out heresy from the minds of the people—a job it continued to do for the next seven centuries. For this Guzman's followers earned the title "the Hounds of God."

PHILIP THE FAIR AND THE DECLINE OF FAITH

The symbolical turning point was the reign of Philip IV, which began fifteen years after the death of the saint-king Louis IX. Philip was called the Fair because he was handsome, not because he was just. For he used any means, fair or foul, to enrich the monarchy. He taxed the clergy for half their annual income, and when the pope objected, Philip accused him of witchcraft and sent troops to assault his summer residence in Italy.

Philip determined that the pope would be stationed where he would remain under French control, in Avignon. Thus commenced the seventy-year schism called the Babylonian captivity. It weakened the spiritual power of the Church because the monarchs of Europe, remembering the Investiture Conflict, were quick to move in and reclaim the rights they had lost.

Philip also removed one of the most ancient bans in

Christianity, that on usury. Heretofore only non-Christians such as the Jews could officially lend money on interest. Now that Christians could do so legally, there was no place in the community for the Jews, and soon most of them were ejected from their old centers.

Philip eliminated the Knights Templar and sequestered their property. The Knights had been founded in the first decades of the twelfth century to keep open the roads and sea lanes to Jerusalem. Their commanderies straddled the known world, and their international contacts made them as wealthy as the Jews and even more powerful. After much planning in secret, all the Knights were arrested in 1307 and turned over to the Inquisition.

Thus were three of the most important agencies of international contact emasculated: the curia, the Templars, and the Jews. France, and with it the rest of Europe, closed itself off and became insular.

THE HUNDRED YEARS WAR, 1337–1453

Shortly after Philip's death a dynastic argument started a war that was to last four generations. It was a war not between nations but between feudal lords, the English and the Burgundians opposing the French, who at one time lost almost one-third of their territory.

When the war began, the population of France was about three times that of England and her international prestige and prosperity were greater. Her chief weakness was chronic disunity, while the strength of the English lay in their centralized administration and a line of able rulers.

It was when the English attacked Orléans—the largest remaining French stronghold—that Joan of Arc turned the tide. Joan, a commoner who heard voices commanding her to save France, so inspired the dispirited troops that victory came to the French. She is better known today than she was in her time, when her final sacrifice was received with foppish indifference by those who were most in her debt. Yet in halting the English she changed history and thereby came to symbolize the romantic spirit of France.

Feudalism was badly weakened by the war, a sense of nationalism appeared, and kings began to make their claims of divine right that led in time to the French Revolution. The countryside had been laid waste with a savagery which had not been experienced since the time of the Vikings. The prosperity of France, once so great, was undermined for centuries and did not fully recover until the eve of the Revolution. Intellectually, France ceased to lead Europe and scholars no longer flocked to Paris as the center of wisdom—and were not to do so again until the time of Louis XIV.

The architecture of France, both artistically and spiritually, reflects this massive and terrible decline.

THE BLACK DEATH

It must have been some time during 1346 that word first reached Europe of a plague of unparalleled ferocity raging far away in the East. Even in those times of relatively easy travel and spread of news, calamities in China tended to be dismissed with a polite yet detached regret. Reality was soon to unsettle the Europeans. Arriving via the Crimea and the Genoese trading posts, the plague had taken a firm hold in Italy by the spring of 1348. The French, of course, gave it their own name, the *mort bleue*.

There have been three great pandemics in history. The first began in Arabia in 542 and helped to weaken Justinian's empire. The second was the medieval plague which continued on and off until the final terrible outbreak in London in 1665. The last began in Yunnan in 1892, reaching Bombay four years later (where it killed over six million) and finally Suffolk, England, in 1910 (where, mercifully, only a handful died).

It has been said that the medieval plague did not differ greatly from others like it and that the terrible losses had more to do with prolonged malnutrition than any intrinsic ferocity. In one sense the plague was the inevitable fate meted out to people who had bred too fast for too long without providing themselves with the resources needed for such an extravagance.

The death toll from the first visitation was between one-eighth and two-thirds of the population, depending on local

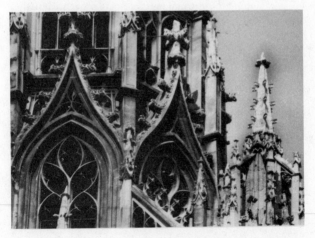

The Flamboyant spire of Saint-Maclou, Rouen.

conditions. Once it had taken hold in a community it returned again and again, mostly with lessened vigor but still conscripting an awful toll. Over the following fifty years, in six repetitions of the epidemic almost the same numbers were killed as in the first visitation. Each successive generation was attacked before it had time to make good the losses of the last. Thus by 1380 the population of France had declined from about nineteen million to little more than eleven million. Life changed dramatically, as one survivor recorded:

> Those few folk who remained alive expected to become virtuous with love and charity toward one another. But no sooner had the plague ceased than we saw the contrary: for since men were few and now abounded in earthly goods, they gave themselves up to a shameful and disordered life.
>
> Moldering in ease, they dissolutely abandoned themselves to the sin of gluttony, and to games and unbridled lechery. Men thought that there should now be an abundance of all things, yet everything became unusually scarce and remained long thus, and most commodities were more costly by twice or more. (*Cronica*)

In spite of much compassion and altruistic heroism, the Black Death left behind a deep pessimism. The emotionalism of the next century, the self-castigation of the flagellants, and the universal melancholy had a lot to do with the lasting impression these dreadful days left on all survivors.

RECOVERY AND THE REFORMATION

The second half of the fifteenth century was a better time for France, but it was not to last. Foreign adventures into Italy, overspending at court, and an old-fashioned army that was no match for the armaments of Spain prevented further growth and contributed to the religious upheavals of the next century.

It was a time of great change, of Henry VIII of England, Calvin and Luther, and Charles V of Spain, who united Germany, the Netherlands, and parts of Italy into one colossal kingdom. The Spaniards captured the French king and held him to ransom, and once again the country faced ruin. With these tensions, religious issues came to dominate all others. The chief grievances against the clergy were their worldliness, their ownership of one-third of all the arable land in France, and their moral laxity. John Calvin helped to instigate the Reformation by returning to Saint Augustine's doctrine of predestination and insisting that God, not the Church, determined who would be saved and who would be damned. He rejected the entire basis of medieval piety by arguing that salvation lay not in miracles, or in the power of relics, but in direct personal contact between the sinner and God.

Calvinism held a special attraction for the bourgeoisie

because Calvin argued that prosperity was a certain sign that a man had been blessed. Here was born the capitalist ethic: that wealth is a sign of grace.

MELANCHOLY

A pervasive sadness clothed the last decades of the Middle Ages. In poetry and chronicles, on tombs, in sermons and documents, one feels an immense melancholy. Huizinga wrote, "Great evils form the groundwork of history," and referred to one of Eustache Deschamps' laments:

Time of mourning and of temptation,
Age of tears, of envy and torment,
A time of apathy leading to damnation.
Age of decline nigh to the end,
Time most horrible which does all things falsely,
An age of lies, full of pride and envy,
Time stripped of all honour or true judgement,
Age of the uttermost sadness which shortens life.

It was a disillusioned time, one that had little in common with the hearty days of the twelfth century but terminology.

Renaissance figures on medieval detailing, south front, Senlis cathedral.

2

FAITH AND THEOLOGY

THE CHANGING FACE OF CHRISTIANITY

The Middle Ages opened with a massive campaign to bring the remaining pagans into the fold. This conversion drive forced changes in the nature of penance that created a situation of great tension: by 1100 people had come to fear that damnation was virtually inevitable. The anxiety this situation fostered was assuaged only by an extraordinary innovation, the cult of the Virgin, which swept all the old beliefs before it. Suddenly, in the lifetime of one generation, the situation had been transformed and salvation was possible. This transformation released enormous creative energies that changed society and produced a new culture. Rightly it could be called the miracle of 1130, for out of the terror that hell was imminent for all came one of the most positive expansionist epochs in European culture.

DIVINITY TRANSFORMED
AND THE NECESSITY OF GUILT

History deals not in eternal truths but in the ebb and flow of events and the ideas which so often direct them. From the point of view of a believer, the evolution of religious concepts can be seen as a gradual progression toward the truth. However, the historian recognizes that our notions are only one phase in an endless tide of ideas, and that even if we are committed to them, we can still examine the evolution of the gods with detachment.

The nature of our gods seems to rise and fall in two-thousand-year rhythms. In the earliest stories the gods had children: Rhea and Cronos, male and female deities, spawned families who made the substance of myth. Then, sometime in the second millennium B.C., the gods of the Mediterranean became infertile unless they cohabited with human beings. The heroes Achilles and Hector were products of divine miscegenation. The most celebrated of these occasions, the best remembered among Christians, is the time God lay with a virgin called Mary.

That conception ushered in a third stage of divinity that has survived another two thousand years. Nowadays God is no longer producing children, for Jesus was the last.

In the distant past most heroes died as a result of some imperfection in themselves, but Christ's death occurred because of some imperfection in us. This, by implication, placed the responsibility for Christ's death on our heads. Though God offered Himself, man carried out the execution and has had to accept the consequences.

The most important consequence has been guilt, and even though many periods have been unaware of the fact, guilt has played an important role in our history. The increase in the collective guilt had to be expressed, and one wonders to what extent the Crusades, the burning of the heretics, and the callous disregard many Christians have for other beliefs may have come from unassuageable guilt. The violence at Vézelay, the repetitive pictures of the horrors of hell, and the almost universal preoccupation with Satan demonstrate the effect of this guilt.

Maybe the ultimate judgment will be that man could not kill God with impunity and so has progressively distanced himself from the spirituality which had lain at the root of most previous societies. Now, two thousand years later, it may be time for our view of God's nature to change again. The historian looks with pleasure for signs of what it may be.

Unlike Asian religions, Christianity does not put much emphasis on achieving spiritual fulfillment here on earth. Perhaps the reason for this is that we were thrown out of Paradise for trying it. We are usually told that Adam and Eve were expelled from the Garden of Eden for eating of the tree of knowledge of good and evil. This is not so; they were chastised and given suffering for eating the fruit, but their expulsion was for another reason:

> And the Lord God said, behold, the man is become as one of us, to know good and evil: and now, lest he put forth his hand, and take *also of the tree of life*, and eat, and live for ever: *Therefore* the Lord God sent him forth from the garden of Eden, to till the ground from whence he was taken. *(Genesis 3:22–23; emphasis mine)*

So the expulsion had to do not with good and evil but with choice and therefore judgment. Knowing that death awaited him, man had the choice to remain mortal or to achieve everlasting life. "And now, lest he put forth his hand, and take also of the tree of life, and eat, and live for ever" are powerful words. Man was about to "become as one of us," which was not acceptable.

Maybe this is why so few westerners have dared the mystic Way, which might have opened the gates of Paradise for them, here on earth.

IMMANENCE VERSUS TRANSCENDENCE

There are two opposite ways of apprehending the spiritual world: one is transcendental and the other is mystical, or immanental. In the first God transcends our world, lying beyond an impregnable barrier that divides Him from us. In the second He is integral in everything, in every rock and seed. In the first the Church forms a necessary connection between us and Him, while in the second we need no intermediary because He is in us all.

Like most religious people, medieval Christians believed that the world of our senses—those things which we can touch, see, and smell—was only a poor reflection of the sacred, that the idea behind each person's own idea stemmed from the Creator, so there was no particular thing or thought that did not reflect the universal.

One response to this dichotomy is to argue that there is an unbridgeable barrier between the world of the spirit and ourselves: God created us and then left us to our own devices. The other view holds that there is no barrier and that God is present and active in everything always. The first view is transcendental, the second immanental.

Christians have, on the whole, preferred the transcendental. Man is the guilty party, unclean from the very act of conception, and God naturally keeps Himself at a distance. Yet the immanental view can be very powerful. It is an unforgettable experience which dissolves the barriers, and all at once we are sharing His ecstasy. At that point we *know* and do not have to theorize. This is the message of the best-known mystics, Saint Francis, John of the Cross, and Saint Teresa, but such private experiences of the Almighty are distrusted by the Church, for they seldom confirm orthodox theology.

The art and architecture of the eleventh century suggest that, for all the faith of that period, the most common outlook was transcendental. However, by the twelfth century the mystical current that had been apparent in the ninth century was taking over the popular imagination. It may be that the daily occurrence of miracles encouraged the belief that God was very close. The relics which wrought these miracles were like particles of paradise on earth, from which it was not a big step to believing that He could be present in all things.

People's gratitude for the Virgin's intercession, which promised paradise to any who worshipped her, probably tipped the scales and induced the mysticism of the twelfth and early thirteenth centuries, at least in the prosperous regions in the north of France. For a short time it was believed—not just by a few saints but apparently by the whole community—that God's presence lay not only in the thought which had brought the world into being in the first place, but also that it continued to exist within the world for all time. The sacred had come so near that Abbot Suger could write of his "immersion in the infinite ocean of eternal light." The spirit was therefore available to all those who were pure enough to see.

The impact that this popular enthusiasm had on architecture was prodigious. The basic characteristics of Gothic as it evolved after 1130, particularly the dematerialization of its substance, were to a large measure the expression of this view. The built form of the church was, in its essence *as well as* in its sensible reality, the Heavenly City. It was no mere allegory, it was actual. The choir was called "the City of the Great King," and Suger subtly altered the words of Paul's Epistle to the Ephesians to read:

> All the building—*whether spiritual or material*—groweth unto an holy temple in the Lord: in whom ye also are builded together for an habitation of God through the Spirit, *that we may more loftily and aptly build in a material way.*

The popular intensity of this mysticism could not be sustained, and from just before 1200 we notice the gradual reintroduction of the traditional view that there was an inviolate barrier between spirit and earth. At the time the Chartres Royal Portal was built, God was immanent in all creation; by the next century He had removed Himself, transcending the world, where He has remained, as far as most of us are concerned, ever since.

THE EUCHARIST AND THE END OF TIME

If a church has a purpose other than the glorification of God, it lies in the ritual of the Eucharist. The ceremony is millennia older than Christ and comes from the banquet at the initiation ceremony, in which the sacrificial victim is dismembered and fed to the celebrants. The mass has essentially the same meaning: Christ is taken apart and fed to His worshippers so that He may be recreated within them. By surviving the killing of another we affirm our own life; therefore, to cannibalize our God is not only to enjoy the benefits of sacrifice but to reintegrate the God inside us.

Where the ancient Greeks looked back to the origin of life, when Dionysus was blasted out of the rocky womb of Mother Earth, the Christians looked forward to the end of life and their final union with God. One view looked back across the endless cycles of time and encouraged a certain fatalism, the other forward to the final moment when all cycles would finish and the material world be terminated forever.

Thus Christians have only this life in which to make good; they have no second chance. Without reincarnation and a belief in the repeatability of things, it must be done now or not at all. Free will adds a deep anxiety that is absent in most other religions, for ultimately only we are responsible. This point cannot be overemphasized, for it divides us from most earlier belief systems. The uniqueness of both

Gothic architecture and our modern technological world owes a great deal to the lonely angst induced by our transcendental beliefs.

Although medieval man believed that miracles were happening every day, the stage had been set for the prevalent belief that miracles are a thing of the past and that salvation is up to us alone. Time is short! Without advance notice God is going to end it all. We had better be ready!

PENANCE AND GUILT

The major spiritual desire of the eleventh and twelfth centuries, as it appeared again and again in charters and wills, was *remissio peccatorum*, the remission of sins so that pilgrim would always be ready for the Last Judgment. To remit one's sins, one did penance, humbling oneself before both God and the Church.

At the time of Saint Augustine in the fourth century, the notorious sinner was excluded from the life of the Church. To be readmitted, he virtually had to promise to live a monastic existence for the rest of his life. There were three stages in remission: the confession, the satisfaction, and the reconciliation. These stages were not as we know them today, for the reconciliation was often an annual event after which *all* the consequences of sin were canceled.

The possibility of this cancellation was an extraordinary claim. In the ninth century the Church was not universal,

Pagan motifs and figures were incorporated into Romanesque sculpture at Aulnay.

for only a relatively small proportion of the people had been Christianized. Even in the early eleventh century only half the population had been baptized, for most Christian communities lay along the ancient trade routes while the remote countryside and hill country remained pagan. In the massive conversions of the next century the attitudes and prejudices of these multitudes could not be ignored.

The old religions did not have the Christian attitude to guilt and sin, so the newly converted wanted to receive absolution in the here and now, at the confessional, rather than have to carry guilt with them while they did penance. Having admitted their fault, they deemed it only just that they should be forgiven forthwith.

During the two difficult centuries after Charlemagne, it was important for people to have their burdens lifted as much as possible. Life was insecure enough without adding to it the load of sin, so from the end of the tenth century absolution was given after confession. The sinner still had to complete the penance demanded by the priest, but he was not excluded from the Church while he did so. Perhaps too many of the newly converted would have drifted away from the Church had they been kept from the mass until they had finished their penance.

But there were unfortunate long-term consequences to this arrangement, which seem to have become apparent around 1100. Being reconciled to the Church may have ended the guilt on earth, but it did not affect the punishment in eternity, for how could man judge on His behalf? It left people without the satisfaction of finality that they had had in the earlier act of reconciliation. One could say that the quick fix left them with a terminal hangover.

Before the cult of the Virgin, people feared that if they had not been able to complete all penance for every sin, no matter how small, before they died, then in front of an impartial judge salvation might be impossible. As Saint Bernard warned, there was little doubt that "few, very few will be saved." Consequently, the overwhelming majority were damned.

As living standards improved, people would have asked why it was that they could improve their lot on earth yet had little hope of improving their chances for heaven. The consequent tension might have been like the problems we create today by advertising lovely things to people who cannot afford them. One has the impression that the violence at Vézelay, and the tempestuous sculpture of Charlieu, Saint-Gilles, and Étampes, reflected this contradiction (see pages 181, 263, and 209).

The tension seems to have reached a climax around 1130, culminating in an ideological blowout that installed the Virgin as intercessor in the great transformation of medieval faith discussed on page 45. As in the story of Theophilus at Souillac, the arrival of the Virgin seems to have saved the day, proving that miracles were not things of the past but a part of the everyday and natural operation of the universe.

FAITH AND THE MIRACULOUS

For medieval man the world was chaotic, and only the perpetual and miraculous intervention of the Almighty could assure order. He was the direct cause of every moment, from the most trivial to the most unexpected. Natural forces were overpowering and uninsurable. Men were terrified of the dark, at times to the point of insanity. Thunderstorms, and above all an eclipse of the sun, brought panic, the entire community rushing into the church for protection and standing as close to the altar as possible. (Shakespeare reflected these feelings centuries later: "The heavens themselves presage the death of princes.") Evil was not an abstract force but a real, omniscient, powerful entity that searched one's private thoughts for weakness. Monks were known to travel in pairs for fear of the devil. According to Saint Bruno, Satan "moved in the air and in the dust that floated in every stream of light; a breath of wind, a turbulence of air, the gust that blows men to the ground and harms the crops, all these are the whistling of the devil."

The end cannot be independent of the means. Although it was a spiritual age, many of those who were able to feel faith most strongly were also ignorant, and thus belief in miracles prospered. For political reasons the Church Fathers had decided that miracles were needed to propagate the faith—and that once the Church was universal, miracles would not be needed. This was like the Marxist promise that after the revolution the "state would wither away," whereas inevitably the state, like the propagation of miracles, grew with use.

A miracle rests on the childlike belief in God's daily intervention. It is the natural impact of omnipotence on substance. In hard times the miracle promised hope. Rival teachers attempted to prove their doctrines by walking on flour without leaving footprints. The trial by ordeal, on which medieval justice rested, was based on the belief that God would intervene on the side of the just.

Once we understand the cause of something that might once have been considered a miracle, it becomes an ordinary event like any other, and the scope of the miraculous is diminished. Firewalking is still somewhat miraculous today, ESP is not.

RELICS AND THE ONGOING MIRACLE

God's will was made visible through miracles, and saints' bones were the intermediaries. Pilgrims traveled enormous distances to visit the shrines where the greatest miracles were performed. The more renowned shrines were crowded with the sick and dying, eagerly searching for a cure. They lay in the nave on their palliasses of straw, surrounded by relatives, waiting for the clergy to visit them. Their presence made the church noisy, energetic, smelly, and exciting. Abbeys and churches vied with one another to possess the most famous relics, as the story of Saint-Sernin in Toulouse shows. Sometimes relics were purchased or given, and surprisingly often they were stolen.

Between the time of Charlemagne and the age of the Crusades we know of over a hundred thefts, many of them bizarre in the telling. A typical account told how Saint Foy was stolen by a monk from Conques. At a special gathering, the monk Armisdus was chosen to visit Agen, where the bones of Saint Foy lay. On arrival he was asked to join the community. He was in no hurry; it took him ten years to gain their confidence. Patiently and, one hopes, not a little guiltily, he waited until he had been appointed guardian of the church's treasures, including the saint's tomb. His opportunity came one night when he was left alone in the church. He broke into the tomb, stole the bones, and on a horse which had been prepared for the occasion, rushed the relics to Conques. The enraged Agen monks pursued, but the triumphant thief reached home with his treasure, and it was received with great rejoicing.

Even stranger than the robberies was the almost universal approval of them by contemporary writers. Condemnation was rare; in nearly every document not only the skill but the virtue of the thieves is praised.

Many stories were in fact made up to enhance the image of a saint. He was a living power, physically present in his reliquary, and quite capable of defending his shrine. So when his relics moved, he moved with them. Therefore, it

Saints on the lintel of Bourges cathedral south door.

was argued, theft against his will was inconceivable. When theft occurred, translation must have been intended, so robbery was only a ritualized technique for ensuring that the saint's own wishes were fulfilled. And the fact of theft demonstrated the real value of the spoils, for it was accepted that no one would take the enormous risk of abducting a saint who could not perform. If people of the time had believed their own stories, the relics of a satisfied saint would have needed no guarding, yet security became as important as display, and the relics at Chartres were guarded day and night by men armed with iron maces.

The dazzling display of wealth, the golden ornaments and silk wall hangings, the brass candelabra and clouds of incense drifting permanently in the air were all meant to impress. The relics were housed in the most sumptuous reliquaries, for only by show could they testify to their powers and invite commensurate gifts. Like altars, they were covered in pure gold that was itself scarcely visible beneath a profusion of sapphires, diamonds, rubies, and emeralds, all enhanced with exquisite designs and delicately worked patterns. The reliquary of Saint Foy at Conques is such a showpiece.

The most efficacious relics included pieces of the true cross, the crown of thorns, and Mary's scarf. There were an enormous number of martyrs, mainly Roman and male. The belief that Christ and His mother were perfect and without sin and had thus risen boldly to heaven meant that their relics were rare and ingenious. There were a number of foreskins, some baby teeth, hair clippings, nail parings, a vial containing Mary's milk, and similar *spolia*. By permitting the dismemberment and translation of the saints' bodies in the early days, the Church opened the door to a lucrative industry that fed on credulity and contributed to the outrages that led to Protestantism. Yet people still stand in awe before Lincoln's top hat or a dummy of Jack the Ripper: such is humanity.

The original number of saints being small and the need great, the bodies were dismembered so that every church could have a share. The parts were proliferated so widely that later on the clergy were unable to verify the hundreds of thousands of relics spread across Europe.

There were enormous private collections of relics, not unlike the art collections of a Guggenheim or a Rockefeller, and the spiritual authority of relics gave political and social prestige. Reading Abbey in England was not founded until 1121, yet within three generations it possessed 242 items, including twenty-nine relics of Our Lord, six of Mary, nineteen of the prophets, fourteen of the apostles, seventy-three of the martyrs, fifty-one of confessors such as Saint Jerome, and forty-nine of assorted virgins.

Abbot Suger wrote of the popular enthusiasm:

As the numbers of the faithful increased, the crowds at Saint-Denis grew larger and larger until the old church began to burst at the seams. On feast days it was always full to overflowing, and the mass of struggling pilgrims spilled out of every door. Not only were some pilgrims unable to get in, but many of those who were already inside were forced out by those in front of them. As they fought their way toward the holy relics to kiss and worship them, they were so densely packed that none of them could so much as stir a foot. A man could only stand like a marble statue, paralyzed, and free only to cry out aloud.

Meanwhile the women in the crowd were in such intolerable pain, crushed between strong men as if in a winepress, that death seemed to dance before their eyes. The blood was drained from their faces and they screamed as if they were in the throes of childbirth. Some of them were trodden underfoot and had to be lifted above the heads of the crowd by kindly men, and passed to the back of the church and thence to the fresh air. In the cloister outside, wounded pilgrims lay gasping out their last breath. As for the monks who were in charge of the reliquaries, they were often obliged to escape with the relics through the windows. *(De Consecratione S. Dionysii)*

Relics could bring great wealth to their owners. They were an indispensable part of life and were often used in taking oaths and ensuring victory on the battlefield. When the possessions of the abbey were threatened or the enemy pressed at the gates of the city, the relics would be taken on an impressive procession amid monks clashing cymbals and blowing ivory horns.

The mantle of the Virgin was taken before both the French and the English armies just before the battle of Bovines, and both were asked to give to the cathedral building fund and to pray that they might have victory. That the French clergy would solicit money from their king's enemies might appear treachery to us, but at that time they had no concept of France as a nation; that idea was not to surface until the end of the fifteenth century. Instead the count of Chartres supported his king and brought his army to fight the English while the clergy of Chartres begged money from both sides.

Consequently, the asset value of a famous relic was prodigious. Before the crusade to Libya, Louis IX pawned the Crown of Thorns with the wily Venetians for enough money to take his troops across the Mediterranean. A well-publicized relic would draw enormous crowds, and with them unbelievable donations. Jonathan Sumption describes one successful shrine:

Herds of animals were offered every day, palfreys, cows and bulls, pigs, lambs and sheep. Linen, wax, bread and cheese arrived, and above all purses full of money. So much money was given that in the evening several men were needed to collect it up and put it in a safe place. The offerings exceeded all other revenues of the abbey combined, so that the abbot was able to build powerful walls and retain a large body of knights and servants. It bought

The abbey of Conques is still hidden among hills a long way from other towns.

the seigneurial rights over most of the neighbouring towns and villages. The monastery was completely rebuilt and henceforth its servants and officials were treated with respect and fear wherever they went. *(Pilgrimage: An Image of Medieval Religion)*

PILGRIMAGE

The pilgrimage is as ancient as religion itself. Consulting the Delphic oracle, the aboriginal walkabout, and bathing in the Ganges at Benares are all forms of pilgrimage. The Christians adopted the system and over the centuries raised it to a new level. Penance had to be done on earth to satisfy the Church, or there would be no road to eternal bliss.

Not all pilgrimages were for redemption or cure. It was also a punishment that was cheaper than sending a man to jail. Murder, assault, and riot often carried the penalty of exile. As the medieval church could control its congregation by denying them confession outside their own parish, to be banished was almost equal to being exiled from God Himself.

Until at least the end of the twelfth century the offender was chained, his possessions confiscated, and he was turned out to wander. Iron collars were placed around the neck, arms, and legs, and a knife or sword used by a murderer was often attached to the fetters as public notice of the crime. Pilgrimages of this sort were sometimes for life, sometimes "until pardoned by God, and the chains should break asunder in front of the shrine." The offender became an outcast, like Cain, "a wanderer and a fugitive on the face of the earth, never to return to his native land."

Typical was the nobleman who had murdered his father. He joined a band of people in a similar predicament, walked to Rome and then overland to Jerusalem, returned along the unbearably hot north African coast to the shrine of Saint Cyprian at Carthage, then hitched a lift in a boat back to Rome. Still unpardoned, he returned to Jerusalem, saw Mount Sinai, and came again to Rome, all in the fruitless hope of some sign from God. It was not until he had walked again through the whole of Italy to the shrine of Saint Marcelin in France that pardon came and his chains fell off of their own accord. The distance traveled was some twelve thousand miles, a journey that would have taken many years without horse or money. Like Tibetan criminals up to recent times, he had been thrown on the mercy of the world; only by being a penitent could he hope for nourishment and even life itself.

> Some of us are usurers
> Others thieves and murderers.
> We sin by self-indulgence,
> By excess pride and lies.
> We who lead a worldly life
> Are drawn so deeply into sin
> That only by the greatest miracle
> Will God have mercy on us.

It was typical of the later Middle Ages that judges stopped demanding religious observances. Banishment might be for five or twenty years to somewhere like Cyprus, and if the criminals came home, well and good. However, just as money could buy salvation, it could also mitigate if not stave off exile.

The most important shrines of the eleventh century were in Rome, Jerusalem, and the tomb of Christ's brother, the Apostle James in Compostela in northwestern Spain. In the eleventh century the route to Compostela became Europe's major pilgrim circuit. It was energetically fostered by the Cluniac order, which acted like a modern tourist agency with its own hospices and lodgings. The monks organized the devout into parties, made up new songs for the way, encouraged new roads and bridges, and published a splendid guidebook. The guidebook was just like a modern one: it explained how much money was needed, described the roads and rivers along the way, recommended clothing, and offered a list of useful foreign words. The route was probably the busiest trunk road in Christendom—and the shrewdest and most successful promotional campaign of the Middle Ages.

One reason for encouraging the faithful on this long and arduous journey was to mobilize public opinion behind the Church in its struggle with the nobility. Another was to recruit people for the Crusades against the Moors, who then ruled nearly the whole of the Iberian peninsula. Saint James's transformation from apostle-brother to warrior-horseman and "killer of Moors" encouraged many knights to stay and fight the infidel. The successful expulsion of Islam from most of Spain was due to this development.

There was a strong millennial fervor at this time, a belief that the world would soon be overthrown and the New Jerusalem installed. Among the poor it was like a cargo cult, promising that the rich would be brought low and the ordinary folk would inherit the earth. All the people felt that some personal sacrifice was essential, and from this feeling came much of the self-abnegation found among the Cistercians. The Church took advantage of both feelings to promote pilgrimages and their military counterparts, the Crusades to Spain and the Holy Land.

A pilgrim visiting Jerusalem might expect the journey to cost him a year's income. How did he raise it? If he were a landowner, he might sell some land to a monastery, just as the crusaders sold their vineyards and chattels to buy armor and horses. Sometimes the land was given as security for a loan; if the borrower did not return, it remained with the Church.

Economically pilgrimages had a powerful and lasting effect by compelling a redistribution of wealth through the loans and sales required to pay for them, and by spreading the wealth of one area into those the pilgrim visited or passed through. This aided the independence of the towns that provided a lot of these funds and thereby opened up the closed society of the eleventh century to the commercialism of the thirteenth and ultimately that of our own day.

More than anything else, travel broke down the insularity of peasant and town communities, habituating people to movement and the sight of new places and customs. The pilgrimages offered scope for change just by displaying it. It was symptomatic of the fascination with travel that one of the most widely read books in the fourteenth century was the account of the journeys of Marco Polo. Yet without the spur of guilt and the fear of divine retribution little of this would have happened, and the immense interchange of peoples and ideas might never have begun.

THE INDULGENCE WAS THE GOAD

The indulgence was a formal promise by the Church that a penance had been remitted. It was a dispensation from the earthly father on behalf of the heavenly father; it did not release the sinner from guilt (only confession and absolution could do that), but it excused all temporal punishment.

The first indulgences were offered toward the end of the eleventh century. For example, an indulgence was offered for visiting the monastery at Figeac that had been destroyed by the Moslems; it was assumed that visitors would make donations, thereby enabling the monastery to be rebuilt. In a pregnant move, the pope also granted remission of half a sinner's time in purgatory if he arranged to be buried in the abbey.

A few years later Urban II announced the First Crusade by offering that "every man who sets out for Jerusalem to liberate the Church of God shall have the *entire penance* for his sins remitted." This was later called the "plenary" indulgence because it erased all the penance due for the sins of a lifetime. It was an extraordinary guarantee of salvation. No wonder the crusaders flocked to the cross—and no wonder that people later demanded the same rights for money rather than the hardship of war.

The concept was not unreasonable: the sick and the maimed needed some way to do penance without having to make a pilgrimage. However, as with any hole in the dam of orthodoxy, what a thumb would stop at the start a dozen carts could not fill a few generations later. During the next four centuries the indulgence became the most popular spiritual tool, eclipsing every other sacred exercise. The system acquired an elaborate apparatus of dispensations and financial alternatives, and this undermined the original spiritual purpose.

Every shrine and bishopric attempted to issue its own indulgences and to offer as much as possible in order to improve sales. In one case a man was assured he would have as much space in heaven as he had on earth, thus promising the barons for eternity all the hunting forests they might require. The unscrupulous manipulation of these meretricious promises, especially during the schism, was possible only where the sacred concepts which had once guided Christianity had been laid aside.

The turning point came in 1352, just after the ravages of the Black Death, when Pope Clement VI allowed the population of Mallorca the indulgence for visiting Rome in return for simply making a payment equal to the cost of the journey. The precedent was ruthlessly exploited by the next pope who needed money and popularity, for ordinary people would pay anything to relieve the anxiety of sin. This was the nub of the problem, and it was perhaps the price paid for killing God.

The indulgence became the cornerstone of late medieval piety. The diocese which could not afford the huge sums Rome demanded for the right to issue indulgences became unpopular. Yet the system drained away money that could have been used locally for charity, rebuilding, and the work of the clergy. By the fifteenth century, otherwise reputable clergymen had no compunction in forging these rights. The Franciscans were the greatest offenders, along with the major cathedral chapters. Each salesman, like an insurance broker, tried to offer his clients a little more than they could obtain elsewhere. Where Urban II had promised one week's indulgence for a serious gift, four hundred years later the clergy were offering fourteen hundred *years* of remission for each time a pilgrim, or even a local parishioner, entered the church and merely viewed the relics! Urban II's guarantee, which sent thousands to the Crusades, would not have brought in a penny by the time of the Reformation.

Instead of being a stimulus to pilgrimage, the indulgence

had become an alternative to it: the journey could be made at home by reading a devotional book that explained the journey. The last step in this sorry and debasing affair was the right to buy someone else's indulgence, or to release the dead from purgatory. Salvation had become a commodity, embracing the now familiar capitalist concept of more for less. The modern world had been born.

RELIGION TRANSFORMED

THE VIRGIN AS INTERCESSOR

In the austere and transcendental world of 1100, extraordinary numbers of people were traveling all over Europe in search of penance. Be it through relics or Crusades, pilgrim needed to confess his sins and complete the full extent of the penances imposed by the clergy if he was not to go to hell.

The situation offered little hope. As sculpture and painting shows, there was little softness in God. He was the all-male arbiter, inexorably certain and judging with such fairness that few could expect to be saved. The Vézelay narthex was probably the last great statement of this view, which disappeared from sculpture between 1130 and 1140, never to appear again with the same austerity or indifference. Thereafter God opened Himself to his feminine side.

The Chartres Royal Portal ushered in a new approach: the Virgin Mary joined the judge and became the Queen of Heaven, ever ready to intercede for the sinner. After Chartres the figure of God welcomes pilgrim as father

The Virgin, north gable, Chartres cathedral.

rather than as judge, and Mary is often seated with Him. Justice has become humane and compassionate.

Her Stories and Miracles

One popular story of Peter and his brother Steven illustrates both the situation and the extraordinary change that occurred. It was an old story that was revised in the 1120s to include the Virgin:

> Peter is a venerated archdeacon, but he is a little greedy, and when he dies he is "led to a purgatorial state in punishment for his faults." Brother Steven is a corrupt judge who misappropriated houses and gardens belonging to Saint Lawrence and Saint Agnes.
>
> When Steven dies he goes to paradise for judgment; there Agnes shuns him, and Lawrence clutches his arm with a grip like that of a manacle. Christ sends him to the bottom pit of hell for his venality, and there he joins none less than Judas, who is being tortured (appropriately) with sharpened nails.
>
> On his way down Steven hears "from a long way off the lamenting souls who had been placed in punishments." These are the souls of the dead, and among them he recognizes his brother Peter. Steven is surprised to find Peter here because he had thought him a good man. Peter replies that he was in fact a little too greedy, to which Steven asks, "Do you hope in the end to achieve salvation?" This unexpected question suggests that even though Peter was a good man, salvation was not inevitable.
>
> Peter's reply is important. He hopes to be saved because he did good deeds for the Church, but only "if my Lord Pope were to say mass for me, with all his cardinals, and if God were generous." Even with the pope working for him, salvation would not be certain.
>
> Meanwhile, back in paradise, a Saint Praejectus had been called in because Judge Steven had given his shrine lots of gifts each year. This put the saint under a feudal obligation to the judge, so first he won over Lawrence and Agnes, who agreed to modify their claims on Steven. Then he had to approach Christ. To make sure that the original judgment would be overturned, he co-opted the Virgin Mary to appeal for him. This is the part of the story that was rewritten to give the Virgin the key role. None of the saints could now guarantee to intercede successfully on their own, and thus appeals for mercy came to be concentrated through one channel.
>
> On hearing Mary's appeal, Christ returned Steven to his body for "as long as required to do penance for his past sins" and to recite a prayer daily. In the original version it was the 118th Psalm, "Give thanks unto the Lord," but in the revised version Mary commanded him to recite her litany, *Beati Immaculati*. On returning to his body, Steven lived the thirty days needed to make good his injustices, including returning the saints' houses to them. He then died "no longer guilty." (*Dicta Anselmi, the "HM" collection*)

The details tell us an enormous amount about the expectations and fears of the early twelfth century. For a minor sin Peter finds himself in some unspecified state (not yet purgatory, for this *state* was not defined as a *place* until the next century) from which he might be saved if enough important people prayed for his release. If not, he would inevitably go to hell, for there was no other place to go. But the rogue Steven, who had been rightly consigned to hell, was saved by being allowed to complete his penance on earth. Peter, poor fellow, had not completed his earthly penance, and in spite of his goodness he was given no chance to do so.

This story was politically attuned to bringing the Church the maximum benefit. The clergy wanted pilgrim to complete fully any penance given him by the priest, and if he failed, it threatened that only through the prayers of the living could he be reprieved. It also warned of the dangers of tampering with any property owned by the saints, for ultimate judgment could depend on them. Further, Mary has no brief to watch over mankind. She must be appealed to specifically and through prayers and gifts reminded of pilgrim's existence and needs. This places the onus on pilgrim to be generous to the Church now, for later will be too late.

The effect these stories were designed to have on the community seems pretty clear. Today we would call the story of Peter and Steven a first-rate PR job. It demonstrates pilgrim's hopelessness when even Peter could be damned, and the enormous relief when it became known that the Virgin could alter the situation. These stories, and hundreds like them, were prepared by the intelligentsia, most of whom were monks. They and the pastoral clergy who worked in the field were deeply concerned with the emotional needs of their parishioners, and it would appear that these miracles were deliberately created to ease their burden.

The Satisfaction of the Mother

The cult of the Virgin was well established by 1140, yet the old motifs and ideas did not disappear at once. It took a couple of generations for the psychological implications to seep into medieval culture. The feminine symbol of the mandorla was still being set around the figure of God the Father and the occasional crypt was being commenced even two generations later. But during the second quarter of the twelfth century a revolution occurred which affected all perceptions and art, and Mary was brought up out of the ground into the sunlight, both literally and figuratively.

In the eastern Church Mary had been worshipped from earliest times. It has even been said that this had more to do with grammar than theology, for in Greek the term for the Holy Ghost, *hagia sophia*, is feminine, thereby introducing a female into the Trinity. On the other hand, the Latin for the Holy Ghost was *sanctus spiritus*, which is masculine, and this made the western Trinity exclusively male. An all-male godhead is extremely rare in world religions—one suspects because it is unbalanced, for we need to respect both sides of our nature, the male and the female. To worship one and deny the other prevented Christians from ex-

Theophilus arranges his contract with the devil on the left, and signs it on the right: Souillac.

pressing both sides of their inner needs. Psychologically we cannot, no matter how biased our cultural attitudes, ignore the two aspects of our anima, the male and the female. No matter how suppressed, both will express themselves in some way, just as the monks who tried to stifle their desires were inevitably assailed by the devil.

One of the more popular legends about the Virgin concerned Theophilus. The story of his compact with the devil, carved at Souillac, showed that if pilgrim prayed to her he could almost certainly expect to be forgiven. The pure and masculine justice of the Christ of Moissac had turned soft, for even the worst sinners could touch her heart. She was known to have protected a Parisian adulteress from the wrath of the woman she had cuckolded simply because she had daily honored the Virgin. Mary was the most sympathetic intercessor of all time, as the prior of Sauxillanges knew: "She is the sovereign remedy for the sick, for she can obtain from her Son all that she desires. She is merciful on our sins and relieves us in all our troubles."

It was the unexpected appearance of Mary in the judgment hall that transformed the Middle Ages. Where nearly everyone in 1100 feared he would be damned, by 1200 the majority could hope to be forgiven for most of their sins. Mary brought hope where there had been despair, thereby releasing people from a great burden. It felt like a fresh love affair, and from this moment on European culture and thought soared, creating in a few short years a new civilization.

Her Immense Popularity

In spite of popular enthusiasm, the Church refused to proclaim Mary's bodily assumption until 1950. This did not

The vitality of medieval culture, the imagination, and the urge to be reborn are encapsulated at Chartres: view of the spire over the south transept.

stop people's believing she was *the* intercessor, nor did it prevent the chapter of Chartres from dedicating the cathedral to her assumption. The belief was never damned as heretical because it was too important and too popular, but it played havoc with the incarnatory activities of the Holy Ghost. Christ could be bodily assumed because He was without original sin. That meant that He had not been conceived through the sinful act of sexual union. As only a virgin birth could ensure total lack of sin, to get the Virgin into heaven next to Him, she too had to have been conceived in the same way. The Holy Ghost therefore had to have visited twice, once to Mary and before that to her mother, Anna.

Cathedrals and abbeys were rededicated to her, especially the Cistercian foundations, for was not Saint Bernard called "the knight of the Virgin"?

At Chartres, in the right-hand door of the western portal, she sits enthroned, frontal and calm. A fully adult Jesus sits on her lap, no larger than a child, and His mother is set around Him like a throne, He on her womb. This is the feminized version of the central tympanum, in which the Father sits within the almond-shaped mandorla (see page 66). This shape has since ancient times symbolized the vulva and hence the Mother. Thus the male sits within the womb in both tympana, proclaiming a feminine foundation to the Trinity.

During the decades before the Virgin appeared in sculpture as the Queen of Heaven, a great chain of miracles began to occur, and relics suddenly turned up: cribs, milk from her breast, locks of hair. The most celebrated is the famous *camissa*, or tunic, which can still be seen at Chartres.

Many apocryphal stories were added to her traditional roles in the annunciation, the visitation, and the nativity. Starting before Mary's birth, the legends amplified the stories of her parents, Anna and Joachim, her birth and schooling, and her marriage. Many of the little graceful touches which we take for granted were invented only at this time: the ox and the ass, and the midwives who, when Joseph ran out of the stable for assistance, turned up uncalled. These stories made her a real woman and mother, allowing her to play the dual role of princess and confidante.

THE MAGI

Just as the life of the Virgin was elaborated, so the stories of people associated with her grew until the accretions hid the originals. At first they were acceptable because they were couched in the symbols of the times.

The Gospels are exceedingly brief on the subject of the magi; in the original the word means no more than wise men. Popular fantasy first increased their number to the mystic three, then made them into kings. For a while they came alone, later they arrived by horse or camel, surrounded by a huge retinue. The details of their presents were enhanced with additional meanings in the ninth century: gold is a gift to a king, frankincense is the symbol of His divinity, and myrrh is used by embalmers for His inevitable sacrifice. In the twelfth century the magi were universalized as all humanity by showing one of them as a youngster in his late teens, another as a mature man of forty, and the third as a wise old man of sixty.

As advertisers have always known, no product exists until it has been named, and since the magi of the Bible were nameless, the deficiency was made up by the pseudo-Bede. Caspar, which means "treasurer" in Persian, became the youngest, who brought frankincense; Balthazar, or "war lord," became the middle-aged man, who presented myrrh; Melchior, the eldest, whose name meant "king," brought the gold. It was not until Europeans began to travel the world in the fifteenth century that the magi were further universalized as the three races of the world, Caspar being light brown (and eventually yellow), Melchior white, and Balthazar black.

Finally, Satan himself entered the scene. The thirteenth-century mystic Mechthild of Magdeburg wrote: "When the strange star shone, Satan came to Bethlehem following swiftly after the three Kings, and looked angrily on the Child, for highest honor was done Him with rare gifts. Satan was in great perplexity."

This brings us to the Albigensians, for it reminds us of their heretical, yet logical, proposition that the Evil One had created the world and that only by God's sacrifice, in which the devil was trapped into killing God Himself, could Good come into it. No wonder Satan was perplexed.

THE SUFFERING CHRIST

As heresy cast doubt on the divinity of Christ, the Church replied by emphasizing His personal suffering. This was an easy way to affect the congregation. The naturalism and expression of emotion showed that Christ had suffered infinitely on the cross, and that only by that suffering could He have brought man to the possibility of salvation.

Early medieval artists generally avoided showing Christ in agony on the cross, preferring to depict Him with eyes open, body calm, His manner relaxed. A board was placed under his feet to avoid the distressful notion that the full weight of the body might be tearing at the pierced holes in His hands and feet. Indeed, the entire reality of nails piercing the center of the palm was iconographic rather than actual. The Romans never made this mistake, for the weight of the body would soon have pulled the nail through the skin of the hand; they nailed the wrist, not the palm, so that the body would remain supported by the sinews and cartilage.

However, from the end of the twelfth century, and especially in the thirteenth as the immanental views declined, the depiction of Christ was changed. He was shown dying or already dead, His eyes closed, His head drooping to one side, the blood pouring from the wound in His side. Even the elimination of one of the nails that fixed His feet to the cross added to His suffering by twisting one foot upon the other. In time, and increasingly after the plague, this modification developed a momentum of its own, for once the door to cheap emotional tricks had been opened, the way was clear for the full exploitation of agony.

THE DANSE MACABRE AND THE DECLINE IN SPIRITUALITY

Though the brevity of human life and the proximity of death was a commonplace of medieval preaching, the post-plague generations seem to have turned it into a central subject. The most powerful impact came from the gruesome and dismal Dance of Death, where skeletal figures, prancing obscenely across the fields, lead bonny ladies and well-fed prelates toward their untimely end, as on the walls of the abbey at La Chaise-Dieu.

This spectral and macabre image played upon a deep layer of fear that was represented in the story of Lazarus, who after his resurrection lived in continual misery and terror at the knowledge that he would have to pass through those dreadful portals yet again.

It is not that the hideous figures with gaping mouth and bowels crawling with worms represented a new idea; but it was only in the fifteenth century that the image became popular, supported by exquisite artistic realism that was able to depict the horrible details of decomposition. It was a sign of the times that people wanted to see the worms and not the flowers which would sprout thereafter.

Throughout the Middle Ages there was an ever-present contempt for the clergy, combined with a great respect for the offices they performed. In the thirteenth century poverty was a virtue and the begging Franciscans were among the most popular orders; by the fifteenth century people were beginning to see that poverty was a social disease rather than a virtuous emulation of the apostles, and hostile poems became popular:

> Let us pray that the Jacobins
> May consume the Augustinians,
> And that the belts of the Minorites
> May hang all the Carmelites.

Typically impudent perhaps, but much laughed over at the time, was the quip made by a churchman during the ceremony of his election as abbot: when the news came that his mistress had given birth to a son, he remarked, "Today I have twice become a father. God's blessing on it!"

Art had come to enhance the material world rather than the spiritual. Where objects were arranged for their mean-

Senlis cathedral south transept, details on the western buttress.

ing, like the sun and the moon that flanked many crucifixions, they came to be selected for their effect, such as the intriguing reflections on a curved mirror or the delicate pattern of false arches and pinnacles placed partway up a wall rather than on the roof where they belonged.

The emotional tranquillity found at Chartres or Vézelay is missing at Rouen. The deep colors of the stained glass have been replaced by a mild gray, the otherworldly figures by well-dressed nobles. The spiritual meanings given to the various zones of the building, to the cathedral as paradise itself, and to the vaults as the canopy of heaven have all drifted into limbo.

It is no wonder that today we understand so little of symbolism, for we are the inheritors of the fifteenth century. Although the twelfth century inaugurated many of the concepts that made today possible, it did so in a spiritual context that is unknown to us. When we returned to these ideas it was within an utterly different milieu in which the essentials were status and profit rather than spiritual universals.

3

SYMBOLISM AND MEANING

SYMBOLIC CONCEPTS AND GEOMETRY

SYMBOL AND ALLEGORY

Symbols are an essential ingredient in all religious beliefs, for they provide the most powerful images in life. With the myths that accompany them, they compensate for what cannot be comprehended. They imply more than their immediate meaning, and the more they imply the more potent they become. Thus in the circle, the cave, and the moon, for example, we meet universals that appeal to all.

Most of us tend to cultivate ideas which cannot be proved. They are the private convictions that give meaning to life and establish our place in the universe. We can stand the most extraordinary hardships when we are convinced they make sense. It is the role of symbols to encapsulate these ideas, and for this reason they go back to the most ancient fantasies and needs of our species.

Symbols raise man beyond the mere material roles of acquiring and spending. They cannot be created consciously, though we may consciously decide to let them into our lives, or to enrich them by applying them to new ideas, as the Church did during the Middle Ages.

Symbol is not the same as allegory. Symbols universalize ideas such as nobility, whereas the knight saving the damsel in distress is allegory. Nobility is an attribute of all people at all times, but the knight is limited both historically and geographically. Only the symbol can approach the universal by integrating ideas into one form that we all respond to.

The more fundamental symbols are abstract, and the first of them is the circle, which contains the essence of many other symbols: the sun and the earth, the heavens and the moon, the movement of the sky and repetitive cycles all appear circular. The circle is formed by a compass turned from a central point, and as it has neither beginning nor end, it suggests the eternal and the infinite. The space within it is one, lying beyond the inevitable changes of corruptible reality. Thus the circle is universally recognized as the symbol for essence and spirit.

The circle may also be thought of as the central point around which the arc of the cosmos has been drawn. God stands at this point and wields the compass that scratches the circle onto the blank mass of original chaos. Illuminators showed Him creating the universe with the dividers—dividing the waters, etc.—just as the master mason would be shown creating the templates.

The second fundamental symbol is the square. It is universally recognized as the earth, as substance. We establish our material security within the four walls of our house or room, within the four walls of the fortress or, ultimately, the four walls of Heavenly Jerusalem itself. Nothing in nature has straight sides and right-angled corners, yet we live in houses and on land bounded in this unnatural way, perhaps because it symbolically satisfies us.

As the circle contains a point, so the square contains a cross. We can place ourselves in the center of the cross and orient ourselves, in the deepest sense, to the center of the universe. It is significant that when we feel uncertain we say we are "disoriented." As human beings we have four directions, two sides, back, and front. When we stand and want to locate the pole, we raise our arms toward the rising and the setting sun and know that our face is looking northward toward the pole star and the axis through the

The circular tower with eight openings behind the octagon with four turrets is set on a square base decorated with rectangles and spheres: Notre-Dame, Étampes.

earth. Thus the cross represents concepts similar to the square.

Symbols can be joined. The circle and cross together suggest the seasonal rhythms of the world, those aspects of earth which partake of the Creator. And each symbol will imply others. The four arms of the cross imply five because, just as the circle has both arc and center and therefore suggests two, so the four arms pointing outward intersect to locate a center and move our attention onto five.

Five is the sum of four, the material universe, and one, the spirit. So the pentagon represents the material sanctified by the divine. It also refers to Christ, as the human imbued with the spirit and as God become man. It is substance and essence united in the one.

One last example (from here on the meanings of the figures can become a little idiosyncratic) is the octagon. In the East it represents the essence of all material creation, for it is formed out of two squares, combining the four of the earth with the duality of its nature. But for the Christian it is seven plus one, seven being the number of earthly cycles, of the vital rhythms of the manifest which, when combined with one as spirit, represents the resurrection, the stage after we have completed our time on earth. Thus the Christian interpretation is time-oriented while the eastern stems from the form itself.

As with form, so with number: we have lost much of our sensitivity to the meanings of the numbers because our education accustoms us to regard number as simply an expression of relative quantity. Yet the meanings for the first four numbers represent truths so profound that there is not a culture or a tribe that has not understood them in a similar way. The number *one* is of course the First Cause. *Two*, the duality, is the essential nature of all created things, coming from the first breath of God in which He conceived of self and other, and from which evolved all existence. It represents the most fundamental cleavage of all, that between essence and substance or, if you like, heaven and earth, yin and yang.

From that duality and the endless patterns of contradictions it engenders comes *three*, the Creative Principle. In every dispute there must be a resolution, as the Schoolmen would say. Three is the number of growth and spirituality, of increase and change. Thus most godheads have three aspects, be they from Egypt, Rome, or India.

Finally, *four* is the material universe, as the square of two. It is the superabundance of duality, the real world as manifested from the spiritual. Hence the four walls around the Garden of Eden, the four rivers of Paradise, the four arms of the church which give it stability and locate it in eternal space and time.

The numbers after four are not as fundamental. Different cultures interpret them in their own ways, and the universality of meanings becomes lost in complexities of interpretation. (For further discussions of specific symbols elsewhere in this book, consult the index.)

The first part of this chapter deals with some of the issues which were incorporated into Christianity from the past, and with the techniques for incorporating them into the building, both by number and geometry. The major issues will be illustrated in the cathedral of Chartres, where they are more clearly expressed than anywhere else. The following part discusses more purely Christian concepts and how they affected architectural style for five hundred years.

ORIENTATION

There is growing evidence that at some distant time in the past most sacred sites were selected, and the temples on them oriented, so that they related to the heavenly powers. By placing the church on top of the most sacred pagan sites, Christian missionaries ensured that the new retained all the virtues which had been acquired by the old. Not only did the new church take over the space and therefore hide the remains of the previous faith from view, but by physically supplanting it, the new appeared victorious over the old.

The clergy often simply followed the orientations or emplacements they inherited. Whether they understood the reasoning or the connections is hard to say, though one has the impression that at least up to the early part of the Middle Ages they did.

As ancient gods lived on mountains, in caves, in trees, and in lakes, shrines would often point toward these things to invite the spirits into the sanctuary itself. The church that replaced the shrine would usually be oriented the same way, as is shown by the fact that few churches were built facing due east before the Reformation. They face every which way, like the winds themselves; some point south, some north, and very few face exactly east. At times they face the midsummer sun or are aligned to some aspect of the heavens. The rising sun on the church's saint's day will often pass through the eastern windows and strike the altar or the western doors. In some places the churches face other churches, as if to share their powers with one another on some gigantic telegraphic line of communication. These connections are called ley lines and were like some manifestation of cosmic powers passing across the surface of the earth.

The cathedral of Chartres, for example, faces 43° north of east, so that in late summer the afternoon sun streams directly through the great northern rose window. This orientation is twisted a little to the north of the most ancient part of the building, the subterranean chapel of Saint Lubin under the altar. The orientation of this chapel is the same as the longitude of Chartres. This is to say, the inclination of the church from a line joining it to the north pole is the same as the town's inclination above the equator. No maps were needed to determine this, nor was any understanding of terrestrial degrees of longitude or latitude. The builders need only have measured the angle to the pole star on any fine night and then aligned the building from the east by the same amount.

This is an ancient idea that appears in other countries and shrines, including Angkor Wat in Cambodia and Borobodur in Indonesia. It relates the sacred precinct to the pole star which marks the axis of the universe, for this star alone remains stationary while the universe swings around it. Symbolically this axis is like a tree, for it links paradise with earth, essence to substance, and the present to the future. In Gothic churches the axis rises through the center of the building and ascends through the opening in the central boss toward heaven. At Chartres this opening is enormous, three times the size of any other. It is like a porthole or door into the cosmos. By orienting the cathedral to the pole star, the builder expressed in plan what this central axis explained in elevation, the indissoluble connection between the site of the cathedral and the axis of the universe.

THE DRAGON AND SAINT MICHAEL

The earthly manifestation of cosmic powers has long been associated with the dragon, which inhabits the fantasies of all cultures. Apollo was installed at Delphi only after his victory over the serpent Python. The Chinese dragon represented the powers of the earth, flowing like water through the mountain chains and down the valleys. No wise man placed himself in the dragon's path, but every wise man sought to benefit from its proximity. The dragon was to be wheedled, not destroyed, for in ancient times the harnessing of the power of the dragon was the essential prerequisite to making any site habitable—especially a sacred site.

When benevolent, the dragon brought fortune and good weather, but until it was tamed it represented the ultimate chaos and the unbridled forces of nature. It was barbarian, lawless, and ultimately death itself: Kali the Creator and Kali the Destroyer with a belt of skulls. The Uroboros swallowing his own tail is guardian of the treasure (which symbolizes our psyche). As set out in the Chartres labyrinth, we have to curb the dragon if we are to grow, just as Theseus had to kill the Minotaur. He who curbs the dragon is a hero, for he has faced and tamed the nether forces of the underworld, the abysmal fears of the unconscious.

Because Christians associated the dragon with paganism and Satan, one of the four powers closest to God, an archangel, no less, was empowered to deal with it. Saint Michael is often depicted standing victorious over the dragon, commanding the prominent hills from which the dragon had once concentrated its powers. Mont-Saint-Michel is one of the most famous of these representations; from Cornwall to Sorrento this saint perches on the tallest peaks.

Hence the many Christian stories of bishops and saints meeting the dragon in combat and forcing it to yield. Just as a stake was used to eliminate vampires, the dragon is skewered by the crook. Thrust through the dragon's heart, the tree becomes the central axis, the navel of the world, connecting heaven to earth. The stake has made the dragon man's servant rather than his master. Thus the myth is in essence the struggle for salvation, and like sin, the dragon has not died. It has been overcome for the moment, but it will return, and Saint Michael will again sally forth to do battle in a cycle without end. Myths such as these make it easier for human beings to cope with the reality of our mortality in a universe that seems to go on forever.

THE SUN AND THE MOON

Between eternity and mortality all life moves in rhythms and cycles that seem to pulse from one extreme to the other. As medieval scholars would say, there are opposing views to every proposition on earth. To every male there is a female, to every good an evil. Is our view of the universe dualistic because our brains are divided into two halves, with their left and right hemispheres each approaching reality from a different standpoint, or are our brains binary because they are the natural and inevitable product of a dualistic world? Whichever it be, the structure of our brain ensures that every observation and every question will be viewed from more than one direction.

We enjoy classifying opposites: for example, almost everywhere we go in the world, whatever the race or lan-

The tower of the sun, north tower, Chartres cathedral.

guage, people feel that the sun is male and the moon female. The moon's monthly cycle more or less coincides with
a woman's periodicity. The moon is the light in the dark,
and in a chauvinistic world it properly reflects the light
from the masculine sun, full of energy and power. So in
Christian times the Virgin was called the Queen of Heaven,
for she was sister to the sun and bride to Christ the Son.
Thus, allegorizing Mary as the moon implies that she as
Church reflected the light from the sun, Abbot Suger's *lux
nova* (see page 101).

If these puns seem confusing or farfetched, they nevertheless lie at the root of much religious symbolism the
world over, for people find them endlessly fascinating and
meaningful. Consider the special significance that Christians accord to Sunday, the day of the sun. Drawings of the
crucifixion showed the sun and the moon each on one side
of the cross, for together they declared the extent of God's
rule over the universe.

This may explain why the two western towers at Chartres
have different heights. The northern tower is taller than the
southern, and although the northern was built much later,
it may have always been taller because the southern tower
is capped with an iron emblem of the moon, the northern with a sun. Thus the towers may have symbolized the
union of the two principles the sun and moon usually
represent, the masculine and the feminine. The solar symbol is over the taller tower, just as the solar year is
longer than the lunar year by eleven days. The differing
heights of the two towers may then reflect the different
"years" that served to calculate the date of the Easter festivals, which were to recur until the end of time, when the
Easter sun would be united with the Easter moon in a perpetual spring.

In the northern hemisphere, Easter celebrated Christ's
assumption and the advent of spring and thus the season of
rebirth, that magical moment when cold and leafless trees
were transformed into sap-filled fruitfulness.

The traditional anniversary of the crucifixion is March
25, which is also the Feast of the Annunciation (being nine
months before Christmas) and the starting date of the
world at the Creation. How neatly this package adds to the
nature of the spring festival and Christ's birth! One might
ask why this important day was not made to coincide with
the equinox. In Middle Eastern tradition one cannot be
sure that the equinox has been reached until *three* days
afterward, which is why the rabbi enters the temple on
March 22 and emerges three days later dressed in new
raiment.

This is also why Christmas falls on December 25 and not
on the shortest winter day, December 22, for His birth
from the womb of Mary—the Christian sunrise—coincides
with the recognizable rebirth of the sun following the dark-
est day of the year. These patterns add great richness to the

The choir of Saint-Denis, showing the axis that passes through the center of the apse and exits toward heaven through the cross on the peak of the roof.

passage of time, and Christians feel calmed and certain in their immutability.

THE AXIS MUNDI AND THE HORIZONTAL

The search for a calm center between contradictions has led some to the eye of the storm, where all the incompatibles of life have been resolved. This blissful place is the *axis mundi*, the vertical axis which joins, according to *Il Purgatorio*, the devil at the center of the earth and God beyond the pole star. Around the *axis mundi* all things move and have their being, but on it the yin and yang of life are perfectly balanced.

At Reims and Chartres this axis may be placed through the crossing, and at La Chaise-Dieu through the apse, to join the church to the Heavenly City. Where there is an illuminated lantern over the crossing, as at Germigny-des-Prés and Laon, it is reminiscent of Jacob's ladder, which connects our world to the spiritual. In a circular building such as Neuvy-Saint-Sépulchre there is only one axis, and that is up. Compare the photograph of Laon on page 121 with the one of Neuvy-Saint-Sépulchre on page 76.

In addition to the vertical axis, there are two horizontal ones. (Figure 1.) Both represent essential aspects of the Christian teaching. The longitudinal axis from the western doors to the apse represents pilgrim's progress along the

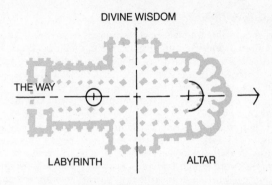

Figure 1. The meaning of the axes at Chartres.

Way from the mundane world at the western entry to the most spiritual at the eastern, where he hopes to meet God at the Eucharist. At Chartres this axis passes over the labyrinth, the symbol of the Way to God here on earth. Because Christ said "I am the Way," this axis represents the Man lying along the length of the building, His head in the apse and His arms outstretched along the transepts, properly called the "arms" of the church.

Just as the longitudinal axis represents the Man and the Way, so the transverse axis represents the woman and the means—or should we say the Virgin and gnosis, or divine knowledge. Mary was the embodiment of *hagia sophia*, or sacred wisdom, and as such she became the patron of the Seven Liberal Arts. At Chartres the old laws, the past, and the teachings of the Old Testament prophets are carved on the north side. On the south are the new law and Christ's covenant, the apostles and the teachings of the confessors. Between the blank walls of the transepts the Way flows like a stream between the banks of knowledge: the boat/nave is stabilized by the outriggers of gnosis.

At Chartres the cross axis of the cathedral intimates the Virgin's role as guide along the Way. She is like Ariadne in the labyrinth offering the rope to Theseus who, like pilgrim, would otherwise founder and be lost on the shoals of heresy.

> Beware, for love alone without knowledge remains unfocused, unaimed, undirected. The consequence is pointless, but through the medicine of knowledge joy is anchored so that love is directed to the Subject of all love.

This was the opinion of the scholars at Chartres since the time of Fulbert in the early eleventh century. It had been questioned by Bernard of Clairvaux, who believed that faith alone was enough. Though he won his argument against Abelard, in the end faith was to be limited by reason in the works of the Schoolmen.

DOORS AND DIRECTIONS

We should imagine the horizontal axes of the church extending beyond the building infinitely in all directions, toward all *four* sets of doors, which Saint John described
when he wrote that the Heavenly City "had a wall great and
high, and had twelve gates . . . on the east three gates; on
the north three gates; on the south three gates; and on the
west three gates. . . ."

Therefore the church, as the embodiment of the earthly
Garden of Eden, had four sets of doors along its four axes.
Those to the east were guarded by "cherubim, and the
flaming sword which turned every way" that God installed
after the expulsion. It was the function of the church to find
the penitent a way past this sword, that "on the sabbath it
shall be opened" (Ezekiel 46:1).

It is an essential characteristic of sacred sites that they be
isolated from the world, with a specific entry point and a de-
finable way through the precinct. At Chartres, pilgrim
enters through the western doors, on which are carved the
basic truths of Christianity: that Christ was born of woman
and was bodily resurrected on death. The resurrection is
the proof of His divinity and thus, in a circular way, proves
that Mary was Mother of God. Christ in the central tympanum welcomes those who believe the truths written on
either side of Him. That is all, it is very simple: believe this
and you are a Christian.

So pilgrim affirms his belief before starting along the
main axis toward redemption at the altar. On the Way he
needs guidance, which is presented in the lateral doors. The
north door is on our left and the south on our right. All cultures have drawn a distinction between the right and left
sides of the body, perhaps because most of us are naturally
right-handed. The right is the positive side, the left is relatively negative or malefic. The right leads us upward, the
left downward; the right reflects the positive aureole of the
right hemisphere of the brain, the left the more critical ca-
pacities of the left hemisphere.

Clocks (but not sundials) turn to the right. All processions, be they Shinto, Hindu, or the Stations of the Cross
(one excludes the Black Sabbath, for obvious reasons),
move from the left-hand side of the church to the right.
Language reflects these ideas, for the French for left has
become our "gauche," the Latin for left our "sinister." One
is "left out" or "left alone."

The sun rises in the east, where we look to the Garden of
Eden and Jerusalem. Its warming rays stimulate ideas of
resurrection and salvation, and the east is altogether the
most positive direction in a cold climate. In the northern
hemisphere the sun passes toward the south, so when we
face the sun it moves from left to right like a procession.
Shadows are cast on the northern side, where it is damp
and chill and the moss will grow. In winter there is not

much pleasure to be had on the north side; it is the devil's, and while this was not true for Norsemen, it was for Christians who remembered where the Norsemen came from.

The early Christians were unable to agree on how to interpret some of these things, but by the time of Chartres they had sorted it out. The south side of the cathedral is the bishop's side, and God's, because it is the sun's, and by analogy the Son's. This is why the sculptures on the southern doors at Chartres represent the events and teaching since Christ, with the martyrs and confessors. It is the New Testament door, and it refers to the new covenant. The northern doors on the left represent the past in the Old Testament figures and allegories of the Church in the stories of Mary and Job.

THE DOORWAY AS VULVA AND PEARLY GATE

No door is merely an opening from one space to another. Our deepest emotions can be moved as powerfully by a doorway as by the sun or the moon, though most of the time habit dulls our sensitivity to its role as the gate which welcomes or excludes, depending on its design. Fundamentally, the door represents both the vulva through which we were born and the threshold of Paradise through which we may be born again.

The origin of the Christian western front is the Roman *castrum*, or castle gate. The arrangement is defensive, designed in the practical way of the Romans to deter an enemy and defend those within. The Christian westwork excludes the satanic enemy and defends the faithful.

In early buildings such as Jumièges, the twin towers resemble a huge keep that has been split open for the instant so we may pass through, like the jambs of some gigantic doorway into the empyrean. In drawings and poems the entry into Paradise through the stars is located in the constellation of Gemini, the twins. They look not unlike the prophets who flank the church portal itself. Jacob's ladder is shown leading up to Gemini with "the angels of God ascending and descending on it" (Genesis 28:12). Even when the wish to cover the church with towers had abated, the two pointed spires at the west usually remained stretching to infinity, assuring pilgrim that the transitory will be connected to the eternal.

The west front need not have the same number of stories or the same proportions as the nave and aisle behind, for it is an independent triumphal entry. The central door is the most important, for it is aligned with the main axis of the cathedral and leads directly to the high altar. It was opened only for processions, burials, and great occasions when the clergy took the relics, their most important asset and the visible demonstration of God's power, through the central door in ritual pomp. To carry the relics out of the security of their sanctified home was an act of trust; the return of the

The west front of Saint-Denis, with three doors, one of the first rose windows, and at one time two towers.

relics was a triumph, like the welcome given the hero laden with trophies and spoils. The modern political parade with its ticker tape and brass bands shares the same roots.

When the great western doors were opened and the faithful looked into the mysteries within, the symbolism was overtly sexual. First the Church was seen as the Virgin and the Bride of Christ. Then, in time, this symbolism was enriched to include Christ's entering the church like the morning sun, piercing the glass of the apse windows, carrying His cross and holding it slanted downward like a beam of sunlight. Seen through the western doors, it would have been like some celestial apotheosis. The imagery and the action were both penetrative. Christ in glory entered into the church, which was Mary, fulfilling her with His ray of light.

Thus the doors form the entry into the Way, the vulva of the mother as sanctuary and home. The relationship was comprehended as the union of heaven and earth, reenacting the annunciation itself, and of the sun at springtime bringing all things to life. The symbolism was so strong that rulers used it for their own purposes.

THE GALLERY OF KINGS

In ancient times the sun was worshipped as the bringer of light and warmth, from which all living things derive their life. Its apotheosis at the spring equinox, which heralded the victory of day over night, and Christ's triumph over death in the Easter rituals were celebrated at the same time. This moment is the sun in victory, or *sol invictus*.

Emperors and kings took this symbolism for themselves: when riding in triumph, they would have the sun displayed over their heads. They too were the *sol invictus*. Thus the German emperor identified himself with the Victorious Christ and was referred to as Christ's Vicar at a time when the pope was merely the Vicar of Saint Peter.

Palaces often had an arcaded opening above their impregnable lower walls. From it the king would present himself to the people in the morning with the sun behind him, likening himself to the epiphany, or the supernatural manifestation of Christ as king. In doing this, the kings increased their own authority by aligning their position with God's. After 1200 the Church used the same idea in reverse, incorporating a gallery of kings over the western doors at Paris and on the transepts at Chartres. In the coronation cathedral of Reims they were moved up to the skyline, as close to godliness as they could get.

The kings look down on pilgrim, detachedly acclaiming his merit or at least loftily implying the merits he may receive when he comes before God. Above the kings is the rose window as the eye of Church and God (see page 121), and above that the twin spires stretch skyward. Every part of the front continued the symbolism of the entry as gateway and hence the meeting place between God's world and man's: the towers linked heaven and earth vertically, the gallery joined pilgrim with the temporal powers and the king's authority with God's, the doors symbolized re-entry into salvation around the axis of the Way to the altar and the eastern gateways. These messages are reinforced in the sculpture.

South porch and gallery of kings at Chartres cathedral.

THE MANDORLA AND THE TREE OF LIFE

The figure of God the Father over the doorways was often, at least up to the mid-twelfth century, enclosed within an almond shape, which was not used around any other aspect of the divinity (see Figure 2 and the tympanum of Charlieu, page 182). This shape is called a mandorla, from the Latin for "almond," and it is constructed from two arcs, each of whose center lies on the opposite arc.

The arcs are generated from circles that represent the godhead. Being formed from two circles suggests the first division into aspects, from which comes the duality of existence: not unlike the meaning given to the number eleven (see the discussion of the labyrinth on page 74). Two equilateral triangles fit inside. The point of the upper triangle represents the First Principle, which bifurcates into essence and substance at its base. From this first duality is derived all manifested creation, represented in the point of the lower triangle. Further, the upward-pointing triangle concerns the masculine sky god and the downward-pointing triangle the underworld feminine aspect (see the discussion of crypts on page 84).

Containing both triangles, the mandorla is the perfect expression of the Creative Principle, fecund and generative, and by implication the opening into the womb of creation. In fact it looks like a vulva, and enfolding God the Father it suggests the mother, thereby balancing the male and female principles. Appropriately, Ambrose calls the Virgin "the temple of God" in his work *On the Holy Spirit*.

It was a significant consequence of the revolution in medieval theology that came with the cult of the Virgin that this motif was used mainly in the Romanesque period. Like the crypt, it had largely disappeared by 1200, to be replaced by another symbolism in the labyrinth.

Where the mandorla, usually placed over the western entry, contains two triangles, the eastern end could be said

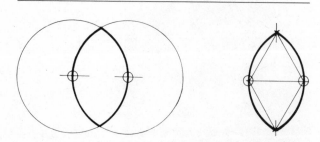

Figure 2. The mandorla, constructed from two circles, and the two triangles within in.

to include six, for we can draw a hexagon within its circle. Now six is the number of perfection (see the discussion of the labyrinth) and is placed at the head of the church, while the mandorla, representing the Creative Principle, is set over the west. Where the mandorla represents the generative principle from which all reality has been manifested, the circle symbolizes the totality that gave it birth. The perfect is at the altar, the manifest by the entry from the world.

The mandorla is often placed over a central trumeau, or doorpost, as at Vézelay. Together they form a vertical axis that is the symbolic equivalent of the axis through the dome or the crossing. This is an *axis mundi*, suggestive of the tree which connects the world to the heavens. Immutably rooted in substance while its leaves wave in the easy fluidity of the sky, the tree partakes of both worlds.

The associations of the tree are rich: Buddha found enlightenment under a tree; on the tomb of Adam as first man Seth planted the tree from which was made the cross to immolate the First Man; the Druids worshipped the oak and the yew, and every religion has had its sacred groves, be they in forests or made of stone.

Inside the church a huge cross was often suspended over the altar, as in Saint-Maclou in Rouen. Thus Adam's tree occupies the choir of the church as another *axis mundi*, an axis through which the mass at the altar may ascend to heaven through Christ's sacrifice on the cross. The tree is similar to Jacob's ladder, just as the twins Gemini remind us of the jambs of the pearly gates. Thus, both consciously and unconsciously, the clergy incorporated into the church the major aspects of their faith and the psychological fundamentals that are common to all mankind.

GEOMETRY: APPLYING SYMBOLS TO ARCHITECTURE

Geometry was overwhelmingly important in Gothic design. It constituted the very principle of its order and esthetic cohesion. Houses and factories can be utilitarian arrangements of timber and brickwork without impairing their function, but sacred buildings have only one essential function, and that is to exemplify the spirit. Therefore every step in the laying out of a sacred building is itself a sacrament. This is traditionally done through number and geometry because there are meanings in shapes and numbers that reflect the natural order of creation. They are seldom consciously part of our lives, so their meanings remain veiled. Yet these fundamentals affect all of us, even when we are unaware of them. For the ancients there was no separation between number and meaning; they were one and the same.

At the basis of number lies the sacred concept of analogy, where all creation, in various degrees, reflects God's image as shadows of the Creator. Erigena wrote that "we understand a piece of wood or a stone only when we perceive God in it," and by logical deduction, when men shape wood and stone using God's proportions and harmonies, He will be perceived in the product itself. This is why the architect, as both the user of symbols and the shaper of the stones that embody them, came to hold such a high position in medieval society.

Some of the meanings are obvious, such as the symbol of the cross in the plan of a church. Some become clear when we know something of numbers, such as the use of seven bays across the Chartres transepts to represent knowledge in the Seven Liberal Arts. Others, such as those used in geometry, are more difficult to understand.

It is generally true that the more meanings we find in a thing, the richer it becomes. Geometry is the queen of meaning because, properly used, it combines form with number and symbol. A circle set around a square unites all the meanings of the circle and the square with those of zero and four. Further, when the circle is outside the square a relationship is suggested between the two which is perceived differently than if the circle were placed inside the square. You might like to draw them and ponder the differences.

Through geometry, and to a lesser degree through number, the medieval architects sought to embody the whole of Christian knowledge, theological, moral, natural, and historical. They tried to give everything a place, and though some were as contradictory as the cycles of the sun and the moon, the masters attempted to reconcile and incorporate all sacred knowledge into the plan. The design of the cathedral of Chartres illustrates this.

Geometry is used in every step in the design of the great south rose at Chartres cathedral. The full elevation can be seen on page 65.

THE GEOMETRY OF THE CATHEDRAL OF CHARTRES

Form and Number

In any church plan the shape of the building—the numbers and the proportions—must reflect the great truths. Two and four are the proper numbers for the west, three and seven for the east. Thus the western doors, be there one or three, fit between the two towers. Two is the number of duality, of the first division in the act of creation between the things of the spirit and the things of the world, between essence and substance. The towers have four sides, which is 2^2, and which symbolizes the material world. Thus pilgrim enters from the western end through the symbols of the mundane from which he has come and between the doors which express the truths he must accept if the rest is to be meaningful.

He then proceeds toward the east, through the nave which is the ark of God's chosen. He passes over one of the critical points in the geometry, on which lies the labyrinth as the exemplification of the Way. His path leads to the crossing, the *axis mundi*, the calm position of rest around which everything has been properly arranged. Through the center of the crossing lies the transverse axis of the Virgin and of knowledge as the guide.

Beyond the crossing lies the inner temple and the chapels. The three largest form a triple crown, for three is the number of the spirit, properly represented by circles. Pilgrim thus moves from the duality of existence toward his redemption in the spirit, from the twos and the squares at the west to the three and the circles at the east. However, there are three doors in the west, just as there are four additional chapels between the three largest in the east. The doors as the entry into the church as the City tell pilgrim of the spiritual world within, while the four chapels remind us that even here this City still had to be made by men from earthly materials. More fundamentally, no symbol is complete without its opposite, and every meaning implies its inverse.

The symbolism of the Virgin required the use of both seven and nine: seven because she is patron of the Seven Liberal Arts, nine because she was in Dante's words "the root of the Trinity." Thus there are seven bays in the nave to the crossing and nine to the western doors. There are seven bays across the transepts and seven chapels. There were to have been nine towers, and there are nine bays from the altar to the labyrinth. (See La Chaise-Dieu for a similarly purposeful use of numbers.)

The Diamonds and Their Lengths

To transform number and form into architecture, the master builders employed geometry, for only then would the layout be orderly, the structural sizes properly determined, and the fundamental meanings made explicit. Only a portion of the cathedral's extraordinary richness can be described here as a demonstration of what should be found underlying the design of every sacred building. The geometry may appear a little complex, yet it will show why the medieval masters, like nearly all architects, were fascinated by the power of geometry and depended on it.

In Figure 3 the basic principles are expressed as three diamonds. Diamonds representing the Trinity would be equal in size, as at Cluny. But for the Virgin they need to be unequal, one for her and two smaller ones for her flanking bodyguards or attendants. Thus she dominates an otherwise trinitarian arrangement, just as her powers to forgive were coming to dominate the judgment hall.

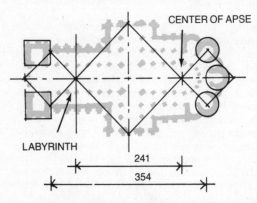

CENTER OF APSE

LABYRINTH

241

354

Figure 3. The first step in the geometry for Chartres cathedral.

The diamond on the left locates the Royal Portal and the squares of the towers and touches the center of the labyrinth at its eastern tip. The diamond on the right touches the center of the apse and locates and encloses the three major chapels. The larger diamond in the middle, which joins the altar to the labyrinth, also determines the faces of the transepts. The importance of the labyrinth may be gauged by the position it occupies in this geometry, as the counterpart to the altar at the west.

The length of the central diamond had been made 241 feet, the distance between the centers of the flanking diamonds 354 feet. (This was not our foot, of course, but the foot of the first master, which was that of the Romans: 294.5 mm.) There is little obvious significance in these numbers. Twenty-four times ten would have clearly related to the twelve apostles, the twelve tribes of Israel, and so on. Thirty-six times ten would seem more appropriate than 354. So why were these lengths chosen? And why was the crossing made a rectangle rather than a square, with sides of 56 feet and 48 feet?

These four dimensions set out the building, and after that the foot unit was never used again. Geometry took over, and every pier, every wall, and all the details were derived from the first units. They were the shouts that launched the avalanche; from them, by skillful and graduated steps, the masters determined every form and part of the building.

In fact these four dimensions represent divine truths in an abstract and more universal way than language, through a system called in Hebrew *gematria*, which is as ancient as number itself. Each letter of the alphabet was given a number: the letter A was one, B was two, and so on to the twenty-second letter, the last in the Latin alphabet of the twelfth century. Considering the number of rings in the labyrinth, this in itself may have been significant.

For example, the phrase *Beata Virgo*, the Blessed Virgin, consists of 2 for the B, plus 5 for the E, plus 1 for the A, and so on to a total of 96. Half of this number was the length of the crossing. In the other direction, the width of the crossing was numerically equivalent to *Maria Mater Dei*. Thus the two liturgical phrases are written into the core of her building.

From point to point the middle diamond is 241 feet long, which number is the sum of the phrase *Beata Virgo Maria Assumpta* plus one (in *gematria* the one as the Godhead may be added to or subtracted from any phrase). Most wonderfully, this phrase is also the dedication of the cathedral. It has been enshrined in the central geometric figure to locate the center of the choir and the labyrinth, and both transept doors are dedicated to Mary's gnosis.

The distance between the centers of the two minor diamonds of 354 feet, so there might be no doubt about who really rules at Chartres, is the Virgin's number as *Regina Coelis*, the Queen of the Sky. Like innumerable mother goddesses had been before her, she is the moon whose year consists of 354 days.

Having worked all this out, the master architect had only begun to create the City of God. His next step was to move out from the numbers to the forms of the building.

The First Geometry

As you stand in the crossing, notice that the bays immediately adjacent to it in the nave and the transepts are not quite the same width as the second and third bays. The reason for this is not esthetic—how could anything in our vision compare to the rightness of pure measure?—but geometric. The master drew two circles around the crossing, of 112 and 96 feet, using the two phrases cited above. *Inside* one circle and *outside* the other he drew the two hexagons shown in Figure 4. All axes and all four surrounding piers were determined from them. Onto them he then added three equal bays, each half the size of the cross-

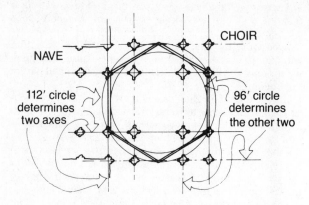

Figure 4. Constructing the crossing and the adjacent bays within the first figure.

ing, and behold—they touched the labyrinth and the center of the apse.

He then proceeded to design the piers and the walls with their buttresses, using a beautiful selection of squares and octagons and incorporating, in sequence, each of the numbers from one to ten. Thus every part of the building, from the piers to the windowsills and from the wall buttresses to the cornices, was derived directly from the first figure of three diamonds. The single statement about Mary and her assumption stood as the foundation for every subsequent design decision. In the end, the numbers and the geometry form an encyclopedia of medieval knowledge.

One of the most surprising things in the cathedral is the reduced sizes of the five bays between the labyrinth and the western doors, as shown in the photo. Yet this apparent mistake was no accident. The geometry of the diamonds fixed the four bays on either side of the crossing, so they could not be moved. If between them and the west front the master had placed four bays instead of five, he would not have had to shoehorn them into a space that was too small. But then the Marian numbers of seven and nine could not have been used. If geometry had not been a factor, all the bay widths could have been adjusted until they were equal; contrariwise, if the numbers had been unimportant, eight equal bays could have been built between the crossing and the western doors. The truth is that both geometry and number were of equal significance and were reconcilable only if there were some distortion to the appearance. If we ever need proof that in a spiritual age meaning mattered more than looks, we have it here. Within three generations these values were to be reversed in the façade of Notre-Dame in Dijon, where artistic issues supplanted the symbolic.

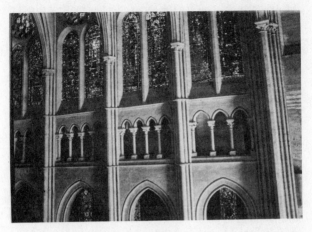

The western bays of Chartres cathedral are smaller than those alongside the crossing for geometric reasons.

The Bent Axis

Having set out the cathedral to geometric perfection, the master architect proceeded to bend the axis by one foot at the altar. You will see this when you stand in the nave and try to line up the window in the end chapel with the arch of the arcade behind the main altar, for you will then have to move some feet to the south.

In more than half of all medieval churches there is a small deflection in the axis, the nave not being precisely in line with the choir. At one time this was thought to represent the head of Christ drooping onto His shoulder while dying on the cross. However, it has been shown in a number of cases, including Notre-Dame in Paris, that the deviation came from the nature of the site or from obstacles that could not be demolished.

Medieval churches were always built in sections, often with considerable time elapsing between each project, and because the old building was shut off from the new during construction, it may not have been easy to align the new work accurately with the old. Abbot Suger tells us they set out the choir of Saint-Denis with the greatest care, yet the axis of the choir is misaligned some 3° to the nave. Can we infer from the care taken in the setting out that the deflection was deliberate? Further, and against all probability, the bends in church axes are nearly always in the same direction, offset to the south of the altar. There are occasional exceptions to this, but their rarity only reinforces what would seem to have been a general rule.

No medieval text refers to this phenomenon, but in India the *Vastu Shastras* instruct the architect to avoid the "vulnerable points" by moving the altar a little to the north of the axis, which achieves the same effect as moving the axis to the south of the altar.

One reason is architectural, for bending the axis avoids perfect symmetry, as do all natural things. Examine a leaf or the two sides of your face, and you will see that in nature nothing is purely symmetrical. The flawless perfection of a doll is lifeless, if not a little terrifying.

Another reason is theological, for the real world is only a poor reflection of the ideal, so it would have been presumptuous to produce perfection on earth.

THE LABYRINTH

In the center of the Chartres nave is the labyrinth. It is the single largest decorative item in the building, larger than the rose windows and larger than the sculptured doors. The arrangement of circles and arcs is not unique to Chartres, for it is found in most of the other labyrinths that survive from the period. The pattern and the location must therefore have meaning, yet no one has told us what it is.

It is not a maze, for we do not become lost in it. It is a singular path which starts on the side closest to the western doors and traverses eleven rings by a circuitous route to finish at the center. You can follow it in Figure 5.

Figure 5. The labyrinth in the nave of Chartres cathedral.

The center is like a flower or a snow crystal with six sides. Six is one of the Perfect Numbers, in which the factors of the number add up to the number itself. (The factors of 6 are 1, 2, and 3.) The next Perfect Number is 28 (you can work out the factors for yourself), and the next 496. It is one of their remarkable qualities that there is only one Perfect Number among the first ten numbers, only one between 10 and 100, and only one between 100 and 1000. Further (but probably unknown to the Middle Ages), there is only one perfect number between 1000 and 10,000.

The factors of 496 can be written as $1^3 + 3^3 + 5^3 + 7^3$, using only odd numbers to the third power. Similarly, the factors of 28 can be written as $1^3 + 3^3$. These correlations were enough to make perfect numbers more than fascinating to medieval scholars.

The problem with the number six, like the six-sided figure, is that it is too perfect. Perfection is not for ordinary mortals. If the central flower, the symbol for heaven as the rose garden, had been left a hexagon, there would have been no way into the center. But by opening the petals, man is allowed into the garden.

The turns in the rings around the center make a cross, symbolizing the four directions which encompass the earth, the four Gospels which contain the whole of Christ's message, the four rivers of Paradise, and so on. There are eleven rings, which is not a Christian number. Certainly there were only eleven true disciples, but you seldom see eleven apostles in art (Cahors may be an exception): Bartholomew was always being brought in to make up the twelfth.

Eleven in Islam represents the *Hu*, the state that is closest to God. Man can go no further without himself becoming God. The *Hu* is the primary exhalation of the One when He first conceives of Himself as both object and subject. It is the initial division into aspects before He continued to the definition of archetypes, then matter, and so on until the whole of creation had been manifested. Even before there were thoughts or words there was this distinction between the "I" and the "Thou." The number eleven in the Arabic notation recently introduced to the West consists of two identical vertical strokes. Looked at from one side, the two strokes become one, so the *Hu* is both the first duality and the All.

It also reminds us of the twin arcs that form the mandorla in Figure 2. The eleven-ringed labyrinth came into use at the very time the mandorla went out of fashion. The mother as the root of the heavenly Trinity was transformed into Mary as the guide to pilgrim's earthly way—a crucial change in emphasis.

With the addition of the center, the labyrinth returns to twelve, the number of completeness: the totality of the year, the full extent of Israel, and so on. The paths and the center represent all that there is in heaven and on earth, which was exemplified in the esoteric meaning of the zodiac, described later in the section on Chartres cathedral.

The first five signs, from Aries to Leo, cover the creation of life and matter; Virgo is the creation of man, and Libra, the seventh sign, is man in essence, his potential and his

Eleven piers in the circular church of Neuvy-Saint-Sépulchre.

powers, including the ego. The next sign, Scorpio, is man's notion of self and the point of choice between spiritual life or death. The last four signs depict the way back to God through understanding and spiritual consciousness. Applying this interpretation to the design of the labyrinth may explain its arrangement.

One enters on the left of the center into Scorpio, where pilgrim makes his first decision for Christ. He then passes along Libra on the left, his ego/essence, which must be appreciated before he can make sense of the rest. The inner rings, representing Taurus to Leo, cover knowledge of the creation of the universe that, when guided in the sequence laid down in the Seven Liberal Arts, gives understanding. The second time he enters Libra he passes along the full half-circle facing east. Pilgrim now reappraises himself, and just as this half-circle lies symmetrically across the main axis of the cathedral, so pilgrim has been set by the Arts on the right course for the rest of his journey. From this firm position he continues on his way to God, following the outer circles until at the end he passes through Libra for the last time, to shed his ego. With innocence he enters the seventh circle, Virgo, to be reborn into paradise, the center which is also Aries, the First Cause and the Creative Principle.

In the center there used to be a brass plaque that was taken up during the Revolution to make cannon. We are told that on it were inscribed the figures of Theseus, the Minotaur, and Ariadne, the king's daughter who helped Theseus to victory. Theseus is pilgrim, the Minotaur his satanic side—and by implication the evils of bull worship from which Christianity had borrowed so heavily. Ariadne is the Virgin, for though she was betrothed to Theseus, she remained a virgin and was left on the sacred island of Delos when Theseus returned to Greece. Theseus voluntarily searched for and finally destroyed the devil, be it original sin or his own inner passions. Having accomplished this, he could have been lost in the darkness were it not for the guidance given him by his Virgin Lady. She holds the string, the thread that leads Theseus not through the labyrinth but out of it. The labyrinth is easy to get into, but knowledge, her gnosis, is essential if one is ever to emerge from it.

The labyrinth therefore represents man's way back to God here on earth. It was placed at the same distance from the crossing as the crossing is from the high altar, and thus it is everyman's equivalent of the altar. God approaches pilgrim at the mass, and in another sense pilgrim approaches God through the labyrinth. The sacred connection lies at one end, the mundane at the other.

CHANGES IN ARCHITECTURAL SYMBOLISM

Reflecting the changes in medieval spirituality, there were three major phases in French architectural development: from Romanesque to Gothic, followed by the International and Flamboyant. The points of change, when Gothic architecture grew out of Romanesque during the twelfth century, reflected the transformation of God's relationship with His creation from being transcendental to immanental. The culmination of these changes a hundred years later marked the return of the transcendental views.

The Romanesque buildings of the eleventh century were like citadels, refuges from the world, offering pilgrim a secure and tranquil environment for prayer. Simple in form and unadorned, they spoke of architecture itself, without embellishment. At this time the vault over the apse—and later all the high vaults and even the galleries—came to represent the Heavenly City. One could say that God and man were separated from one another so that the spiritual was untouched by the earthly and transcended it. Map 1 (page 82) shows the churches in this guide that contain work from this period, known to historians as the First Romanesque.

We might call the following period Decorated Romanesque; it began toward the end of the eleventh century and continued for three generations. The churches of this period are shown in Map 2 (page 92). Change was gradual as prosperity increased and the miracle of 1130 took hold. Buildings became larger and more ornate, and sculpture appeared in the capitals and doorways. It was as though people were seeking a new richness to express their confidence in the future. A new monastic order, the Cistercians, rejected this richness and returned to the austerity of the earlier Romanesque.

In most buildings God's presence could be imagined as

*Even where space
is complex in the
Saint-Benoît-sur-
Loire ambulatory,
the weighty walls
and sharp corners
anchor it down.*

coming from above the sanctuary or from beyond the walls,
and it was during the Decorated period that architecture
began to direct pilgrim toward Him. Pilgrim was lifted up
into the vaults as pointed arches replaced the round, or he
was encouraged to glimpse paradise through the walls of
the flat eastern ends so loved by the Cistercians.

Beginning around 1140, the canopy itself began to descend toward the pavement, as though God were recipro-
cating man's eagerness for Him. In the first phase of Gothic
(up to the 1180s) architecture became increasingly light,
from the choir of Saint-Denis to the Soissons south transept, until for one short magical moment in the 1170s the
City of God appeared to occupy the entire building. The
City appeared like a temple, lightweight and delicate, hovering over the walls of the fortress. God's City lay within the
building, immanent in the world. The churches of this
phase are located in Map 3 (page 102).

Most of the early Gothic churches are in the Paris Basin
because it was there and practically nowhere else that the
revolution in architecture occurred. The atmosphere of the
region was ebullient and confident; it grew on prosperity
and peace and expressed itself in the new style.

In the churches of the second phase of Gothic (from the
1170s to around 1200), shown in Map 4 (page 117), the
upper stories began to levitate slightly. The canopy seemed

INITIAL

William

x william l

---- FIRST TI

fox william fa

fox william l

l Fox, William L.,

resource] : Las Vegas

DATE: 08-18-2006

ON: oc AT TERM: 8 INITIALS:

The choir of Saint-Denis continued the first clear statement of the immanental view: open, spacious, light, and confident in the future.

to be suspended, hanging on the fingerlike flying buttresses and trailing long thin shafts toward the pavement like tendrils, while still connecting heaven with earth.

In the third phase of Gothic (from about 1190 to the 1230s) the canopy began to withdraw, hiding behind screens or lifted to enormous heights where it again became untouchable. The clerestory began to dominate as glass and tracery overwhelmed the interiors. A tension was being recreated between the proximity of heaven and its unapproachable splendor, which was becoming too bright for contact to be maintained much longer. These churches are marked in Map 5 (page 124).

From the early 1220s this conflict was being resolved. The elements that had once made indissoluble contact were gradually eliminated, among them the many towers and the lantern over the crossing. This was when the clerestory began to lift off with the canopy, sometimes taking the triforium with it, while the rose was absorbed by the windows and the roof was simplified into a lid. The churches of this fourth and final phase of Gothic are cited in Map 6 (page 130).

The Rayonnant buildings erected after 1230 and before the war are shown in Map 7 (page 132). The detailing has become complex but repetitively mannered and uncertain, with clever ways of appearing to unpeel the wall so that the City of God was distanced from the structure and the canopy separated from the congregation. Elegance was often more important than strength. When this new style was adopted beyond the Paris Basin, as at Clermont-Ferrand or Saint-Urbain at Troyes, it was the Rayonnant manner that predominated.

After plague and war had laid France to waste, there was a final burst of energy that now seems more like a frenzy for its own sake than a deep spirituality. Walls and windows were decorated so that a shimmering energy appeared to pass like an electric field across the surfaces. The churches from this Flamboyant period are located in Map 8 (page 137).

In one sense Gothic adapted a two-thousand-year-old style to a new purpose not intended in the original. Similarly, as heaven became transcendent again, the Gothic style that had been evolved to express the immanental view was modified in turn to express the views it had been created to deny. At each change old motifs appeared in new clothes.

In nearly all the medieval churches we need to use our imagination if we are to have much feeling for what they were like a thousand years ago. Today we see them bare, the plain stone walls and piers occasionally retaining a scrap of paintwork. In the north side of the choir at Chartres the altar of the Virgin may give some idea of what the interiors were like originally. As every chapel and every altar would have been in the Middle Ages, it is surrounded by candles, perhaps a couple hundred of them, flickering in their uncertain light. Gold and precious stones shone with an eerie iridescence, the copper and bronze of the candelabra and giant candlesticks reflected the candlelight, and

Extraordinary richness in the carving of the capitals after 1130, as the exuberance for life appeared in the stone: Châlons-sur-Marne nave.

over all hung the lazy plumes of incense. The interiors were like jewels themselves, reflecting the words of Saint John that the Heavenly Jerusalem

> was of jasper: and the City was pure gold, like unto clear glass. And the foundations . . . were garnished with all manner of precious stones. . . . And the twelve gates were twelve pearls. (Revelation 21:18–21)

The walls were hung with tapestries, carpets and rushes covered the paving, and of course the disarming glow of the stained glass suffused everything. There was always music. Large choirs and musicians were constantly employed, not only during the masses but for processions to the relics. Important visitors would be heralded by fanfares and shouts of welcome. The church was alive and the focus of all activity.

THE FIRST ROMANESQUE: 1000–1100
The Citadel of Peace

Pilgrim is protected, kept in his place, and shown the Kingdom

Throughout the Middle Ages the Roman Church insisted that salvation could be obtained only through its ministrations, as in the story of Peter and Steven. It insisted on remaining the intermediary between God and man. This relationship was expressed in the forms of the nave, which was for the people, and the choir, which was for the Church. The nave was square, cubic, and rectangular, the eastern end was round, cylindrical, and spherical; the square symbolized the earth and the circle the celestial. In some places, such as Nevers, the transepts and the crossing exaggerated the barrier between the congregation and the Church, but both zones were kept separate from God's world. Many techniques were tried to achieve this.

The earliest medieval church was a protective place. The plainness of the enclosing walls and vaults and their cool tranquillity suggested a changelessness and timelessness that induced feelings of peace. It was a citadel of faith, designed to be a fortress and a refuge. Castles and fortifications were constant reminders that the wall, and particularly the plain wall, was intended to protect those within and to keep other people out. The towering plain surfaces of the church walls give a similar impression, and in the eleventh century, when men still remembered the insecurity of the previous two centuries, it was a powerful image of protection.

As citadel, the enclosure safeguarded pilgrim from the daily insecurities of life, bringing him the peace to experience the City of God with an immediacy that was not possible outside. The interior was bounded and secure; as in the

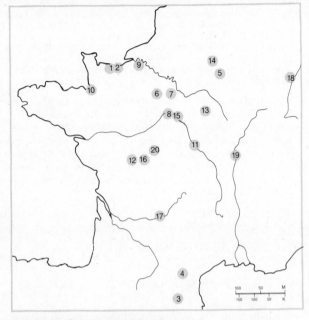

MAP 1 Churches of the First Romanesque

1 CAEN, nave of the Church of Saint-Étienne
2 CAEN, Church of la Très-Sainte-Trinité
3 CANIGOU, Benedictine Abbey of Saint-Martin
4 CARCASSONNE, nave of the Basilica of Saint-Nazaire
5 CHÂLONS-SUR-MARNE, nave of the Church of Notre-Dame-en-Vaux
6 CHARTRES, crypt of the Cathedral of the Assumption
7 ÉTAMPES, crypt of the Church of Notre-Dame-du-Fort
8 GERMIGNY-DES-PRÉS, Church of la Sainte-Trinité
9 JUMIÈGES, ruins of the nave of the Benedictine Abbey of Notre-Dame
10 MONT-SAINT-MICHEL, nave of the Benedictine Abbey of Saint-Michel
11 NEVERS, Church of Saint-Étienne
12 POITIERS, Church of Saint-Hilaire-le-Grand
13 PONTIGNY, nave of the Church of Notre-Dame
14 REIMS, nave and crossing of the Basilica of Saint-Remi
15 SAINT-BENOÎT-SUR-LOIRE, choir of the Benedictine Abbey of Saint-Benoît
16 SAINT-SAVIN-SUR-GARTEMPE, Church of Saint-Savin
17 SOUILLAC, choir of the Abbey of Sainte-Marie
18 STRASBOURG, crypt of the Cathedral of Notre-Dame
19 TOURNUS, narthex of the Church of Saint-Philibert
20 VIC, Church of Saint-Martin-de-Tours

Chartres crypt, nothing distracted one's concentration on the spirit.

The Church called itself the Bride of Christ in order to institutionalize the bonds between God and the clergy from which the Church gained its authority. At a time when power went to those who fought for it, the Church needed all the support it could get to hold its own. As the New Jerusalem had come, in John's words, "down from God out of Heaven, prepared as a bride adorned for her husband," the Church magnified this role by showing the Godhead hovering over the altar, blessing the work of the priests. The half-dome over the apse was often painted with the figure of

Germigny-des-Prés from the south, with plain walls, small windows, and simple forms.

God the Father, as at Paray-le-Monial and Vic. This stimulated the belief that Christ looked down on His Bride and was actually *within* the edifice.

Thus a painted heaven hovered over the circularity of the choir, which lay apart from but on the same plane as the four-squaredness of the nave. Nearly all Romanesque buildings utilized this formula in one way or another. As can be seen at Conques and Toulouse, there is no clerestory and the light filters in from hidden sources within the gallery, hinting at another world beyond the man-made interior. At Paray-le-Monial and Souillac the cornice moldings that are usually placed on the top of the external walls are used on the inside to suggest that the sky-as-heaven is above the enclosure (see page 88). In all of them pilgrim was offered a glimpse of the City of God, unseen but vibrant, just out of sight beyond the enclosure. Its glory was reflected in the light praised by Abbot Suger, but it was not physically present within the sanctuary.

Thus separation in Romanesque is both horizontal and vertical, above and beyond our space, be it eastward through the enlarged window of Saint-Benoît-sur-Loire or upward through the accentless empyrean of Cahors. After 1200, when transcendence returned once more, the separation became more vertical than horizontal, as is best observed in the Saint-Denis nave, but the church of the 1100s was an impenetrable fortress, as in the crypt of Chartres or Canigou.

THE CRYPT AND THE MOUNTAIN

The function of the crypt is little understood. It was occasionally used for the bodies of saints or to house in safety

The light from above the Toulouse south transept comes from windows that cannot be seen, and it enters the church through brilliantly decorated arcades.

the more portable relics, but its real purpose may have been more psychological than practical. The crypt is the subterranean part of the church; physically, it is the foundation of the sanctuary. In ancient religions people would worship in caves because, unlike anything built above the ground, they are enclosed by the most massive thing on earth, the mountain. Nothing feels more secure than, and in the history of mankind nothing has had the same ancestral connotations of home as, the cave set into the mountain, represented by the crypt with the church above it.

Remember how we felt when as children we crept into the local cave. The atmosphere was awesome and secure: we were back in the womb with mother. Thus it was that the worship of the Mother Goddess took place in caves, even when they had to be constructed of stone, like the barrows of Malta. Church crypts feel enormously peaceful and calming to the nerves. When we give them time to work on us, we may emerge from their cool darkness with a heightened awareness and sensibility. They epitomize the tranquillity to be found in most Romanesque buildings.

When we look downward into the blackness or the deeps we tend to relate psychologically to our past, to dark and hidden things, to old memories and the unconscious. Conversely, when we look upward toward the sky we open ourselves to inner growth and lighter thoughts, directed

Saint-Denis crypt.

toward the future rather than the past and toward consciousness. Up is to the attic of the mind; down is to the
cellar. We go up the mountain and down into the cave.

Wells are often found in crypts, as in Chartres and
Tournus, and almost never on the main floor of the church.
The well is "the fountain of paradise that waters the earth"
in Alcuin's phrase, while for Jung it was symbolic of the unconscious, for wells are deep, their waters dark yet cool and
nourishing.

The cave is generally felt to be female, as are the earth
which encases it, the seas around the earth, and the ships
that ride on them. Because the mountain and the sky are
male, the rain becomes the seed that fructifies the female
earth. The fruit of the earth is their progeny. In the *second*
story of creation in Chapter Two of Genesis, God created
the earth and the plants and then "caused it to rain upon
the earth." It had not been seeded, in fact.

The cave is the opening within the earth which permits
us to enter into the earth's most secret recesses. It is the
primeval Mother, the source of life, and the original paradise, and although the feminine aspect was missing from
the all-male Trinity of the eleventh century, it could not
be eliminated. It had to appear somewhere, no matter how
disguised, and it became manifested in the crypt, which
supplied the emotional counterpart to the male judge
upstairs.

To our observation that Christ was visible in the apse
over the altar should be added that the crypt lay under the
choir and supported it. Above the altar was the Father and

below it the Mother, enfolding and nurturing the Bride as parents guard and guide their children. The symbolism is as elemental as the needs it satisfies.

The impulses which led to the building of crypts and to the worship of the Virgin were, at source, the same. With the cult of the Virgin, the masculine Trinity was transformed into a more balanced tribunal and the need for the cave disappeared. Within a couple of generations no more crypts were being built in France.

The entry into the church is to the church what the cave is to the mountain: the entry into the Mother. All these important aspects seem to come down to the same thing: the building is tall, strong, and protective like the father of the family, while the entry and the crypt are enfolding, calming, and soft like the mother.

IMMOBILITY AND ALTERNATION

Most interiors were divided into compartments by large shafts that corralled one bay from another. Even in buildings intended for flat wooden ceilings which did not need these shafts, such as Jumièges, they were carried all the way up the wall so the divisions could not be forgotten. The shafts tend to immobilize the observer, anchoring him in a state of well-being and stillness.

The Scholastic search for clarity is reflected in the shafts which define the structural function of each part, so there would be just one column under each arch or rib. Shafts were not merged into one another but were undercut and separated from their neighbors with sharp arrises that maintained their individual identity. Similarly, arches were separated from their supports by capitals, piers from the paving by bases and torus molds, windows from walls by drip molds and string courses.

Hence the different sizes of the aisle bays and nave bays could not be disguised but had to be expressed somehow. Aisle bays were normally half the width of the nave, and if they were to share piers, one or the other would have to be rectangular in plan. However, a long rectangular aisle would have impelled pilgrim eastward as if in a tunnel, in conflict with the passivity induced by the shafts in the nave. This knotty problem was resolved by making both the nave bays and the aisle bays square and downgrading the importance of each alternate pier, as it supported only the aisle vaults.

Alternation was in fact a neat compromise that maintains a slow, measured rhythm in the space, one that we sense whether we are walking along the nave or just looking from bay to bay. As we know from later designs in which all the nave bays are rectangular, we tend to skip from one to the other like a stone over water, taking it all in rather rapidly. But when the space is divided into square bays—and this is particularly noticeable in such domed churches as Souillac—we tend to stay for a while in each space, centered on the wholeness of the square plan.

It is as though pilgrim had to be slowed down and prevented from jumping, in his enthusiasm, straight into paradise. He was forced to wait and do penance; now was too soon.

THE HEAVENLY CITY

God had always been seen to be present in the relics and the altars. A canopy called a ciborium, which was placed over the altar like a rajah's palanquin or an Egyptian ceremonial fan, attested to its importance and was symbolic of God's special protection. A ciborium was carved above the Virgin on the western door at Notre-Dame in Paris, and there was another at Chartres before it was broken off. It was often made from richly embroidered cloth, domed in form, to represent Deodoris of Tarsus's description:

> two heavens, one visible, the other invisible, one below, the other above: the latter serves as the roof of the universe, the former as the covering of our earth—not round or spherical, but in the form of a tent.

In time the vaults above the ciborium acquired the same protective symbolism as the ciborium itself, for as the abbot of Saint-Remi, Pierre de Celle, had written, "where should one treat of the tabernacle of Moses, if not in the tabernacle itself." The church was literally fulfilling the prophecy of

> the holy city, new Jerusalem, coming down from God out of heaven, . . . And I heard a great voice saying, Behold, the tabernacle of God is with men, and he will dwell with them, and they

The arches over the saved in the Conques tympanum representing the Heavenly City encouraged the idea that the spirit could inhabit architecture.

shall be his people, and God himself shall be with them. (Revelation 21:2–3)

This was the great promise and hope for which the medieval church prepared itself and its congregation, for that day when "there shall be no more death, neither sorrow, nor crying, neither shall there be any more pain." At a time when the Second Coming was believed to be imminent, the Church naturally incorporated something of the tabernacle of God that was to precipitate this longed-for moment.

The tabernacle was imagined to look like a sumptuously decorated parasol tent, for Isaiah had written that He "stretcheth out the heavens as a curtain, and stretcheth them out as a tent" (Isaiah 40:22). From the inside the light coming through the skin, especially when the skin was made from richly woven or painted material, would have been seen to glow like stained glass. This may have inspired the invention of painted glass that recreated this translucence in more permanent materials. Similarly, the invention of the rib may have been inspired by the curved lines on the undersurface of the tent.

Vaults came in two types: those that centered themselves over you and those that led you somewhere, be it up or along. Domical vaults, and to some extent six-part vaults, are centering devices (see page 108), while barrel and groin vaults and their successor, four-part vaults, are directional (see page 119). The latter type would seem to have represented the tabernacle, the domical type the night sky.

THE DOME AS HEAVEN

At Cahors and Souillac we naturally tend to gravitate toward the center and look up, and the dome seems to rotate around us rather than hang independently above our heads like a rib vault. Having no corners that let us define its form, it looks as if there is nothing there. This is why the connection between the dome and the night sky is particularly strong. Just as the stars seem to rotate around the observer, the sphere of the dome appears to locate itself directly above us. This may be why we refer to the "vault of the sky." The fulcrum is emphasized by the hole normally found at the top, for we feel ourselves ascending like an arrow through it to the light beyond.

Normally the chamber under the dome is square in plan, or more appropriately a cube, in memory of the earth. It is supported not on shafts but on massive boxlike piers and arches which hold our gaze within each dome. Seen from underneath, the curved pendentives are not unlike the stretched material of a tent held down at the corners.

The word "dome" shares roots with some of the most basic elements in our lives. It stems from the Latin for "house," hence "domicile" and "domestic." This is not the house in the suburban sense; rather it means the house as

The domed nave and choir of Souillac.

protection, from which comes "dominus" for "lord," "madonna" for his "lady," and our "dominate." The Italian for cathedral, "duomo," emphasizes that in essence the home is a spiritual place. It thus links the most powerful images of security with the eternal heavens.

THE VAULT AS TUNNEL

The effect of the barrel vault was opposite to that of the dome, for it acted like a tunnel, leading pilgrim from the nave toward the east. Barrel vaults rise out of the vertical planes of the walls, and as they curve over our heads they constantly return our attention down the walls to ourselves. The pavement and the earth itself is the start and end of any movement. We are swung back from the center, unable to rise too high, kept from flying, as if there were a lid over our heads.

In some cases (Beaulieu and Moissac) there are no windows, so there is no hint of spring or autumn, of rain or shadow. The interior has been turned into an artificial sealed cave like a gigantic crypt. Where there are clerestory windows (Saint-Benoît and Saint-Savin), the barrel vaults and their arches still do not allow our gaze to wander beyond the confines of the enclosure, but return us whence we came.

Thus pilgrim is immobilized and grounded, held within the tunnel to be led in the correct direction. The transverse arches and the shafts leading up to them may slow down the action, without stopping it as happens with alternation in the piers. When the vault is pointed, however, as at Le Thoronet and Cluny (see pages 281 and 199), a vertical element creeps in. This was enhanced when groin vaults were used in the high vaults at Vézelay, but it became over-powering when the groins were replaced with ribs.

THE FIRST RIB VAULTS

Groin vaults were first used over aisles, where the creases on the surface prevented pilgrim from getting the impression that heaven might be occupying these lateral and lowly spaces. Moving them upward into the high vaults to some extent repeated this sensation, but as they were further away and usually well lit, the *combined sequence* of vaults was more important than the space collected under each one. Together they became like tents, tied down to the earth by their shafts.

If the groins had been painted, they would have looked like ribs. Indeed, the first ribs were created for their visual effect, not for structural reasons. It was a neat builder's device to tidy up the creases of the groin, for it had proved quite difficult to arrange the curves of the groins in a pleasant way where the widths of the sides differed. Around 1100 someone in England hit on the idea of covering the groin with stones which could be set along a good-looking curve and the cells fitted in between. The idea caught on quickly, yet it was thirty years before it was realized that the rib could act as an arch as well as a cover mold. From that moment a new structural esthetic became possible.

In the rib vault, line is more important than surface. Our

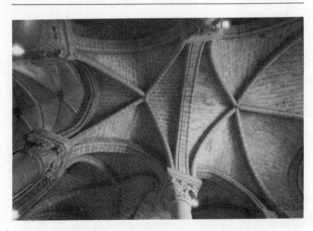

The fine ribs of the Saint-Denis ambulatory spread a thin web of movement across the surfaces.

gaze does not center on one place but wanders across the building, up and down from arches to shafts and along from one bay to the next. The general direction is upward toward the boss, especially where the ribs are pointed, but once there, the urge returns to follow the lines elsewhere, to the shafts and down to the floor or onward to the next bay and its boss. The rib vault is dynamic and restless.

The two representations of the heavens, the dome and the rib vault, thus reflect two different approaches to the eternal, the active and the contemplative. Ribs excite us to movement, the dome to stillness.

The north of France avoided the dome. Even over the crossings of Laon, Braine, and Chartres, where domes were possible, rib vaults were used. It was not that the north denied the image of heaven resident in the dome, but that the vault expressed those ideas differently, preferring to impel pilgrim to action rather than restrain him. Under the domes of Cahors and the barrel vaults of Aulnay nothing much was asked of him: pilgrim was stilled and given a tranquillity missing in the outside world.

This may have had something to do with the nature of each society. Where the north was outward-seeking, exploring, crusading, and inventive, the south and west was a more peaceful community and more pleasure-seeking. The troubadours came from here, heresy found hospitality, and the rigors of the feudal system were less heavy. It may be significant that after the feudal contract was imposed on the south by the northern barons, no more domed churches were built.

THE DECORATED ROMANESQUE: 1070–1160s
The City of God Moves In

Pilgrim is caught up in the drama

Where in the First Romanesque the relationship between man, church, and God seemed static, in the decades before 1100 deliberate connections were being made between the three. The stillness and immobility fostered in the churches built before 1100 were transformed in piecemeal fashion to lift pilgrim up into the vaults. This was done by introducing pointed arches over thin columns, with fluted shafts, interesting paintwork and sculpture, and decorated doors and jambs. All these new details inspired the eye, especially in the Cluniac monasteries, while the Cistercians continued to build in the old manner—but with new techniques that were to play a large part in the Gothic transformation.

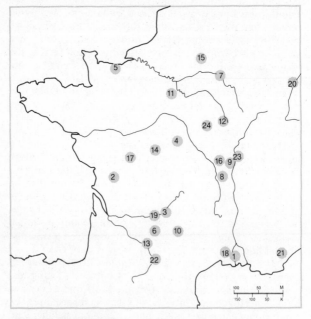

MAP 2 Churches of the Decorated Romanesque

1 ARLES, Church of Saint-Trophime
2 AULNAY-DE-SAINTOGNE, Church of Saint-Pierre
3 BEAULIEU-SUR-DORDOGNE, Church of Saint-Pierre
4 BOURGES, transept doors of the Cathedral of Saint-Étienne
5 CAEN, Church of la Très-Sainte-Trinité
6 CAHORS, nave of the Cathedral of Saint-Étienne
7 CHÂLONS-SUR-MARNE, portal sculpture of the Church of Notre-Dame-en-Vaux
8 CHARLIEU, ruins of Cluniac Abbey of Saint-Fortunat
9 CLUNY, ruins of the Abbey of Saint-Pierre et Saint-Paul
10 CONQUES, Benedictine Abbey of Sainte-Foy
12 ÉTAMPES, nave portal of the Church of Notre-Dame-du-Fort
13 FONTENAY, Cistercian Abbey of Notre-Dame
14 MOISSAC, Cloister and Church of Saint-Pierre

15 NEUVY-SAINT-SÉPULCHRE, Church of Saint-Étienne
16 NOUVION-LE-VINEUX, Church of Saint-Martin
17 PARAY-LE-MONIAL, Basilica of le Sacré-Coeur
18 POITIERS, nave vaults of the Church of Saint-Hilaire-le-Grand
19 SAINT-GILLES-DU-GARD, Church of Saint-Gilles
20 SOUILLAC, nave of the Abbey of Sainte-Marie
21 STRASBOURG, transepts of the Cathedral of Notre-Dame
22 LE THORONET, Cistercian Abbey of Notre-Dame
23 TOULOUSE, Basilica of Saint-Sernin
24 TOURNUS, Church of Saint-Philibert
25 VÉZELAY, narthex and nave of the Basilica of Sainte-Madeleine

THE VERTICAL CONNECTION: THE CITY OVERHEAD

The esthetic impact of round arches is totally different from that of pointed arches. The round arch is self-contained; our glance moves up one side, over the top, and down the other side in one easy movement. The movement within a pointed arch, on the other hand, starts from both sides at once and proceeds jointly to the apex, to flow on and out of the form in the direction of the heavens.

The round arches in the cloister of Le Thoronet induce a horizontal action.

Being self-contained, round arches divide the space horizontally at the capitals, while pointed arches unify it into one wholeness, and the capitals only make you pause sufficiently to absorb the horizontal forces before, reinforced by the inherent verticality, the arches urge you to proceed upward.

Later architects eliminated the capital altogether, molding column, rib, arch, wall, and roof into one gigantic web. The result was powerful and unified, but the tonal subtleties and sensitive interplay of the twelfth century were lost.

At the same time that pointed arches came into use, shafts were made thinner and taller, especially around the ambulatory. At Paray-le-Monial they are so thin, and the arches over them so stilted, that the vaults of the apse seem to float, creating the illusion of the City of God hovering within all the upper parts and not just in the vaults. It is as if the pavement were a springboard for the elegant shafts whose tips just touch the butterfly weight of the ciborium-like canopy over the altar.

One other verticalizing element was the lantern tower over the crossing. Where the tower lacks windows, as at Strasbourg, the lantern is a dark tunnel leading nowhere, like one more lid on the space. But when windows are set into the lantern, as in Germigny-des-Prés and Conques, the light opens up the center like some distant intimation of God's interest. Before 1130 this was the strongest vertical-

The pointed arches in the screen between the towers of Notre-Dame, Paris, excite a vertical action.

izing device used, for unlike the domed apse it brought the heavenly light right into the building, suffusing the space with His presence. (See the photo of the lantern at Laon on page 121.)

THE HORIZONTAL CONNECTION:
THE CITY BEYOND

Just as the squareness of the nave symbolizes the earth, the circularity of the round apse symbolizes the heavens. As a circle it has a center, through which passes the *axis mundi*. Once within the circle one is protected—a ritual that every schoolboy knows. It is the sacred grove beloved of the Druids, surrounded by trees that have their roots in the earth and their arms in heaven.

In the tenth century a passage was set around the apse with chapels off it so that pilgrim could perambulate around the choir without approaching the high altar. Cylindrical columns, usually carved from single blocks of stone, were placed between the apse and the ambulatory. They were such an important part of the scheme that columns from earlier churches were often saved and reused, and Abbot Suger was prepared to import them from Italy at great expense. Each column was a circle, and each encircled the circle of the apse; because the circle is the symbol of the One, roundness was repeated and emphasized all about the eastern end.

The round apse with its semicircular dome shields and protects the altar, as in Souillac (see page 89), and when the dome sits above a triforium or a row of windows it is like some stilled cocoon hovering overhead. It is essentially inert, capping the horizontal relationship between the nave and the choir.

Intersecting lions on the trumeau at Moissac.

To bring movement into the apse the Cistercians popularized the straightened eastern wall to make a rectangular eastern end. They were particularly devoted to the Virgin and may have decided to invite heaven inside, in a mystic way, rather than leave the City hovering just overhead.

The flat wall attracted the monk's attention horizontally toward the eastern windows and invited God's attention *in to* his world, while the circular apse directed his attention *up to* God's. One reinforced the distinction between our reality and His, the other assured us of His presence in our world at all times. (As if to make sure, the Cistercians also favored the rose window as God's eye looking in.) During the second half of the twelfth century the flat eastern end became the dominant form in the Soissonnais and remarkably popular elsewhere; compare Mantes-la-Jolie (page 111) with Laon (page 121).

The circular chevet attached to a rectangular nave represents the marriage between the circle and the square. Because the rectangular choir misses out on this conjunction, it may have been argued that as He was mystically within the building, the union of spirit and matter had happened at such a fundamental level that the squareness of the church needed no circle to symbolize its spiritual connection.

It may have been the Cistercians who forced architects to face the real value of simplicity just at the time that a new direction was needed. Any builder employed by them had to rethink his assumptions, and as Le Thoronet shows, skill was largely concentrated on putting meaning into geometry and on exquisite stonework. The masons had to focus on the forms alone rather than on what was carved into them. One has the feeling that many key ideas were honed there and that in the Paris Basin these ideas fell on fertile ground.

THE CONNECTIONS WITHIN: IMAGES IN THE STONE

Stone carving was reinvented during the eleventh century after a hiatus of some six hundred years during which the skill had all but disappeared. Some think that Roman models were responsible for the resurgence, but these models had been visible for hundreds of years without stimulating much. From the aisle sculpture at Saint-Sernin in Toulouse, the advance was breathtaking: the Cluny choir and the Moissac cloister, both near the turn of the century, then the extraordinary work at Beaulieu, Vézelay, Saint-Gilles, the Moissac porch, and all that immense variety of work in Burgundy. This enormous output culminated in the great thirteenth-century portals of Chartres, Paris, and Reims, which make France the most astonishing repository of extant medieval art in Europe. As Fil Hearn wrote, Romanesque sculpture is "singularly alluring to twentieth-century eyes. Its formal abstraction, its grotesque expressiveness, and its imaginative treatment of spiritual themes appeal to us with the immediacy [of] the art of our own time" (Romanesque Sculpture).

This art was public in the most intimate sense, for it dealt exclusively with the religious concepts of the time in a way that could be shared immediately with everyone. Beginning in reliquaries and altars, it soon put figures of God and His saints and apostles *into* the building rather than onto its surface as a painting. To reinforce this difference, most figures were surrounded by architectural settings which integrated them into the stonework and shared with them the monumentality of the building itself (see page 95). Thus the images fostered the view that the spirit actually impregnated the material edifice, laying the groundwork for the Gothic immanental view. Placed around doorways, the figures were like an admonitory welcoming committee that simultaneously threatened and encouraged pilgrim each time he entered the church.

The first sculpture in architecture appeared on capitals, such as the fine examples at Neuvy-Saint-Sépulchre, Cluny, and Saint-Benoît, and it is worthwhile observing them with some care (binoculars are a great help). They are often carved with biblical stories, as though they were three-dimensional equivalents of the wall paintings which surrounded them.

In these austere interiors the capital provided the only

sign of life in the stone by bringing the vitality of nature's leaves and animals inside. The symbolic importance of the capital was that it covered the transition from the vertical of pier and wall to the curves of arches and vaults. The domed vault symbolized the sky-as-heaven while the rectangular and planar walls symbolized the earth. The capital was in one sense the point where the two aspects of God's creation met to produce the everyday reality of our world, pulsing with life, vital and varied. Capitals are a touch of Paradise which enliven the junction between the imperfection of our world and the perfection of the spiritual.

The invention of the rib at this time added decoration to the vaults just as shafts and cunning moldings were adding it to the doorways. Along with pointed arches, these things introduced movement into Romanesque interiors.

THE GREAT WELCOME: DECORATING DOORS AND WINDOWS

Having neither frames nor tracery, Romanesque windows do not disturb the solidity of the wall, and the smaller the window, the more protected the interior appeared. The wall is the primary element, the openings merely punctuations; even where the doorway is large, the round arch isolates it so it does not dominate the wall but merely penetrates it.

As times changed and the Virgin was softening the judge to let the sinner in, the sculptor was softening the edges of the openings which let the penitent in. Decoration was placed around doors to make the entry more magical yet more humane. Then similar shafts and patterns were placed around the windows so that they looked like doors— but doors leading toward the horizon to welcome God in the same way the real door welcomed man. The light coming through these windows was the mystic light of paradise, which played a key role in stimulating the invention of Gothic. The window-as-doorway became a leading motif in nearly every building, as in Nouvion and Aulnay, growing until it replaced the wall itself with patterns of tracery that became the most important design element of later centuries.

The cornice around the edge of the roof was also decorated. It finished off the silhouette of the building at the skyline. If the cornice had been straight and unadorned, as in modern offices, there would have been a distinct cleavage between the edifice built by man and the heavens in the sky. The decoration of the cornice has given an electric charge to the upper edge of the building, so it looks like a balcony to heaven.

In western France, and indeed in all the areas controlled or influenced by the English, decoration had a lighter and less intensive feeling than in the east and north. It is delightful, full of humorous and inconsequential carving. Mad

South porch, Beaulieu-sur-Dordogne.

little figures, distorted like acrobats or rude as peasants, are full of intricacy and plain fun. This sculpture did not have the same symbolic significance as that in Burgundy, but it was happier, like the courts of the southern nobles.

THE MIRACLE OF 1130: THE GOTHIC REVOLUTION

Without the impetus to recreate architecture which came out of the cult of the Virgin, the masters would probably have continued ringing changes on the same Romanesque motifs for centuries. The force needed to revolutionize tradition is so enormous that only the most energetic communities can manage it. It took the militaristic, aggressive, guilt-ridden, yet mystic societies of the north to do this. The elegant humanism of the south and west, both happier climes to live in, changed little.

Ideas in art do not move in simple progression, and the interface between the changing aspects is often so hard to define that historians understandably make things simpler so they may be comprehensible. But the interface is both complex and more interesting than is often thought.

The decisive features of Gothic architecture are not the pointed arch, the great height, or the cross-ribbed vault. What most of us have been taught ignores the facts. The ribbed vault had been invented in England in 1100, and the twelfth-century builders from western France (then ruled by English kings) handled rib vaults with a skill and delicacy that was unsurpassed by their Gothic contemporaries.

The great abbey church of Cluny, started in 1088, is immensely high and its arcade arches all pointed, while in the clerestory of Chartres, completed around 1220, the arches over the windows are round. Not only that, nearly every church in the Île-de-France up to 1230 is squat, with vaults that start at the base of the triforium, so there is almost no room for a clerestory at all.

Most of the motifs used in Gothic architecture are found in the Romanesque, as at La Trinité in Caen. Except for four key inventions, the earlier Gothic buildings can be distinguished from Romanesque by the thinning of the shafts and ribs, their gradual emancipation from the wall, and the liberation of the spaces around them. Gothic derived from a fresh view of structure that bypassed the decorative experiments of the previous fifty years. From it came the four key inventions that took architecture far beyond its Romanesque model: the flying buttress, used at Sens about 1160; the wide window that replaced the wall, first used at Chartres about 1200; the tall clerestory, used at Soissons in 1210; and tracery, evolved at Essômes and Reims around 1215.

Gothic was not invented in a series of linear steps, each evolving from the last. It was a jumpy process, with key ideas being tried in many places, shared and discarded, before the final mix was set. Once consolidated around 1240, there were few significant changes for over two centuries.

The flying buttress had been invented to the southeast of Paris around 1160 and used in a couple of Île-de-France buildings a little later. Some Parisian builders were interested in lightweight construction, and it was therefore natural for them to adopt the flying buttress so that they could make the walls even thinner and taller. The result was a totally new type of structure, unheard of in masonry

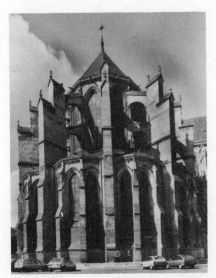

Soissons cathedral, the first mature Gothic cathedral, big-windowed with multiple flying buttresses, triforium, and four-part vaults. See the interior on page 119.

construction anywhere in the world before this date: the skeletal frame.

At Braine the northern builders inserted a triforium into the elevation which seems to have stimulated them to go higher, as can be seen in Longpont and the Soissons choir begun shortly afterward. One of the most important moments seems to have come when the northern builders saw the potential in the skeletal structures being developed to the southwest, to combine the flying buttress with the triforium. This was first achieved at Chartres, and it was the supreme moment of medieval architecture. From it came the classic cathedral form, so that Chartres is rightly known as the Parthenon of France.

Meanwhile, the double window with surmounting rose was being developed in two areas. In the Oise to the north of Paris the frames were simple splays so that the windows were like cuts through the wall, while along the Marne the frames were articulated with shafts so that the edges were emphasized. From the former came the windows at Soissons, from the latter the aisle tracery at Reims. At the same time the windows were widened until all vestiges of the wall had been eliminated between the buttresses. This was an invention of a master from the Laon area, though his first chance to use it occurred at Chartres.

In about 1210 the flying buttress stimulated an eastern builder from the Marne to heighten the clerestory windows dramatically. At Orbais the sills were lowered below the vault springing to make the upper glass area as tall as the aisles. This separated the vaults from the lower zone and began the visual isolation of the upper and lower parts of the building in reflection of the changes then occurring in religious ideas.

It was not Paris's role to make these inventions, but it would weld them into a single statement after they had been perfected elsewhere. When these different streams were conjoined at Saint-Germain-en-Laye and the Sainte-Chapelle, the classic Gothic as we know it was born, to be exported from France after 1240.

The first step in this extraordinary process occurred around 1140, when the canopy began to descend toward the pavement, turning the whole church into a delicate temple. The significance of light in medieval cosmology played a crucial role here.

3

46 96

44

2

3613 1984   1983

N6310.43

FOLLOWED BY: flushing
FROM: b13102758 Fluss...   flutre fe
resource] / Donna Fluss, Donna
CATALOG DATE: 08-18-2006
FUNCTION: oc AT TERM: 8 INITI...

0259 >

FIELD: 100 1 |aFojas, Cami
INDEXED AS AUTHOR: fojas camil...
MESSAGE: ------
PRECEDED BY: ------
FOLLOWED BY: foix gaston
FROM: 6089 Fojas, Camilla,
                  resource] / Camilla,
                  08-18-2006
                   TERM: 8 IN-

|aFox.
fo...

THE FIRST PHASE OF GOTHIC: 1130s–1180s
Ethereal Light and Space

Pilgrim meets God on almost equal terms

LIGHT IS THE SPIRIT

In medieval times all matter could be arranged in a hierarchy from the most solid to the most translucent. Light, which was at the top of this scale, was untouchable. It passed through substances without changing them and, most important, it drove out the darkness. Together these allegories placed light closest to God Himself, for it was God's breath made visible and the radiance of the angels.

Thus it was argued that truth could be most readily perceived in light. Abbot Suger wrote that "the dull mind rises to truth through the material, and seeing the light, is resurrected from its former submersion." His writings show how the twelfth century worshipped light: "Bright is that which is brightly coupled with the bright. And bright is the noble edifice that is pervaded by the *lux nova*, the new light."

The words *lux nova* also refer to Christ as "I am the light of the world" (John 8:12), so the radiance and spirit have become one. Suger calls the stained glass "most sacred," while the reflection of light in beautiful gems transported him into "some strange region of the universe which exists neither in the slime of the earth nor in the purity of Heaven." Light for Suger was undoubtedly colored.

Light was used in the later eleventh century, at Conques and Saint-Benoît, to show that the world of the spirit was not on our plane. It may have been in the galleries overhead, beyond the brilliant windows in front, or even above the whole building shining through the lantern, but until the walls which hid the City were themselves transformed into sparkling visions of heaven itself, the spirit remained out of touch.

STAINED GLASS AND PAINTED WALLS

Painted walls and vaults are inert, even where the flickering shadows of the candles give some impression of movement, for the action lies on the surface. There is no energy within a painted wall; on the contrary, it is like looking dimly into the furthest recesses of a dark cave and half-seeing the dramas of the other world.

In Vic or Saint-Savin one has the impression, when the candles flicker and the potential for autosuggestion is greatest, that the personages of heaven and hell begin to move and may even come down from the wall if only one could look a little more intently, with a fraction more light, or if one could tear oneself away from the present. Yet heaven is

MAP 3 Churches of the First Phase of Gothic

1 CHARTRES, Royal Portal of the Cathedral of the Assumption
2 CHARTRES, Church of Saint-André
3 ÉTAMPES, choir of the Church of Notre-Dame-du-Fort
4 LAON, first choir of the Cathedral of Notre-Dame
5 MANTES-LA-JOLIE, Collegiate of Notre-Dame
6 ORBAIS-L'ABBAYE, ambulatory of the Church of Saint-Pierre et Saint-Paul
7 PARIS, choir of the Cathedral of Notre-Dame
8 REIMS, choir of the Basilica of Saint-Remi

9 SAINT-DENIS, narthex and choir of the Basilica of Saint-Denis
10 SENLIS, Cathedral of the Assumption
11 SENS, Cathedral of Saint-Étienne
12 SOISSONS, south transept of the Cathedral of Saint-Gervais et Saint-Protais

not within the building but far beyond it. Remove the candles and the incense, and the images would be seen for what they are: mere paintings.

Stained glass is completely different. Its illumination comes from outside, so that all the heavenly light comes through the glass itself, with a timeless uncertainty. Where the wall painting reflects, and is therefore transcendental, stained glass is immanental. Glass walls are luminous, as though the old painted surface had come alive: it is matter transformed from within.

Thus the stone window made of alabaster is the ultimate in the immanence of light. It is no longer found in France, but it is still used in some Italian and Spanish churches. Stone as glass, so pure, so ethereal that the light can pass through it; as stone symbolizes the rock of the earth, so

The painted barrel vaults of Saint-Savin-sur-Gartempe.

light symbolizes the creative process. The union of the two, like God's first creative act into substance and essence, must have appeared as the most magical symbolism. Von Simson wrote:

> In a Romanesque church, light is something distinct from and contrasting with the heavy, sombre, tactile substance of the walls. The Gothic wall seems to be porous: light filters through it, permeating it, merging with it, transfiguring it. The windows are structurally and aesthetically not openings in the wall to admit light, but *transparent walls*. They seem to deny the impenetrable nature of matter. Light, which is ordinarily concealed by matter, appears as the active principle; and matter is aesthetically real only insofar as it partakes of, and is defined by, the luminous quality of light. In this decisive aspect, then, Gothic may be described as transparent, diaphanous architecture. (*The Gothic Cathedral*)

The proof of this is that the amount of light transmitted through the windows is usually too poor to read by. Light did not, positively not, mean physical illumination, at least not until the churches of later centuries were glazed in grisaille. Because of this misconception, we may be disappointed by those buildings which still have their original glass.

The interiors of Notre-Dame in Paris, Chartres, and the Sainte-Chapelle are unexpectedly dark, yet there can be no doubt this is how they were meant to be. Notre-Dame, more

The choir of Vézelay is full of light.

than the others, is dark as night. Even when it has been cleaned, the glass filters out most of the light and we are left with little more illumination than we would get from the stars and the moon.

Perhaps instead of reading "light" for Suger's *lux*, we should think of "glow" or "radiance," for when we compare the glass of Saint-Denis with the painted walls of Vic we can see exactly what he was advocating. The glass seems to be pulsing with an energy that comes from deep inside the material.

Suger's exaltation of light was shared by many, and wherever the light came in, the presence of God was felt. Pierre de Roissy, chancellor of Chartres, expressed this well:

> The paintings in the church are writings for the instruction of those who cannot read: divine writings, for they direct the light of the true sun [i.e., the Son] into the interior of the church, and thus into the hearts of the faithful, thus illuminating them. (*Manual on the Mysteries of the Church*)

But from the middle of the thirteenth century the colors in the glass became less intense. Grisaille was often used, with pictures which could be read clearly. The story in the glass was now more important than the quality of the light. The great windows made the church into a hall in which the prayer book could be read with ease and one's neighbors recognized. God had ceased to lie within the building, which was no longer a manifestation of the City of God but merely the chamber in which one worshipped Him.

Although churches were turned into glass cages, the glazing was never carried down to the floor. The aisle walls remained solid and impenetrable. Stand outside Chartres and notice the smooth weightiness of the walls that is emphasized by the depth of the window reveals and the enormous width of the buttresses: there is no way to see in; the nave is impregnable.

From the inside it is the same, for the walls rise twelve feet before reaching the first pane of glass. We walk within a dark passage bounded by unbroken stone surfaces. The symbols of earthly security are everywhere implied in the lowest story, and with it we associate its necessary companion, the fortress. In one sense these walls represent the lay powers which support and defend the Church, just as they protect and support the rest of the structure.

As light brought solid materials to life, it demonstrated the spiritual essence that lay within all things. It was immanental, for the Creator was seen to reside continuously in all that He had created. Thus to find the essence within the substance was to find God. This led naturally to a new and revolutionary method of designing through the axes rather than through the mass.

THE WALL AND THE AXIS

In Romanesque architecture the wall was the primary structural element. When the architect set out the building, he saw the structure as the thickness between the inner and outer faces. All the loads and oblique thrusts were to be absorbed into the mass of the wall. One way to see how thick the wall ought to be was to draw a square within the space of the building so that the sides located the inside plane of the wall. A circle would then be drawn around the outside of this square, and the external face of the wall placed against the circle. Thus, no matter how big or how small the building, the wall thickness would always be proportional to the span.

After 1100 the master began to design the wall around one or more theoretical axes lying *within* the thickness of the masonry. The axis had no dimension; it existed only in the imagination of the architect, but around it he could "see" the masses needed for the building. The plan of the entire building came to be represented by a grid of axes instead of by the actual thickness of the walls and piers. The stonework therefore clothed a divine concept—and became something divine in the process. The axis, abstract and immaterial, generated the built forms. Thus the building was the substance and the axis its essence. This view is both devout and dialectical. The axis is its immanental form.

The process is the same as God's in creating the universe. First He had an idea—the word, or essence, from which He extrapolated the substance. Similarly, the building was designed out of the essence, which lay in the primal act of its design and represented the way in which cosmic space was originally derived from the cosmic center. There-fore it could rightly become the spirit's building on conse-cration. The Heavenly City could exist in it because, in a sense, the master had approached the design with the cor-rect rituals. As Dionysius the Areopagite said, "the mason looks at the archetypes, grasps the divine model, and makes an impression of it in real material" *(De Ecclesiastica* IV.3).

Structurally the consequence was momentous. The loads of the building, and the diagonal thrusts from the vaults and from wind loads, acted on the building along these axes. To visualize one was to imply the other, which is clearly demonstrated in the intersecting flyers of Chartres.

Since the axis was the essence, the loads and dynamic axial thrusts came to be visualized as part of the spirituality of the building. In some cases the loads were conceived as pure energy *rising* within the buttresses as well as de-scending to the ground. The thin shafts on the inside that join the piers to the vaults seem to support the vaults and, by a quick blink of the eyes, seem to hang suspended from them.

As the energy was thought to ascend and descend simul-taneously, the masonry came to reflect this inner move-ment, as can be seen clearly in the bases of the columns. They are like miniature windows into the period, demon-strating the growing mysticism up to 1200, and thereafter its decline and final extinction.

Intersecting flyers between the choir and the south transept of Chartres cathedral clearly show how the thrusts from each direction were conceived as passing independently through one another.

THE COLUMN BASES

The base of the column is usually made up of two projecting rings, or tori, set around the bottom of the shaft, and an indentation between them called a scotia, which was carved to the same depth as the column and no deeper. The Romanesque torus, to the left in Figure 6, looked like two ropes tightened around the column, as though they were holding a piece of wood from splitting. Below the torus is a square base. The circular upper part reflects the column, the square lower part the footing. It is a convenient way to sit one on the other without any integration between them, and it is also symbolically appropriate.

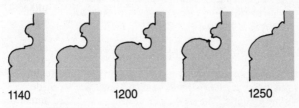

1140   1200   1250

Figure 6. Evolution of the column bases between 1140 and 1250.

Starting in the 1130s in the Chartres western doors, the scotia was bent downward and twisted a little so that it would hold water when it rained. A few decades later the lower torus also began to move, to bulge up and outward so that it was no longer a half-round but elliptical. By the 1180s the upper torus mold began to change too, but rather than turn, it buckled in the middle. The sequence can be followed from left to right in the drawing.

The bases look as though they were being *squeezed* by the tremendous loads above them, as if they had been made of plasticine rather than stone. To have shown this gradual deformation under pressure, the masters must have perceived the energy within the stone, which must have come alive to express the forces within it, more like some organic material than rock.

The last stage is equally significant. The scotia kept turning under "pressure," and the opening into it continued to become smaller. Each step in the process was like one more excruciating weight imposed upon the pier. By the 1220s the slot into the scotia was so small that it would have been difficult to insert the chisel.

Then, some time in the 1240s, the scotia snapped shut

Base to one of the nave piers of Chartres cathedral. The buckling effect is visible on the left.

and disappeared. The recess between the tori had been squeezed out of existence, and the base was reduced to a simple cushion. The new torus covered the different shapes between the circular column and the square base, just as it had in 1100. The stone had returned to stone, and the inner energy had evaporated.

The transition from a transcendent God to an immanental God and back again is well illustrated in these bases. The essential energy in the stone was apparent from the time of the Royal Portal, became more intense as the rest of Chartres cathedral was being constructed, and had disappeared by the middle of the century. With the closing of the scotia, God had become transcendent again.

This may have been the first time that the structure of stone buildings was conceived in such an abstract way. We are used to the concept, for it has been part of western structural practice for many generations, but at this time it was unusual. The wish to reduce matter to energy seems to have satisfied some deep need in medieval people, for the method gradually spread to the rest of the building: first to the vaults and their shafts, then to the flying buttresses and the tracery in the windows, and later to all surface decoration.

THE CANOPY OF PARADISE

Whether the use of axes suggested putting lines on the vaults as ribs or whether both reflected a common need, the evolution of the vault into a suspended canopy depended on devising some technique for levitating its weightiness so that it would appear to float like a tent. Indeed, the image of the tent as the tabernacle of Moses may have set the scene, for medieval drawings often showed it as a paneled tent that would have looked like a vault from inside.

All rib vaults induce an upward movement within the interior. At Saint-Benoît the vaults in the nave and the tunnel-like barrel vaults in the choir can be compared. The pointed junctions and steep profiles of the nave lead the eye up and out of the building. To return our gaze after it has reached the apex is an effort. Rib vaults reinforce not the earthiness of God's place but its ethereality. The concept is audacious; it would have been incomprehensible to the eleventh century, when the choir was built.

There were two types of rib vaults, and each had a different effect on the space. One was six-part, as in Laon and Notre-Dame in Paris, and the other was four-part, as in Braine and Chartres.

Four-part vaults have two diagonal ribs with four curved cells between them. Six-part vaults have one additional rib passing through the boss, but parallel to the transverse arch. The transverse arches and the encasing walls lie over the axial grid that defines the bays, and in one sense the vault reflects their presence in the air.

In a four-part vault the ribs are framed by the axes; in a six-part vault the ribs tie groups of axes together like a topknot, looping across the building to collect vast chunks of space. Each vault is thus discrete and does not lead the eye toward the altar but concentrates our attention on each apex. A six-part vault is rather like a dome, but instead of suspending an opening in the sky, it is a parasol that extends its tassels down to our level.

The psychological importance of this arrangement can be

The rib vaults of the Reims cathedral ambulatory.

The six-part high vaults of Mantes-la-Jolie, each inflated like a tent.

gauged at Tournus, which has the cheapest and most logical vaulting system devised in the Middle Ages, yet was cop-
ied by none. Tournus shows that logic and economy were
beside the point compared to meaning, for its vaults are visually separated from below, thrust up and out of reach,
whereas the builders wanted paradise to be integrated into
the material structure.

Ribs do this; their curved lines disguise the mass and
lead us upward, while plain surfaces only block our vision.
In the repetitive cells of the four-part vault, no one axis or
arch is more striking than another. They form a sequence
of undulating volumes, each centered within the grid. Together they are not so much a sum of parts as a synthesis
that unites the entire vault into one canopy. By attaching
each rib to its own shaft, the zone of the vaults extends
downward over the surface of the walls and carries with it
the meanings it symbolizes. Thus vault and shafts together
join the tabernacle to the church.

THINNING THE SHAFTS AND WALLS
UNDER THE VAULTS

Just as a ciborium was supported on posts over the altar,
and the canopy carried above the king was mounted on
poles held by honored retainers, so the parasol of the City
had "support," though no one would have been misled into
believing that these very thin shafts actually carried the

vaults. At this time they were not carved with the masonry of the wall but were laid as separate vertical *en délit* stones so that a shadow would be cast between them and the wall.

This makes the shafts appear independent of the structure; they look as though they were hanging like ropes rather than pushing up. The idea was first broached in the nave of Fontenay, where the shafts seem to slide down the faces of the piers, supporting little baubles on the ends. It is as if the piers were blocks of rock growing up out of the ground while the shafts were tassels hanging from the vaults like a Chinese lantern. The vaults have become so lightweight that they resemble cloth, with cords hanging from them, pretending to be stone but in real vision the tabernacle of God.

In seeking ways to show that the church was God's temple, some builders reduced the thickness of the wall and the structural members so it would look more tentlike. At Mantes-la-Jolie and Saint-Remi the thin wall is like a curtain: gossamer, limpid, and tranquil. The wall is no longer a boundary, so we easily sense the spaces *on the other side* of the wall. The church is no longer a fortress, yet it feels more secure because it never suggests there may be any threats nearby.

The effect is peaceful and nurturing. We are at rest without being immobilized or driven dramatically into the air. We are left to wander or meditate in tranquillity. These deli-

The walls at Mantes-la-Jolie are paper-thin.

cate structures exemplify the very essence of the period, mystic and immanental, suspended and secure in the knowledge that God was very near. The buildings levitate just a little on the inside, an effect that was also pursued outside in the upper stories and the flying buttresses. For one short, magical moment in the 1170s the tabernacle seemed to occupy the entire material edifice. It was like a temple hanging within the walls of the fortress, so that the City lay within the sanctuary.

The thin walls, the smaller shafts, and the larger windows somehow had to be compensated for structurally, for though the interior might *appear* to be floating, it was still made of heavy stones that had to be upheld. This was achieved in part by increasingly sophisticated and careful workmanship, in part by creating the illusion from the inside that the elements were small and at the same time retaining large supports behind the walls where they could not be seen. By thinning the members and lightening the vaults, the piers did not need to be as thick, and though the buttresses became bigger to take on the loads that had once been carried by the walls, the overall mass of masonry was considerably reduced.

As the quantity of masonry was lessened, the impact of the winds and the outward loads from the vaults became critical factors in the design. The massive walls in Romanesque buildings were usually enough to withstand the lateral thrusts, and as the inner wall had been virtually eliminated, all the loads were concentrated on the external wall. The perimeter wall remained thick, and the lateral thrusts were transferred onto them in a very simple way: by the first of the four key inventions of Gothic, the flying buttress.

FLYING BUTTRESSES AND DEMATERIALIZATION

The flying buttress is a pier placed some distance from the high vaults and attached to the clerestory by an arch: hence the term "flying." As long as the pier was big enough to absorb the lateral thrusts, the building would be stable, which is why these piers are larger in the direction of the thrusts, like buttressing walls. The larger the span of the vaults, the greater the thrust, and so it was a wide building like Sens that stimulated the invention of the flying buttress in the 1160s. The initial purpose was purely structural, for the flyers cannot be seen from the ground. But within a generation their esthetic potential had been recognized.

At Conques and Nevers the wall of the clerestory formed a barrier between the house of God and our world. We are outside, the house is inside. Compare these buildings with Chartres or Beauvais, where the flying buttresses form a lofty cage around the perimeter. They screen the clerestory, hiding the walls so that the precise outline of the most symbolically spiritual part of the building cannot be defined.

It has been pointed out that the steeply sloping flyers at Bourges are far more cost-effective than those at Chartres because they use less material. This is because the flyers at Bourges are very steep and direct the loads to the ground as directly as possible. They look like the gigantic stays of a tent, pulled down to earth and unmistakably structural.

In contrast, examine Chartres or Beauvais from the east: the flyers seem to rise above the edge of the roof like gigantic elbows thrust up and outward. They do not appear to be stabilizing the walls so much as dangling them, like great fingers pointing into the air to hold the church from their tips: the fingers of God suspending the dematerialized and glazed splendor of His City, vibrating just above the heads of the faithful.

A similar effect has been achieved on the inside. The stained glass makes the interior dim, as in moonlight. Entering from daylight, we must wait awhile for our eyes to adjust, the contrast is so great. By the time they do, the cones of our eyes that deal with night vision have come into play, including the violet rods which respond to starlight and to shadows during the day. This imposes a sense of unreality on what we see and dematerializes the interior. The effect is somewhat psychedelic.

Like the flyers, the illumination disguises the solidity of the interior. It appears weightless, as if made from some substance other than stone. Medieval people knew the

The flying buttresses in the choir of Saint-Remi, Reims, seem to dangle the walls from their tips.

building was made of stone, for they saw it being built. Yet it was felt that on consecration God became immanent in the church and transmuted its base materials into the immateriality of the tabernacle. Both the flyers on the outside and the thin *en délit* shafts suspended from the vaults on the inside helped to concentrate this illusion in the clerestory, where heaven is most palpable. The lower level is visibly solid and remains part of our world.

THE DRUM AND THE INNER TEMPLE

Compound and circular piers turn up in the earliest buildings, the former at Germigny-des-Prés, the drums at Canigou, and both at Jumièges, though it will be seen to be significant that cylindrical piers disappeared almost altogether after 1240.

In addition to the symbolism of the circular piers around the altar, and the slower rhythm they impart to bays with alternation, drums create an architecture of space, while the compound pier emphasizes the surface. The medieval principle that each element should clearly express its purpose is better enunciated in the compound pier than in the drum, for each of the shafts in the pier supports its own arch or rib.

Thus the compound pier is an intimate part of the structure. It appears as solid as the shafts, and the shadows between them hold one's gaze on the pier. It is not possible for the eye to simply slide around it, as can happen with the smooth curves of a cylinder.

Even heavy drums, like these at Orbais, emphasize the space around them rather than their mass.

In a manner of speaking, the surface of the drum is slippery. Space around the drum is more important than structure, and although we know that it holds up the building, there is nothing for the eye to grip; we sidle past without attachment, and the space on the far side is continuous with the space we occupy. The drum does not subdivide volumes but passes through them. Thus the interior stretches from one exterior wall to the other, and it looks as though the columns have been lowered into it, as one might lower a bridge into a pool of water.

It is significant that half-drums were seldom attached to the terminal walls to finish the arcade. Instead, the multiple shafts used on the adjacent aisle walls were repeated on the ends. The walls form a single enclosure, and the drums remain distinct from the walls, as though they had been inserted within them. As in Saint-André in Chartres, they are like extensions of the upper floors rather than supports resting on the lower. This scheme first appeared to the north and west of Paris in the 1140s and was most popular in the Royal Domain between 1180 and 1220, exactly coinciding with the most immanental period.

Being isolated from the encasing walls, the drums and the upper parts they support seem like a jeweled reliquary set within the safety of the enclosure. The outer walls remain solid, forming a secure cage around the temple. Thus the drum helps to transform the entire interior into a sanctuary: this is the image of the temple within the fortress.

Drum piers lasted about as long as the belief in immanence. Thereafter they were seldom used, and after a somewhat brief use of the *pilier cantonné* (which is still a drum of sorts), nearly all piers reverted to the compound form of earlier days. (It is interesting to note how many Romanesque forms were reemployed in the later Middle Ages, disguised of course in the trappings of the new Gothic. Both were theologically transcendental epochs, as one might suspect.)

THE SECOND PHASE OF GOTHIC: 1170s–1200
The Temple Within the Fortress

Pilgrim sees the World beyond this world

THE ABBEYS EXPERIMENT
WITH THE SUSPENDED TABERNACLE

The classic architecture of Chartres, and from it the international Gothic which followed, evolved from innovations made in four abbeys to the east of Paris. All four looked for ways to design the triforium as an intermediate zone between the spirit and the world; they aimed to make the upper stories a replica of the Heavenly Jerusalem floating like the ultimate promise over pilgrim's head. There were two approaches, the continuous triforium at Braine and Longpont around 1180 and, in the following decade at Saint-Remi and Orbais, the triforium attached to the clerestory. All used drum piers and projecting flyers to pull the building into the air.

The solution devised at Braine was the most immediately successful, and it was used in nearly every major building for fifty years from Chartres to Reims. However, the Saint-Remi scheme lasted longest, for once the clerestory windows had been extended down to the triforium at Saint-Denis, the two stories became indissolubly united.

THE TRIFORIUM
AND THE CANOPY OF PARADISE

At Braine and Longpont the gallery was replaced by the continuous triforium, which is an articulated hollow threading through the slender vaulting shafts to create a horizontal movement that binds the bays together. The effect resembles weaving; the triforium appears to pass behind the shafts like an unbroken cord, and all loads appear to flow past or through it. The continuous triforium became a centralizing motif in its own right and tied the building together in the horizontal plane. It allowed the builders to increase the height without seeming to be too extreme, and to abandon the six-part vault because it denied the threading horizontality of the new triforium.

The remnants of the blind triforium in the nave of Longpont.

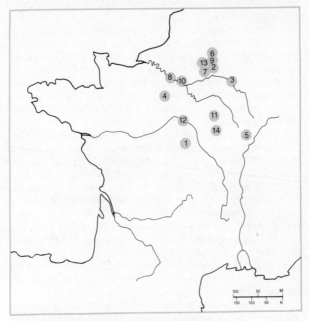

MAP 4 Churches of the Second Phase of Gothic

1 BOURGES, choir of the Cathedral of Saint-Étienne
2 BRAINE, Church of Notre-Dame
3 CHÂLONS-SUR-MARNE, later parts of Notre-Dame-en-Vaux
4 CHARTRES, lower stories of the Cathedral of the Assumption
5 DIJON, Church of Notre-Dame
6 LAON, west façade and towers of the Cathedral of Notre-Dame
7 LONGPONT, ruined Cistercian Abbey of Notre-Dame
8 MANTES-LA-JOLIE, west façade of the Collegiate of Notre-Dame
9 NOUVION-LE-VINEUX, nave of the Church of Saint-Martin
10 PARIS, west façade of the Cathedral of Notre-Dame

11 PONTIGNY, choir of the Church of Notre-Dame
12 SAINT-BENOÎT-SUR-LOIRE, nave vaults of the Benedictine Abbey of Saint-Benoît
13 SOISSONS, lower stories of the choir of the Cathedral of Saint-Gervais et Saint-Protais
14 VÉZELAY, choir of the Basilica of Sainte-Madeleine

As the height of the vaults increased, the triforium anchored the building in the air, so to speak. The center of gravity was raised above the aisles and set into the darkness of the triforium, like an elevated foundation that seemed to lift the building off the ground.

The effect was momentous. When the clergy at Chartres looked for builders to reconstruct the cathedral after the fire, they found them from the region around Braine. Hence, within a few years of Braine's being completed and opened for inspection, a similar scheme was designed for Chartres. This new canon was to influence every major building commenced during the next generation and a half. By 1200 all the classic Gothic cathedrals and more than fifty other important churches had been designed with triforia, and the gallery was dropped for good.

At Chartres you are not impelled toward the altar with the same force as you are at Conques, nor are your normal perceptions of reality disturbed as they are at Saint-Urbain. Yet the choir soars. It pulls us up out of the mundane, demanding our commitment to the spiritual Way. It is the scale that does this, as can be seen by comparing the triforium in the Soissons choir with the one built only a decade or so earlier in the south transept.

In his *De Proprietatibus*, Bartholomaeus Angelicus argued that there were three levels to the cosmos: the celestial world, the elemental, and the lesser. The first was the Idea and the archetypes; from it condensed the middle level which housed such collectives as the four elements, the ether and the stars, and thirdly the individual manifestations of this middle zone. As the church was a microcosm of the universe, the triforium could be identified with this middle level just at the time that theologians were deciding that the purgatorial state (as occupied by Peter in the story) should be redefined as a place. This new status for purgatory is implied in the geometry used to set out the triforium at Chartres.

The triforium was a major innovation in unifying what the Romanesque had kept separate. It did not interfere with the vertical thrust of shafts and clerestory but, curiously, enhanced it in spite of its horizontal nature. The concept is subtle; it depends for its effect on the most carefully balanced detailing so that the triforium emphasizes the vertical by reminding us that the horizontal still exists, even at that level. In contrast, the suggestion at Dijon that the triforium actually passes through the structure is profoundly disconcerting.

The triforium also separated what the Romanesque had kept together. The Braine elevation divided the clerestory from the aisles, and although the tendrils of the canopy still hung down to touch the capitals of the drums, this intermediate zone began the process of separation that by 1240 was to remove the upper stories permanently from the lower.

ASPIRATION

Height

The urge for height that marks the mature Gothic style had been pursued before, in Jumièges for example, and Cluny, whose barrel vaults reached 98 feet (29.5 meters) above the pavement. But the passion to push the vaults higher and higher so that they seemed to gather everything within the building up to themselves was a purely Gothic phenomenon. This passion began in the 1170s at Notre-Dame in Paris, which was taller at 107 feet (32.6 meters). Then Chartres reached 118 feet (36 meters) in the early 1200s.

Bourges and Reims, both vaulted after 1220, advanced only another forty inches in height. Amiens, roofed in the 1240s, rose to 138 feet (42.1 meters), and Beauvais, the tallest of all, reached 157 feet (47.9 meters). The royal cathedral of Notre-Dame had started the passion for height which has been called the Age of the Colossal.

Most buildings in the area adjacent to Paris are squat, the clerestory windows reduced to small roses. Even those built as late as the 1220s and 1230s are dark and cavelike. They have none of the lofty exhilaration found in the contemporary churches being built only a few miles to the east and, except for their detailing, are more like the churches of an earlier century. This is why the Chartres and Soissons cathedrals, the tallest churches after Paris, were built by architects from the north and northeast, not from Paris.

To see the staggering difference that height meant, in works only a few years apart, compare the south transept at Soissons with the choir. As vaults were considered to be the tabernacle of the City, to push them so far up was also to push them far away. Though we call them soaring and feel ourselves elevated by them, height also began the process which culminates in Saint-Urbain and Beauvais of *removing* them from our sphere. Heaven appears so far out of reach that we stand abandoned beneath its splendor.

We may certainly feel uplifted by the vaults, but remember that art is appropriate to the period of its creation, and after the confident intimacy with God that came from the south transept, the Soissons choir is forceful, urgent if not a

Soissons cathedral from the west. The three stories of the south transepts can be glimpsed through the aisle arcade on the right, and the great height of the choir can be grasped from the wall over the opening into the transept.

little demanding, and comparatively uncertain. The thin piers push the triforium far away, using the same technique as in the Paray apse. The vaults seem suspended even though well supported. Over the altar the urge upward is particularly encouraged by the polygonal apse, as the ribs and shafts pull upward toward the giant boss over the pointed ribs and the bright glare of the windows. The choir is like a gigantic tube open along one side to let us in, then to push us upward.

Towers and the Low Roof

Height was not important on the outside until toward the turn of the century. Even at Chartres the roof was originally intended to be low-pitched as it is at Laon, where we are more conscious of the wall than of the covering.

Instead, also around the 1170s, multiple towers were installed along the skyline. Only at Laon were more than a couple completed, where they turned the rather horizontal building into a vertical one. The towers would have electrified the silhouette like a ring of thrusting fingers around the enormous spire in the middle, which was also the great tree connecting earth with heaven, the *axis mundi*. They state to the world that in this building a stupendous effort is being made to reach into the sky, an effort that one would expect to be successful. They resemble a giant socket prepared to plug in to the celestial current.

The jagged skyline of the Braine south transept creates a vertical pulse along the elevation.

Laon cathedral looking past the lantern to the great eastern eye.

The low roof increased the apparent height of the towers by exposing more of them above the ridgeline. The effect is restless compared with the simpler roofs of later buildings. The 1220s saw the decision to scrap the towers and replace them with tall and simple roofs. Chartres and Reims were both begun before then; the latter was intended to have seven towers, while Chartres would have had nine.

The central tower covered the lantern which illuminates the crossing and emphasizes the central axis of the building that connects it to the heavens. The light that materializes through it makes all other spaces less important. At Laon or Braine, unlike the dark lantern at Strasbourg, you are not brought down to earth, nor are you thrown upward as you are at Beauvais.

It is one of the strongest immanental aspects of the 1170s, where pilgrim is bathed by God's light, pouring in from above and spreading outward in ever-widening ripples. Where the vault is the canopy of Paradise, the lantern is the baldachin tent, surrounded by a continuous luminous clerestory.

INTIMACY: THE ROSE WINDOW LETS HIM LOOK IN

Architects fell in love with the rose window. Awesome in its intricacy, majestic in its design and stained glass, it was the most emotionally stunning part of the building.

The rose may have been introduced into France by the Cistercians or Abbot Suger, probably from Italy. The abbot placed it over the western front at Saint-Denis around 1150 (see page 64), while the monks may have set it into the transept walls of Pontigny a little earlier. Within a few years, around 1160, the Cistercians had installed a full-width rose over the eastern end of the abbey of Preuilly, which is between Paris and Fontainebleau.

The rose was not easy to integrate into the rest of the design. If the rose remained small, as on the Senlis west front, it was difficult to stop the wall's dominating it; if the rose were enlarged to the full width of the nave, it tended to conflict with the verticalizing effect of the shafts. More important, the very concept of a stable, centered unit denied the Gothic wish to submerge all the parts into the rhythms of the whole.

Yet the rose gave the building a vibrancy and tension that was lacking in all buildings without it. In the same way that when we stare into somebody's eyes we feel both intimacy and surveillance, the rose encouraged a childlike trust perfectly in keeping with the architecture of Pontigny or Le Thoronet.

Because the circle is the symbol for the one, without beginning or end, these "eyes of God" are also His doorways. Laon demonstrates that wherever you are in the building you will be aware of God's enormous presence looking down at you, especially as the figure of Christ is usually placed in the middle of the rose. These windows let our wandering spirits out just as effectively as they let light in. Through them God looked in on the priest at his task, reminding him of his role in the mass, and examined pilgrim as he left the mass. As Peter of Lincoln wrote, they are

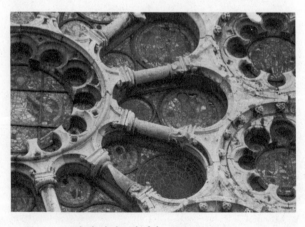

Chartres cathedral, detail of the west rose.

the eyes of the church: rightly the greater is the bishop, the lesser the dean. From the north is the devil, from the south the Holy Ghost; toward these the two eyes look. For the bishop faces south that he may receive the one; the dean north, that he may avoid the other; one looks to be saved, the other lest he perish. (John Harvey, *The Medieval Architect*)

THE THIRD PHASE OF GOTHIC: 1190s–1230s
Detaching the Canopy

Pilgrim is dominated by glass and tracery

ENLARGING THE WINDOW

Up to the end of the twelfth century, windows were nearly always single openings; even where there were two or three in a bay, there remained some particle of wall around them. But where the window stretched the full width between the buttresses, nothing of the wall was left. This was a momentous concept, and the dynasty of great glazed windows that stretched across three centuries from the Sainte-Chapelle to the Senlis clerestory is descended from them.

The concept developed out of the use of axes, for if the building could be conceived as a grid of abstract lines, it would in time be obvious that if all the loads descended where the line through the wall met another across the bay, then all that was needed was a pier-sized buttress at the intersection. The wall was no longer required. From inside, the stonework was reduced to the shafts themselves, and the material edifice dissolved into the glass. The walls had become truly diaphanous.

The first example may have been the Saint-Remi triplet-windowed clerestory just before 1200, though the future lay in the double lancet, used in the Chartres choir aisles just afterward and then applied to the clerestory in Orbais about 1205.

At Saint-Remi the vault capitals were placed below the windowsills, the normal procedure for the time. This attached the vaults to the lower parts so that in its symbolic role as the tabernacle, the canopy connected with our world underneath. But at Orbais around 1205, and then in Soissons and Chartres just afterward, the capitals were moved upward—or, if you prefer, the sills were shifted downward—so that the vault was suspended between the windows, floating the upper stories on a bed of light.

This shift extended the glass zone underneath the capital, as though slicing the tabernacle off from its supports over a shimmering glass cage. The light of God as it occupied the full width of the walls left almost nothing of the structure, and that which remained looked less and less material as the splendor of the illumination dominated the interior.

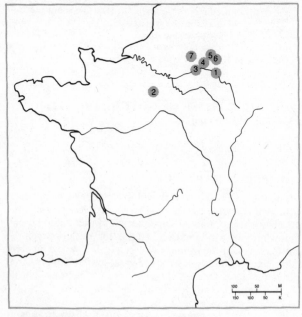

MAP 5 Churches of the Third Phase of Gothic

1 CHÂLONS-SUR-MARNE, upper parts of the choir of the Church of Notre-Dame-en-Vaux
2 CHARTRES, lower stories of the Cathedral of the Assumption
3 ESSÔMES-SUR-MARNE, Church of Saint-Feréol
4 ORBAIS-L'ABBAYE, Church of Saint-Pierre et Saint-Paul
5 REIMS, ambulatory of the Cathedral of Notre-Dame
6 REIMS, upper parts of the choir of the Basilica of Saint-Remi

7 SOISSONS, clerestory of the Cathedral of Saint-Gervais et Saint-Protais

In the darkness of Chartres the stained glass produces such a glare that the edges of the stone under the vaults seem to dissolve. Wondrous and spectacular as the effect is, it was the first step in removing the City from the architecture of the church. The second step was the invention of tracery, which made the windows more eye-catching—at a price.

PLATE AND BAR TRACERY

While not one of the essential inventions of Gothic, tracery turned out to be one of the most spectacular and the most popular. It was used in every country where the style has had any influence. Walls of ancient buildings would be demolished to make room for these extravagant patterns, even though they made incongruous bedfellows with the older work: on the north transept at Laon the builders were in the

South side of the choir, Chartres cathedral.

process of inserting a grand new traceried window when, fortunately, something made them stop. The remains of one jamb can still be seen on the western side.

The patterns of tracery are so eye-catching that the windows became the esthetic center of gravity, wresting attention away from the vault and arcades and directing it toward a two-dimensional translucence rather than the three-dimensional architecture. The wish to dematerialize the building that began at Dijon, and which came to dominate architectural thinking after 1230, found the most useful tool for its purposes in tracery.

The evolution of this concept can be followed in two phases. Around 1190 the clerestory windows of Saint-Remi and the Soissons south transept were divided into triplets. The middle light (the middle opening in a window with three openings in it) was made taller than the others in order to fill the space under the vault. But there was no room for a rose unless the central lancet was to be shorter than the others, and this may have been symbolically unacceptable.

In 1202, in the eastern sanctuary aisle windows at Chartres, twin lancets with a small rose over them were extended the full width of the bay and an arch carried over the window to support the vaults (see above). The stonework between the lancets and the arch was built not like a wall but out of thin stones placed vertically, as there was nothing for the stonework under the arch to do except sup-

Choir of Orbais.

port itself and the glass of the rose pierced in it. Stones set like this are called plates.

In time more openings were cut through the plates to form an assembly of circular holes with odd-shaped solid areas in between, culminating in the western rose at Chartres, designed in 1215 (see page 122). The holes were the primary part of the design, the solids secondary, and this is particularly clear when viewed from the inside.

Another type of tracery, called bar tracery, reversed this process. Instead of arranging a pattern of holes and surrounding them with stone, the stone itself was arranged in patterns and the spaces between them filled with glass. The glass occupies the odd shapes, not the stone, which is in thin pieces, or bars. The stages in this transformation can be followed from the Orbais clerestory and the Essômes transept chapels to the first real tracery in the eastern chapels of Reims before 1220.

Bar tracery helped to change architects' perception of form. In earlier work the shape of every element, be it window, chapel, or porch, was derived from circles, squares, and triangles. Wherever you looked, every part related to geometric forms generated from one or more middle points: windows and doors were designed around a central axis, and so were piers and other elements. Buildings were an assemblage of such forms, and in one sense the wall was just the infilling between them.

Yet tracery made the little spaces in between almost as important as the geometric spaces which defined them.

These noncentralized forms were something new in medieval architecture. In a sense they were geometrically accidental, the result of other actions. Their shapes conformed to no precedent. For the first time, the indeterminate was allowed equal prominence with the determined.

The consequences in later centuries were to be enormous. The very presence of tracery made the opening dominate the surrounding wall. As the window increased in size, a new aggressive esthetic was born in which the building became merely the frame for the window and its tracery, rather than an enclosure for the temple. Tracery was the first step in producing two-dimensional patterns that would, in the next generation, be extended over nearly all surfaces. Stained glass in large single openings, as in Étampes and the Chartres aisles, has a powerful effect because nothing interferes with its impact. But tracery placed a screen in front of the light, pushing it behind the pattern.

Thus tracery removed Suger's *lux nova* from intimate contact with the church, just as the tall clerestory removed the vaults. From the Saint-Denis nave onward the two combined to replace immanence with a glowing but untouchable transcendence.

Tracery in the chapel windows of Reims cathedral.

THE TRIFORIUM ABSORBED

It is the nature of the classical stage in architecture not only to present to perfection the aspirations of the times but to contain the seeds of the future. Innovations that had been brought together so happily at Chartres were altered in this third phase of Gothic. The balance began to change, particularly in three of the elements which had helped to bring it together only a few years before—the triforium, the vaults, and the windows.

At Chartres the triforium separated the clerestory from the aisles, but at Saint-Remi in the 1190s and at Orbais the triforium was attached to the clerestory by extending some of the shafts into the mullions of the windows and omitting the string course between them.

This idea was repeated at Reims and Essômes in the 1220s. A couple of decades later, in the nave of Saint-Denis, the wall behind the triforium was replaced with windows and integrated into the clerestory. Additional small shafts were added around the panel containing the triforium and clerestory, which pushed it back from the plane of the wall. Together these changes did two things: the purgatory of the edifice was merged with the heaven, and at the same time both were subtly removed from our world.

Step by step the celestial paradise withdrew itself, the

The nave of Saint-Denis from the west.

great windows became more magnificent, and the triforium became its support. The arches of the triforium and the pointed gables placed over them looked like the skyline of the Heavenly City. This idea was also used in the carved townscapes on the baldachins over the embrasure statues and in the row of gables alongside the western doorways at Reims.

This City, especially when lit from behind, was part of heaven, silhouetted in its light, but simultaneously tending to remove that light further from us, for it was becoming obvious that our world definitely lay below God's. This distinction was not as clear at Orbais, and it was nonexistent at Mantes-la-Jolie, while the Saint-Denis nave and Beauvais show how far this estrangement had gone in fifty years.

All the elements that had grown out of the immanental mood were transformed after 1220 as people lost their mystic sense. The reintroduction of the compound pier and the absorption of the triforium into the clerestory ended the distinctiveness of the Braine format, while the widened windows and elegant tracery came to dominate the spaces.

THE FOURTH PHASE OF GOTHIC: 1220–1230s
Simplification and Repetition

Pilgrim is returned to his place

In earlier phases of Gothic the enclosure of the church was continuously broken up or prised open. The simple rectangle of Nevers or Canigou was dismembered by the flyers and the towers, and internal regularity evaporated in the bright glass and staring rose windows, in the central lantern and the incredibly thin members.

All this was changed in the decades following 1220, when the elements that had grown out of the immanental mood were transformed. This date is as important as that of 1130: it was the start of a process that was to continue for a generation.

Towers and lanterns were first eliminated in the 1222 redesign of Chartres. In Soissons, Chartres, and Reims the crossing was vaulted over and the lantern became superfluous, as one heavenly zone is enough in any church. Instead of having the light flood into the center, it was excluded by a protective lid at the same height as the other vaults. This sealed the interior and placed a capping on spiritual ambition.

Without a lantern the interior was like the closed system then being created in philosophy, in which Albert Magnus and Thomas Aquinas were attempting to argue every aspect of faith by reason. Neither was a welcome change, for by overdefining their boundaries, they took the mystery out of things and limited dreams and promises.

When it was important to emphasize the verticality of the

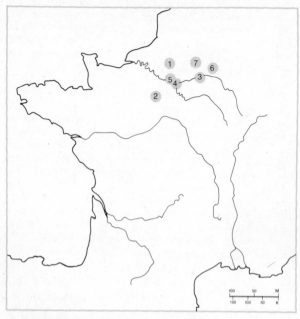

MAP 6 Churches of the Fourth Phase of Gothic

1 BEAUVAIS, choir of the Cathedral
of Saint-Pierre
2 CHARTRES, last parts of the
Cathedral of the Assumption
3 ESSÔMES-SUR-MARNE, clerestory of the Church of Saint-Feréol
4 PARIS, enlarging the clerestory of
the Cathedral of Notre-Dame
5 PARIS, the Sainte-Chapelle
6 REIMS, upper parts of the Cathedral of Notre-Dame

7 SOISSONS, crossing vaults over
the Cathedral of Saint-Gervais et
Saint-Protais

towers, the roof had been kept low, but it was with an almost audible sigh of relief that the pitch of the roof was increased when the lantern was eliminated. At Chartres the
clergy were even prepared to pay a huge sum for additional
flying buttresses in order to raise the roof. The effect was to
tone down the silhouette of the building so that it was less
stimulating to pilgrim. Did the clergy wish to discourage
him from taking salvation into his own hands? Had the fantastic enthusiasm of the previous century been too disturbing, or had the passion and cruelty of the Albigensian
Crusade so reinforced the Church's authority that pilgrim's
hopes and initiatives had to be curtailed and his presumptuous belief that he could have followed the spires to heaven
ended?

Whatever the reasons, conscious or unconscious, a lid
was being placed over the faith, limiting it and keeping pilgrim in his place. The simplified roofs and the towerless sil-

*Chartres
cathedral
north rose.*

houettes, as well as the heavy rhythms of the uniform piers and the weighty triforium, came to dominate. At Reims the triforium is also a lid, for it is taller in proportion to the whole than at Chartres, and the members are distinctly heavier. All in all, there was less excitement and promise in the new architecture.

The transept roses at Chartres show how the eye of God was changing at the same time. From being an independent centered pulse of energy, the northern wheel was absorbed into the windows underneath so that it no longer held pilgrim in its core but dissipated its aim in a breathtaking extravagance, a radiant glory of complex glass and tracery. The northern rose is not a telescope into the City, or God's eye, but it is a brilliant tapestry, and as the splendor of the rose increased in later buildings, the direct spiritual connection with God disappeared behind a screen of color.

RAYONNANT: AFTER 1230
Fragmentation and Illusion

Pilgrim floats across a decoratively overloaded surface

Rayonnant was based on three devices refined to the nth degree: the Dijon technique of peeling the inner skin off the outer shell, the Essômes method of joining the triforium to the clerestory, and the idea of tracery. In the mid-thirteenth century all three were applied almost indiscriminately to

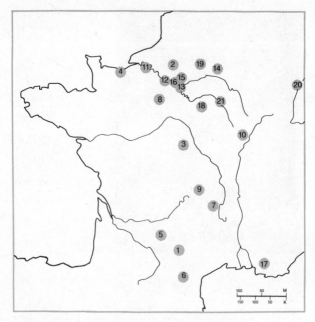

MAP 7 Churches of the Rayonnant and the Export Style

1 ALBI, Cathedral of Sainte-Cécile
2 BEAUVAIS, Cathedral of Saint-Pierre
3 BOURGES, west façade of the Cathedral of Saint-Étienne
4 CAEN, choir of the Church of Saint-Étienne
5 CAHORS, choir of the Cathedral of Saint-Étienne
6 CARCASSONNE, Basilica of Saint-Nazaire
7 LA CHAISE-DIEU, Church of Saint-Robert
8 CHARTRES, Vendôme Chapel of the Cathedral of the Assumption
9 CLERMONT-FERRAND, Cathedral of Notre-Dame
10 DIJON, west façade of the Church of Notre-Dame
11 JUMIÈGES, ruined choir of the Benedictine Abbey of Notre-Dame
12 MANTES-LA-JOLIE, southwest entry of the Collegiate of Notre-Dame

13 PARIS, transepts of the Cathedral of Notre-Dame
14 REIMS, west façade of the Cathedral of Notre-Dame
15 SAINT-DENIS, nave of the Basilica of Saint-Denis
16 SAINT-GERMAIN-EN-LAYE, Chapel of Saint-Germain
17 SAINT-MAXIMIN-LA-SAINTE-BAUME, Basilica of Sainte-Madeleine
18 SENS, Notre-Dame Chapel of the Cathedral of Saint-Étienne
19 SOISSONS, north transept of the Cathedral of Saint-Gervais et Saint-Protais
20 STRASBOURG, nave of the Cathedral of Notre-Dame
21 TROYES, Church of Saint-Urbain

every element. Tracery covered the walls at Carcassonne; in the Paris transepts the rose window joined the lancets underneath; and the peeling process became enormously sophisticated in Saint-Urbain in Troyes. The detailing was refined by increasing the number of shafts or roll molds, by sharpening their edges, and generally increasing the brittleness.

The illusionist world of Rayonnant begins at Saint-Germain-en-Laye, where the windows and buttresses have been detached from the vaults and the walls pushed out of sight behind a screen. Forms have become crystalline,

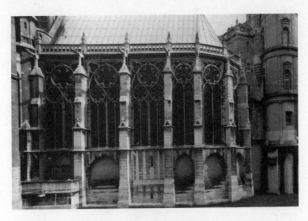

The square windows at Saint-Germain-en-Laye do not reflect the presence of the vaults behind them.

sparkling, and translucent rather than solid and regular. Architecture has consolidated itself—and in the process become a little boring. There is now a controlled uniformity, for each bay of the aisles and the central vessel is vaulted in the same way, each shaft explicitly sustains one single function, each window tracery is reflected in its neighbors and in the various levels. Although the construction was done in as many campaigns as in earlier buildings, the directors of the work maintained a greater control.

The search for wholeness and the gradual elimination of diversity represents an abiding decline from earlier ideals. In the robust days of the twelfth century men stood nine feet tall, extending themselves, unconcerned with neighborliness. It was enough that they believed their designs were correct for them to be built. There is too much good manners after 1250 for dreams to appear more than skin-deep.

The distinctions between the functions of the elements began to blur toward 1240. The hitherto separate moldings were fused or brought so close together that their identities were lost. The projection of the impost was reduced, the scotia in the torus disappeared, and the window shafts moved closer to the wall shafts while the junctions between them became so fluid that the shafts tended to merge into a single bundle of functionless roll molds.

The skill is fabulous, corners are sharp, profiles intricate, and the diamond has replaced the square to emphasize the corners rather than the sides. The thin shadows etherealize everything, like the most delicate cage, and texture covers all surfaces without emphasizing any.

It is hard to focus on one spot, for the strong light displays the edges of the stone and one's concentration is

Two layers of tracery at Saint-Urbain, Troyes.

weakened. The clarity of God's light no longer transmutes the wall but confuses it. What had once been separated into spiritual and temporal is now both. At Saint-Urbain layers of tracery have crept across the walls and additional layers have moved in front of the windows. Arcades cover the flying buttresses, and one cannot be sure where the structure is to be found. The air passes through and behind members that were once solid and were known to be crucial to the stability of the building.

As the triforium was absorbed into the clerestory, and both were pushed higher into the sky, the City moved further out of reach. The surface again became more important than the space, and the sacredness of the church was lost in the decorative overload. The illusion took root at so deep a level that we lost contact with both earth and heaven. The youth of Gothic was over.

THE EXPORT OF A FINISHED PRODUCT

After 1240 the architecture evolving in the Paris Basin was adopted by royal patrons throughout the continent because it combined a costly grandeur within a religious setting. The reputation of the French monarch as "the king of earthly kings because of his divine anointment, his power, and his military eminence" (as Matthew of Paris wrote in the later thirteenth century), gave French culture an aura that other monarchs were quick to copy.

The French were conscious that they were the most vigorous and enterprising race in medieval Europe. They had organized the crusading movement and had supplied most of its fighters and leadership. They had established their feudal system in Greece and Palestine, in southern France and Sicily. It was their destiny, one would think, to be the inspiration of Europe.

The new architecture was called the *Opus Francorum* well into the fourteenth century, and everywhere we find traditional local detailing being modified to take the latest French profiles for tracery and vaulting. As economic conditions worsened in northern France, some masters traveled to other regions in search of work, just as a hundred years earlier the Paris Basin had attracted many of the finest sculptors and masons. It is no wonder, when we consider how international this style became, that John of Salisbury called France the most civilized country of his time.

There is a difference between the Gothic of Laon and Braine, and the Gothic that others so enthusiastically received. The latter came from the Sainte-Chapelle and Reims. It was more crystalline, harder-edged, and had less substantial detailing. There was more glass and less structure, greater undercutting of moldings and less solidity.

The apse of the lower chapel, the Sainte-Chapelle, Paris.

Where early Gothic was both of this earth and within the spirit, the exported Rayonnant, or Court Gothic, was intellectual and extravagant.

Yet Gothic was never, in spite of Clermont-Ferrand and Carcassonne, natural to the south of France or to Italy. The architecture there remained mural, small-windowed, and massive. Perhaps it was the intensity of the sun and light which encouraged the dark, maybe Gothic could have been produced only in a feudal society, or perhaps the Classical influence was too strong. Whatever the natural tendencies, the takeover during the Albigensian Crusade played no mean part in alienating the south against all things northern while removing the excess wealth that might have sustained a new architecture.

With the creation of an exportable style, much of the vigor and inventiveness seems to have gone out of French architecture. The Rayonnant style of the courts does not speak to the soul as did the earlier works of Chartres and Saint-Remi, of Étampes and Essômes.

FLAMBOYANT: AFTER 1450
Playful, Inventive, and Skillful

Pilgrim is isolated from God

There was a long hiatus in construction that reflected the deeper tragedy of France from the mid-thirteenth century to the mid-fifteenth century—depression and overpopulation followed by war and plague, eight generations with little prosperity or security. Then new wealth after the war imparted an energy to the old illusions and gave rise to new ones.

Architecture, as is its nature, remained large in scale and

Vault of Albi cathedral south porch.

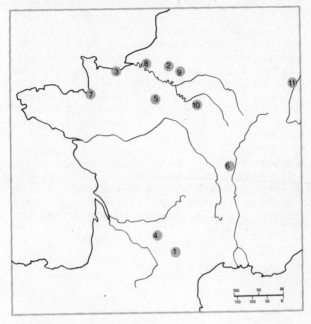

MAP 8 Churches of the Flamboyant

1 ALBI, south porch of the Cathedral
   of Sainte-Cécile
2 BEAUVAIS, transepts of the Cathedral of Saint-Pierre
3 CAEN, Church of Saint-Pierre
4 CAHORS, cloister of the Cathedral
   of Saint-Étienne
5 CHARTRES, west spire of the
   Cathedral of the Assumption
6 CLUNY, Bourbon Chapel of the

   Abbey of Saint-Pierre et Saint-Paul
7 MONT-SAINT-MICHEL, choir of
   the Benedictine Abbey of Saint-Michel
8 ROUEN, Church of Saint-Maclou
9 SENLIS, transepts of the Cathedral
   of the Assumption
10 SENS, transepts of the Cathedral of
   Saint-Étienne
11 STRASBOURG, lateral chapels of
   the Cathedral of Notre-Dame

costly to create. The Flamboyant style grew out of the crystalline Rayonnant, continuing its surface patterns which
disguised any remaining solidity. But there is an almost
pathological dread of clarity. Ambiguity is endlessly pursued, and whereas all the elements were once integrated
logically and lucidly, they are now dissolved in the shimmering air. Where the visual impact of Reims is rich and
magnificent, tricks and stylish fashions become the mode,
tending toward lavish ornament.

All is concentrated in the vaults, as in Strasbourg and
Beauvais: they can be like woven nets hanging over our
heads. The ribs need not rest on the shafts but are ended off
before they meet the structure. The edges of the vaults may
be kept a little way from the walls, bypassed by the shafts
which go on to support some real roof overhead.

The thin arches and the diamond geometry began to
twist and curve, turning back on itself to weave and wave
like shimmering flames of pure energy. The tracery at

Saint-Maclou undulates with such vigor that one has to withdraw a little not to dance with it.

Flamboyant is the end of a great tradition. We do not deal with it in the depth we dealt with the work of the earlier centuries because its grasp of symbols was less clear and it was expressed less coherently than the tradition at Saint-Denis or Chartres. Our own times are approaching, and the meanings are less well observed. The architecture itself is quite superb, exquisitely carved, designed with verve and imagination. However, this guide is concerned not with the esthetics of the churches but with their meaning.

Paradoxically, Flamboyant makes us passive. The active pilgrim of the twelfth century has been turned into a passive worshipper. The building no longer encourages him to participate in its symbolism, so he remains a spectator of the performance, immobilized by the architecture swirling restlessly around him, offering him little to still the soul.

4

THE MASTERS
AND THEIR
METHODS

It is amazing that small medieval towns could have erected their own cathedrals, for even Chartres had only 9000 inhabitants in the thirteenth century. If we had built Chartres cathedral in 1985, it would have cost almost $300 million. The destroyed church of Saint-Nicaise in Reims cost 25,000 livres; the king's total annual income, from which he had to run and defend the whole of his territory, was only eight times that much.

It has been estimated that during one century more than 2700 churches, chapels, and cathedrals were built just in the Paris Basin—about twenty-seven every year! In this same century, more than eighty cathedrals and one hundred major abbeys were built in France. In 1100 the Cluniac order had thirteen hundred daughter houses plus an equal number of parish churches. The total building cost must have been staggering!

The immensity of this achievement in construction can be appreciated only in the context of the times, the limits to medieval technology and site organization, the real difficulties of weather and fund raising, and the part each factor played in determining the ultimate form of the buildings.

TECHNIQUES, TOOLS, AND TEMPLATES

A large building site would have employed well over four hundred people, organized around a number of workshops and yards, with covered sheds for the masons, smithies, and carpenters and great cranes for lifting the stones. At Chartres there were four yards, one on each side of the nave and a second pair flanking the choir. They were not in immediate touch with one another, and to make communication more difficult, at one stage the master's office was at the triforium level in one of the towers.

How then did the master mason, working alone or occasionally with a partner, manage to control this enormous team? How did he instruct the workers to cut a block to a certain size at the quarry, so that it could be fashioned for a particular function, and ensure that it was finished properly, sent to the right place for lifting, and laid the right way up?

The quarryman needed instructions, as did the carter who carried the stones the twelve kilometers from Berchère-les-Pierres. The foreman at the site needed to connect the stone on arrival with the instruction for a particular shape, and after it had been cut the gang of men who erected the stones had to know where to put it. In all, four separate groups were occupied with each stone—without benefit of telephone or photocopier. More than two hundred stones were being quarried, transported, carved, and erected each day! And then there were the prodigious quantities of scaffolding and mortar, iron for the windows, and lead for the roofs.

The accuracy of the carving and the efficiency of erection testify to their organizational skill. But how was it done? No one person, not even an architect, could control such a multitude unaided. The key lay, then as in Roman or Chaldean times, in two things: the foreman and the template.

Building teams are divided into specialist groups or gangs, and when the project is large there may be a number of gangs within each discipline. It has been found over the centuries that the optimum gang size is between eight and a dozen. Among the masons this would include four or five carvers, a couple of apprentices, a few laborers, and a foreman.

It is the foreman who understands the work and maintains daily contact with the master. He takes possession of the stones as they arrive from the quarry, and he ensures that each is delivered to the right erection gang. It is the foreman who constitutes the most precious core of any building organization. In lean times the master could let everyone else go, for he could always employ more masons or laborers, but the key men would have worked together for much of their lives.

The instructions to the foreman came in the form of templates. Templates were full-size replicas of the stones to be carved, cut out of thin sheets of birch wood, and usually marked with an identification number. There were also detailed plans of vaults and elevations of tracery with each stone marked on them. The carvers worked from the templates, and the erection gangs used the identification marks to place the stones.

If you are at Chartres as you read this, look carefully at the stones of the buttress next to the western entry door, or stand underneath one of the crossing piers and look up the 75 feet (23 meters) to the vaults. The accuracy is impressive, for each stone has been cut to within a millimeter of the template. Then remember how hard this stone is. Try scratching it with your thumbnail; even a key will not mark it. Of course the stone has had time to harden over the years, but even so, the limestone from Berchère is one of the hardest.

As the template was the key, it had to be accurate. Without our copying techniques, they used geometry to set it out. Their sort of geometry was dictated by their tools, which were those that every architect used until quite recently: the compass and square, the straight edge, and proportional dividers. Used with care, these tools are totally accurate.

They used the compass to construct a right angle and a 45° angle, and if they wanted to join two lines inclined to one another, they usually did it with a compass and rule. Thus their geometry was based on those figures which could be constructed with straight edge and compass: the square, curves, the octagon, the equilateral triangle, the hexagon, and the circle. Today we use the drafting board, the T-square, and the set square, and so we are more comfortable designing in rectangular blocks. Our work, like theirs, is in part a function of the tools we use.

There are two reasons for using geometry. Imagine the average building site, covered in mud, the templates perhaps left in the rain or even inadvertently tossed on the fire, and imagine that one vault has been completed and covered up before the next one was ready. How would you replace the lost template for a rib? This urgent difficulty can be resolved if you follow the same geometry every time you design it, and thus geometry is primarily the tool of replication.

Second, imagine the engineering problems involved in an age without techniques for calculating stresses and loads, when the builder had to design a beam that would span twice the distance that had ever been covered before. They used rule of thumb calculations, employing geometric and

Individuality and repetition in the gables on the south side of the Chartres cathedral choir.

numeric ratios that were not unlike our rules for brickwork footings in small buildings.

Because a master was taught by his master rather than in a central school, there were few rules common to the trade. Thus there was no point in one master's leaving his templates behind when he quit the job, for the next master would not be able to reproduce them. So the departing master took them, and his successor made new ones according to his personal geometry.

Consequently the shape of many moldings changed on the arrival of a new master. The change was not necessarily a drastic one, but it was apparent enough to be recognized. You can see an example of this at Chartres if you stand outside the entrance to the crypt on the south side of the choir and look up at the transept. Between the aisle window and the tower there is a gallery with straight lintels. Examine with care the cornice under this gallery and the projecting drip course just over that, and you will see two rather obvious examples of changed templates.

All masons worked from dawn to dusk, for artificial lighting was not very good. Summer working times were twice as long as those of winter. They had more holidays than we do, and even though the winters were cold and wet, they lost less time than one might expect because the lodges were enclosed and heated. More time was lost during the harvest, when many of the laborers were called to the fields. Employers would provide gloves, at times hats in summer, and boots for the autumn rains. Laborers were as jealous of their conditions as the modern worker, and their guilds looked after family benefits, pensions for widows, and the education of children.

In many other respects the medieval building site was not markedly different from today's, except that there was no machinery. Hammers and saws were used instead of power tools, barrows and hods rather than hoists, and there were many more people. They had mallets and chisels, rasps and axes, just as our fathers did.

The cranes were among the most interesting devices. There were innumerable types, from the small winches to the massive double-wheeled monsters capable of lifting two tons. Men would walk inside the wheels and slowly raise formidable masses to the topmost height of the cathedral. Some of the stones in the roofs and parapets weigh a ton or more and were lifted and set in place at heights of 150 and even 250 feet (45 to 75 meters)! At Chartres there were at least four of these giant cranes and possibly a dozen smaller ones, which together would have had to raise some forty-five tons of material a day.

The great cranes may have made one lift every fifteen minutes during a twelve-hour summer day, except in the event of breakdown or other hazard; two stones per lift would have been a fair average. The mortar, rubble, and timber would usually have been lifted separately by the many lighter cranes scattered around the perimeter of the job. At that rate they would have needed at least three erection gangs working around each crane, and thus there may have been some confusion at the unloading platform unless it was well organized.

One has to think hard to escape the modern world, but try to visualize making the ropes that would support a ton or more when all you have is hemp, rarely bitumen, and the skill of your hands. Consider making a pulley from one block of wood and setting it over a hand-wrought metal axle. Then put a ton on it and see how often it will turn before it sticks or breaks. It can be done, of course, but the skills needed are impressive.

In all ways these men demand our respect—for their organizational skills, for their ability to cut and place intractable materials, and for the imagination they showed in solving problems that we too would find difficult.

THE MASTERS

The master is he who devises the form of the building without himself manipulating its matter.

Thomas Aquinas

One is fascinated by the numerous changes in the moldings of medieval churches and the endless alterations to such basic elements as windows and piers, even where side by side, as in the Chartres cornice. One constantly finds that corbels differ on opposite sides of the same door, that but-

Changes to moldings indicate where changes to templates, and therefore changes of masters, occurred. The shape of the triforium cornice and (less noticeably) the small drip over it were both altered in the east side of the south transept, Chartres cathedral.

tresses shrink and grow from bay to bay. In detail there is little homogeneity.

Changes often indicate breaks between building campaigns, for few buildings were constructed in one effort. Because funds were hard to obtain, the men could work on the site only when there was money in the chest. Thus nearly every church contains the work of many masters, each pursuing his own ideas and using his own men for as long as there were funds. Each master worked in a personal manner, with his own preferences for certain shapes and ideas, for particular and usually unique rules of geometry, and with his own foot unit.

It is surprising that so much appears so unified in spite of the differences. Of course, age and a common material make a difference, and the builders shared an image of what a church ought to be. It was not like trying to mix Frank Lloyd Wright with Bernini, for they were assembling variations on a common theme.

To find so many differences in a single building may seem surprising, for we are so used to forward planning and strong site control that it is hard to conceive of any other way of getting great buildings constructed. In the Middle Ages two factors mitigated against our methods of today.

The first was insufficient financing. Not the lack of money, for that seems to have flowed in for some projects in enormous quantities, but the lack of those financial tools that provide bridging funds against future income. They had no banks, so that when the money—the actual coins, gold, and jewels—ran out, there was no alternative to stopping the work and sending the builders away. At Chartres this happened almost every year for over sixty years. It was not because the builders could work only during the season, for in some cases they would spend only a few months on a campaign, in other cases many years.

The second factor was the mortar. It was made from lime, not cement, and it took at least three months to set and more than six months during very cold winters. Under arches and vaults the formwork could not be removed until the mortar had hardened; on a small building there was often nothing more for the builder to do but leave the site. This was standard practice.

As this was happening on every building site, at least up to the mid-thirteenth century, the same contractors worked on many buildings, laying a few courses on one church, a wall somewhere else, then a porch roof on a third. Their lives were a constant round of small contributions to many places: it has been calculated that fewer than a hundred contractors were responsible for all the major building works in the Paris Basin during the century of the great boom, and each of them worked on parts of at least forty buildings. The architecture of France is thus like a patchwork quilt made from a few pieces of material used again and again in random order.

The builders often traveled great distances. Because there was so little major work going on in the diocese, all the masters who worked on Chartres had to be brought from elsewhere. One came from the Remois, four from the Soissonnais, and at least two from along the Oise River. They were chosen from just those areas where nearly all the building work in France was being concentrated at that time because they were the men with experience.

Seldom after 1100 were buildings constructed by members of the clergy. Experience became essential as the complexity and technical daring of the architecture evolved. When the clerics did their own building, it was because they were isolated or poor. When monks are mentioned on the site, they are usually listed as unskilled labor, and one is inclined to suspect that they may have been more of a hindrance than a help. In one case out of ten when a novice appears in the chronicles it is because he fell off the scaffolding or in some other way did himself damage because he had not the skill to be careful.

The architect was a professional. He was a man of the world, widely traveled, often well-read, the friend of princes and bishops from whom he gained an understanding of those Scholastic procedures found in his works. He earned enough to be in the same rank as the knights, and he was envied by many, even the clergy. His perquisites might include eating at the abbot's table, the use of a horse or two, and a gift of fine robes. He was famous for the competent professionalism and curt orders which became a byword in French literature whenever a writer wished to describe a man who did things well and with superior assurance. He enjoyed a prestige unequaled then or since.

By the thirteenth century, the most important signal of the architect's high role was that he could be buried in his own church, just like the richest patron or the founding bishop. It was as close to being a relic as medieval man could become, short of sainthood. Perhaps of equal significance, in one case his wife was also buried in the same church and given her own inscription.

In the north transept of Reims cathedral is the tomb of the master mason, Hughes Libergier. He is an elegant figure with cape and gloves and the tools of his profession. He is framed by a canopy and, like a bishop, attended by angels. This is no simple tradesman but one of the personages of the land, well thought of and rich enough to afford such a monument.

Even during his lifetime his name could be inscribed in the largest decorative item in the cathedral, the labyrinth. He had his portrait carved alongside the founding bishop or king. Pierre de Montreuil was called a *Doctor Lathomorum*, an appellation usually reserved for top scholars. The architect's social position had become so exalted that he was criticized for his vanity. For the architect, and only the architect, was capable of erecting paradise on earth. The church was a visible slice of heaven. Not even the bishop, save for a fragment of time at the elevation of the host, could claim to have brought God to earth. Yet the architect was doing this every day.

THE DESIGN PROCESS

Normally the first master employed on a project would have prepared a design, perhaps with a drawing or a model. However, there were probably no working drawings as we know them, no details or specifications, and when the first master moved on, only the model remained to tell the next builder what was expected of him. At times contracts stated that the new work was to be just like that of another church, and then the builder could visit it, make sketches, and do his best to repeat it, but in general only the barest directions were passed on from one master to another.

Over the years changes were made in the design. Even a cathedral like Chartres, which was built speedily, would have appeared out of date by the time it was half finished. The clerestory in the model of 1194 would probably have been like the one at Braine, with large single windows, but in 1211 the chapter decided that the ideas of seventeen years earlier were too antiquated and that the present scheme with its double lancets and rose window would be more appropriate.

Alterations on many levels to a chapel in Chartres cathedral: for example, the buttress set over one of the crypt windows, reduction in buttress widths and their centers, and the changes to the corner buttress.

The unity of the buildings, in spite of the changes, comes mainly from their geometric methods. The sizes for all the larger elements were derived from the plan, and all details were then derived from these elements. For example, the thickness of the exterior wall came from the span across the nave, the size of the mullion from the thickness of this wall, while the rebate in it was determined from the overall width of the mullion. Thus each part of the building evolved though a graduated set of extractions, each one based on the last, until at the base of all stood the ground plan itself. For this reason the whole edifice looks of a piece.

The creation of a Gothic building resembled the growth of a tree. The seed knows it will be an oak, and in the multitude of oaks growing in a forest we recognize that each is an oak, no matter how individual. But site and circumstance will determine how any one tree will grow. The particular form of the individual tree, straight or twisted or perfect, will depend on the type of soil, on storms and drought. Thus each master followed his own vision of the form "church," allowing the circumstances as he found them and the funds and ideas available from his client to direct the manner of his solution.

It was a sensitive and varied approach to architecture. Fluid and adaptable, it engendered the best from these men. As now, there were few geniuses, but where our great architects appear only in the occasional building amid a sea of general mediocrity, in the Middle Ages the most creative men would enliven one level or another of nearly every building. The ordinary was constantly enriched by talent. This is one reason why medieval architecture is both so varied and so beautiful.

We must give thanks to their contractual system, their *ad hoc* finances, and the slow-setting mortar.

WHO WERE THESE MEN?

The names of four of the masters who worked on the cathedral of Reims were once inscribed around the labyrinth. In the center only one archbishop was named. Yet we still have the names of most of the senior medieval clergy, for they signed charters, issued public edicts, and engaged in the political events of the day. Their names survived the centuries because they were written on parchment, yet it is rare to find a builder writing his name on the building. It seems relevant that medieval graffiti are full of crosses, ships, or tools, but almost never reveal the men who drew them. Men expressed the thoughts passing through their heads but did not sign their work. What was being drawn was more important than who was drawing it.

At the bottom of the arches over the Moissac tympanum are two tiny figures, probably the two sculptors who collaborated on the portal. Both are furiously active, their bodies twisted; the one on the right carries the mason's mallet in

Three masons' marks, which were tallied at the end of each day, since the workers were paid by the piece.

one hand ready to hit the chisel in the other, as if working on the decoration of the stone that holds him. The other figure is clean-shaven, the strong movement of his arm having brought him face to face with the observer. He is younger than his companion, though not as swarthy. All that is missing is their names.

We are told repeatedly that the medieval artist worked anonymously for the glory of God. This is a sentimental tale propagated some time ago by the clergy, and it is not born out by the facts. We have the names of more than three thousand architects and many more sculptors, illuminators, and metal workers. We also have inscriptions that indicate their healthy respect for their own skills. Few medieval architects signed their names, just as today few house painters or joiners sign their works: it is a matter of skill, not ego.

The sensitive, aristocratic face of Saint Maurice on the south porch of Chartres cathedral, 1204.

Nevertheless, at Issard the sculptor incised, "God has created everything; as man has remade everything. Natalis made me." Gilabertus of Toulouse reminded people that he was a "well-known man," and Gislebertus of Vézelay proudly wrote his signature on the work he executed at Autun.

Patrons recognized the value of the best men. Artists who were serfs could gain their freedom with their skills, and when freed their status was higher than that of most other workmen. To keep them in an area, craftsmen were occasionally exempted from all forced labor and at times given special protection while working on a project. But there was no distinction between artist and craftsman. This was an innovation of the Renaissance.

No medieval sculptor refused a commission because he felt it might impair his artistic integrity. The architect would design a cathedral and a hydraulic organ. The painter would illuminate a manuscript and paint banners for the tournament. One of the finest painters at the Burgundian court in one week added the finishing touches to two dining-room chairs, repaired and repainted an apparatus for surprising the guests with showers of water, and decorated the inside of the royal galleon.

These men did not have the assertive self-consciousness of a Michelangelo or a Cellini, yet they still wished to be remembered, as Villard de Honnecourt asks in his manual on building practices: "Villard de Honnecourt salutes you and asks all those who will work in the various categories spoken of in this book to pray for his soul, and to remember him."

We see the individuality of the artist in such little things as gargoyles, corbel figures, the treatment of a face, the handling of a gesture. Viollet-le-Duc, who restored so many of these buildings, explained:

> Secular art was like freedom of the press, an outlet always ready to react against the abuses of the feudal state. Civilians saw in art an open book in which they could boldly project their thoughts under the cover of religion. Sculpture possessed a democratic sentiment, a hatred of oppression.

There was also some ribald sculpture, which would certainly not have been encouraged by the Church: the projecting bum at Dijon through which poured the rainwater, the dwarf attempting self-fellatio on the Chartres west front, and innumerable scenes on the undersides of stall chairs.

FUNDING

The enormous cost of the building boom between 1130 and 1230 relative to the medieval economy was staggering. Yet the money was found without the support of modern financing techniques or great banks.

Kings and barons met much of the cost, and just as important were the gifts of the pilgrims. Other sources were deathbed gifts, altar offerings delivered in produce as well as in money, special offerings made on feast days, and indulgences. One routine was to send relics on tour with rousing preachers hoping for miracles. In one case a man who had been raised from the dead accompanied the bones that had caused this wonder, helping in the collection of a great deal of money. Many French churches made their fortunes in the religious revival of the twelfth century. The flood of relics which reached the west after the 1204 sack of Constantinople drew immense sums from the pilgrims.

At first the building boom stimulated the economy, except where the church and merchants were at war, as in Reims. Once built, the cathedrals and churches could do little to restimulate the economy, compared with other forms of construction, such as bridges, which contributed directly to economic welfare and growth. There are good reasons to believe that towns like Beauvais and Reims crippled themselves to build their cathedrals, whereas the construction of a daring bridge near the St. Gotthard Pass hastened the transformation of southern Switzerland from the dead end of Germany into the threshold of Italy.

For a hundred years there seems to have been an unassuageable enthusiasm to construct. No one waited until all the funds had been promised; they just pushed ahead without fiduciary issues or bank loans. They had the faith that no matter how inappropriate the location or the size of the project, God would somehow provide. We climb to the dizzy heights of the towers at Laon only to find at the top that the treads of the staircase have been continued a few risers above the roof, ready for the next stage. These spires would have soared ever upward, like the towers of Babel, to touch God Himself.

The masters and their men worked on these buildings in a way that we would find hard to emulate in the twentieth century, for we have neither their vision nor their geometry, our labor skills are different, and without their fundamental certainty that God would see that His work was done, it is doubtful that we would undertake such projects at all, let alone entrust each of them to such a diverse cavalcade of masters.

The great cathedrals were entirely the product of the Middle Ages, of their audacity and trust, of their sensitivity to the work of those who had gone before. They accepted—and indeed made a virtue of the fact—that a building was more a process than a project. It was a natural growth which might take more than a generation to evolve to its final form, an accumulation of historic events in stone that, like a living organism, evolved toward a common image of the Heavenly City while at the same time reflecting something of each man's personal vision.

5

DESCRIPTIONS OF THE CHURCHES

ALBI, Cathedral of Sainte-Cécile

Department of the Tarn, 76 km (47 miles) northeast of Toulouse; Michelin map reference 82/10

1282–1330	Eastern end constructed, followed by the west, which was completed by 1390. The western tower was completed in 1480, when the building was consecrated.
1519–1535	Southern entry porch added.

THE CHURCH (begun 1282)

The only truly original masterpiece in the south is the fortified cathedral of Albi, which owed too much to the circumstances of its creation to have any influence in the north where inquisitors were rare. Yet there is nothing to prepare one for the startling impact it makes, particularly when one approaches it from the southwest by crossing the stream just below, passing under the railway bridge, and mounting the escarpment.

The old cathedral was ruined during the Albigensian Crusade and slated for demolition as early as 1247. Even though the heresy had been officially eliminated, distrust and suspicion persisted. Bishop Bernard de Castanet, one of the most terrible of the inquisitors, determined to rebuild the cathedral and devoted to it a large part of the fortune he obtained by confiscating Albigensian property. Instead of easing the tension, he perpetuated the hostility for his own ends. The fine art of extortion was his special skill, and when the funds ran out in 1299, a new witch-hunt was started against twenty-five leading citizens. It was not surprising that construction was continued shortly afterward, nor that the bishop made it a castle.

Sainte-Cécile's long, red-brick walls are as smooth as a fortress. This impression is driven home because the traditional square buttresses were changed into round ones, as used in castles. Castle bastions are rounded because the great stone-throwing siege engines could dislodge the ashlar in the corners of square towers and thus bring down the whole. This was so well known that the bishop's intent would have been clear to everyone: never again in this area would the Church be defeated. During the Protestant revolts in the seventeenth century, in spite of a strong resurgence of heresy as the old Cathar beliefs returned, Rome managed in the end to retain control over much of southern France. The message of Albi had been learned well.

Unlike the churches of the north, the roof at Albi is not visible; the building seems all wall. A building with a dominant roof affects us differently than does one with a parapet. The roof, with its large projecting eaves, protects us from the elements and gives a cozy, warm, and dry feeling. The storm and mists can surround us, yet we *know* we are safe.

The wall offers a different kind of security. Like the battlements of a castle, the wall protects us from horizontal forces, from man and society. Where the great roofs of the north, those of Chartres and Reims, protect the church from the elements, the fortresslike walls of Albi protect it from the people.

THE SOUTH PORCH (1519–1535)

The porch on the south ascends in layers of lacelike stone resembling a huge processional canopy, easily demonstrating why the delicate, flamelike spikes have been called Flamboyant. Yet, like the church itself, the long stairway is defensible.

The porch is a clever addition, for the rounded brick buttresses in the cathedral have been repeated in its outer piers. The gables and tracery carved around the drums rise and curve simultaneously, and they speak an infinitely more delicate language than the brickwork. The style of decoration is not natural to stone; it is more like pottery, plaster, or icing. Architecture has moved a long way from the majestic art where structure dictated most decorative forms.

The carving is exceptional. It is extraordinarily difficult to set out this sort of work, for it requires a patience and a geometric skill far beyond the ordinary. How would you direct the carvers to cut the stones? You have no photocopying machine, no computer graphics; you have only your compass and rule, square and proportional dividers, yet with these simple and eternal tools you are to cut templates that will be so accurate, and so easy to understand, that each stone will precisely fit the next. Approach the pillars and look carefully at the joints between the stones. How many errors do you see? How often is a detail on one stone even a millimeter offset from another? Almost never.

Technical skill at the end of the Middle Ages was superb. The amount of work being done was fairly small, and it was as if the thousands of masons and builders of the twelfth century had been reduced to a few dozen, into whom all their skills had been distilled.

ARLES, Church of Saint-Trophime

Department of the Bouches-du-Rhône, 36 km (22 miles) south of Avignon; Michelin map reference 83/10

1130–1140	Cloisters added onto Carolingian nave, which was rebuilt just afterward with the western façade and its sculpture.
1400s	Sanctuary added.

Arles was the third most important city in the Roman world during the time of Constantine. Aspects of Roman life and customs continued here well into the Middle Ages, when some leading families could trace their ancestry to imperial senators and aspects of Roman law were still in operation. Cities had continued to function during the worst years of the ninth and tenth centuries even though they were much reduced in population. The size of Roman Arles can be gauged from the dimensions of the amphitheatre, which seats 25,000 people.

This enormous structure still stands on the highest ground of the town. Saint-Trophime lies below, overshad-

Western porch, Arles.

owed by the immensity of the ancient buildings. (In the twelfth century many more of the ruins would have been standing.) The lintels on the upper floor of the amphitheatre are enormous and weigh many tons; anyone working on the little church below would have gazed on these ruins with awe and wondered at the magicians who floated the great blocks into place when he was capable of building only with small stones weighing a few pounds.

Neither the architect nor his patron could escape his Roman heritage. The west front of Saint-Trophime, like that of Saint-Gilles nearby, owes more to Roman gateways and sculptural arrangements than to anything in the north. The repetitious moldings, the almost identical figures in serried ranks with equal spaces between them, often with the Roman device of a second row of figures behind the first represented only by their heads, are all indicative of the persistence of classical motifs.

Yet it is not a triumphal entry like Saint-Denis or a stage set like Saint-Maclou. It is almost domestic in scale, even though some of the figures are more than life-size. Rather than offering pilgrim a splendid vision of eternity and glory, it merely expounds the rules. There is no feeling of relaxation. In the north one has the impression that the Church is secure and can afford to loosen up, but in the southern and Germanic areas it seems uncertain of itself, determined to allow no room for misdemeanor. Faith is a serious game.

The frontal, wide, and somewhat threatening figures stand protected and isolated in their frames but ready to pounce, as indeed they did a little later during the Albigensian Crusade. There is more skittishness in the animals than in the people. The animals often turn and gambol across the surfaces and around the bases, as if all living energy passed through them. But the saints and Christ on the tympanum are stern and remote, guarded by terrible lions. They seem to be totally concerned with their own affairs, parental rather than fatherly. There is little here of the humanity found at Chartres.

AULNAY-DE-SAINTOGNE, Church of Saint-Pierre

Department of the Charente-Maritime, 83 km (51 miles) southwest of Poitiers; Michelin map reference 72/2

1130–1160   Church built from east to west. The upper
             parts of the tower added in the fifteenth
             century, the spire rebuilt in the eighteenth
             century.

Aulnay lay on one of the pilgrimage routes to Spain. The church is very much of one piece, built fairly quickly, then mercifully left untouched for eight centuries. It is a perfectly preserved example of a small parish church of the pe-

Cornice over entry door, Aulnay.

riod, and the architecture is therefore wonderfully unified.

The groin vaults covering the aisles are set just under those in the nave, as in Le Thoronet and Beaulieu, so that the central space is unlit and gives the effect of a dark hood hanging over the pavement. All the light comes from the ground-floor windows, in aisles and apse, and one feels somewhat overawed by the dark vaults above. Presumably these vaults would have been painted, as at Saint-Savin-sur-Gartempe nearby, the figures moving and shifting in the lamplight, like a shadow-puppet presentation of the heavenly drama. There are two planes, ours and His. God's is like a lid above us, enclosing and not a little awesome; ours has doors garlanded with sculpture to welcome pilgrim, and similarly decorated windows that one suspects were to welcome Him in the same way. Thus the light entering on the horizontal plane offers the promise, while the remote and somber vaults contain, protect, and warn. It is a strange combination.

The window reveals are covered with plants and fantastic animals, with men bent double with their hands under their legs, clothing twisted as if being wrung out after a shower, crazy leaves and flowers. Some of it is religious, most of it just plain fun. No wonder Bernard of Clairvaux had opinions on this:

> But in the cloister, under the eye of the brethren who read there, what profit is there in these ridiculous monsters, to what purpose are those unclean apes, those fierce lions, those monstrous centaurs, those half-men and those hunters winding their horns? Here is a four-footed beast with a serpent's tail; there a fish with a beast's head. Here again the forepart of a horse trails half a goat behind it, or a horned beast bears the hindquarters of a horse. In short, so many and so marvelous are the varieties of shapes on every hand, that we are more tempted to read in the marble than in our books. For God's sake, if men are not ashamed of these follies, why at least do they not shrink from the expense?

As can be seen at Saint-Benoît, either you concentrate your whole being on the Way or you may lapse—here, into jollity. Maybe the Chinese sages were right to believe that laughter was the Way to the Dao, but it was not to be the Christian Way. Bernard and those of the more serious north were to stamp their intellectualism on the happier southern clime.

The magnificent doors were put up before much of the nave, an advertisement as effective as any modern billboard. They showed the people the colossal richness that could be theirs when the money came in.

Some capitals tell the story of Samson, whom the Church considered a prefiguration of Christ because he sacrificed his life for his beliefs after he had been subdued by his enemies. He is shown as a superman, slaying a lion with his bare hands, for heroic combat with a single adversary was one aim of knighthood.

Other capitals carry elephants, birds, and fantastic creatures, all with symbolic meanings. The griffin, for example, has the head, wings, and claws of an eagle with the body of a lion, and it represents their combined qualities, watchfulness and courage. The griffin with the elephant also stood for Adam and Eve. It has a very ancient lineage, having been the winged bull of the Assyrians, and even earlier, the sphinx. It is a mountain creature, hating horses and copulating mysteriously back to back. People believed that elephants mated this way too, and it was also theorized that the elephant had to return to paradise for conception so that the female could take of the tree and give the seed to the male. Hence its synonymity with Eve.

BEAULIEU-SUR-DORDOGNE,
Church of Saint-Pierre

Department of the Corrèze, 70 km (43 miles) northeast of Cahors; Michelin map reference 75/19

1100   Construction started at the eastern end. The sculpture of the south porch dates from around 1130, the western tower from shortly afterward.

The church is almost totally devoid of windows; there is no light inside, no taste of the revolutionary concepts to come from the north, no hint of the writings of Abbot Suger that through light pilgrim would find the Way. It is an enclosure, a sealed envelope for meditation.

Without windows, the church admits nothing from outside, neither sun nor moon, neither flowers nor the perfume of springtime. Day or night would pass unnoticed. It is a totally artificial environment. Of course, when one enters from beneath a brilliant southern sky, the coolness and obscurity within are very attractive. The barrel vault directs our attention toward the east, as at Saint-Benôit-sur-Loire.

We have no comprehension of how tall the vaults are from the outside, where the low roof disguises the vaults rising up into the roof itself. When we enter, the interior comes as a shock: it is awesome. The southern porch adds to the effect, for the arch over the sculpture is so massive that the church walls adjacent to it are scaled down. All in all, one is meant to be surprised and impressed by the interior.

The sculpture over the porch is astoundingly good, carved by the same crew that worked at Moissac. The doorway has an overwhelming sense of authority and high drama. The trumpets blow, and each creature responds according to his fate. The figures are in tension. Even the blessed crawl, push, and pull with urgency, while the terror of the damned is agonizing. Yet the symmetry and stillness of the arrangement imposes a profound acquiescence in the observer.

There is no sign of Mary. As at Vézelay, all is male, apocalyptic and judgmental. But notice the small figures to the right of Christ. Henry Kraus suggested that some of them may be Jews who, from their gestures, are about to expose their genitals to show that they were circumcised like Christ. Why is this happening on Judgment Day, for what status would they have? They are fulfilling the words of the New Testament in which all mankind must be judged, the dead as well as the living, Jews as well as Christians. The former would be tried by Mosaic Law, the latter by the Book.

This is the lone example of Jews attempting to get into the final act, probably because anti-Semitism was a powerful force in the Middle Ages. Although Saint Bernard could write that "We are told by the Apostle that when the time comes all Israel shall be saved," and although Christ was genetically half Jewish, a hatred of these people was one of the major emotional outlets during these centuries.

BEAUVAIS, Cathedral of Saint-Pierre

Department of the Oise, 76 km (47 miles) northwest of Paris; Michelin map reference 55/9,10

1225	Fire ruined the old building and the chapter decided to rebuild the choir, though the sanctuary walls may have been begun around 1200. Work progressed slowly until the triforium was started just after 1250. The high vaults completed in 1272.
1284	Collapse of some vaults and flying buttresses. Repaired and strengthened to 1324.
1500	Work resumed on the south transept, the north starting a decade later. The north finished in 1537,

the south eleven years later. The crossing tower,
which had been raised with a prodigious spire,
collapsed in 1573. The nearby vaults and piers
were immediately rebuilt.

THE CHOIR (ca. 1200–1324)

The ecstasy of height! Even we who take tallness for
granted are moved to awe by the illustrious grandeur of
Beauvais. Never before had medieval builders pushed an interior to such heights, and never again would they try to do
so. Yet it is not just the height that is awe-inspiring, but the
sense of movement that goes with it.

The viewer is not imposed upon, although the building is
imposing. We are taken aloft ourselves, lifted ever so
slightly off our feet and eased into the vaults. It is hard to
focus on any one spot for very long. The glazing behind the
triforium dissolves the edges of the inner arcade and its
tracery, as at Carcassonne. The uncertainty this produces
weakens our concentration, and we move upward from the
triforium to the unbelievably thin mullions that divide the
panels of glass from one another. Even here the intensity of
the light and the conflicting patterns of the armatures leave
a trail of uncertainties until frame and void become almost
interchangeable.

To escape this uncertainty we grip the edges of the ribs
and allow ourselves into the ultimate realm, the vaults. The
tension induced by this upward journey is relieved by the
simplicity and planar solidity of the vaulting cells. With relief we realize that the heavens are there, tranquil, and in
one sense knowable. We are here on earth, tangible and
solid, and Paradise inhabits the vaults; in between, all is uncertainty and movement, dissolved outlines and edges made
fragile by attenuation.

The canopies of Braine and Chartres, where the vaults,
clerestory, and triforium together constituted the other
world, have been withdrawn. Heaven seems to have been
restricted to the umbrella of the vaults alone, which were
then pushed as far from the earth as possible. Height may
have become a passion because people still longed for the
City to be within the church but would not believe it possible. So it was pushed far away, above the dissolving tracery
of the triforium windows.

The windows seem to represent the unknowability of
things. This was the time of Thomas Aquinas, who was or-
ganizing every aspect of theology into a total cognitive system. Aquinas tried to make God knowable and was banned
for the attempt. Meanwhile the masters were suggesting
that not only may God not be knowable, but the Way also.
The last labyrinth was made at Reims at about this time.

The flyers outside are like pinnacles of steel stretching
into the sky. When covered with snow, each edge and shaft,
each separate gable and capital stands out, individually

prominent. The snow accentuates the key elements while disguising the core. The effect on the outside is now one with the inside: real weight and structural function are concealed behind screens of such filigree nothingness that our judgment and experience are suspended. This towering fantasy shimmers into the sky, as little made of quarried rock as the wedding cake is made of dough. The decoration is like icing, applied and cosmetic, gorgeous.

The flyers are the work of the 1260s, contemporary with Saint-Urbain in Troyes and sharing some of its mannerisms. The faces of the buttresses are no longer plain but are decorated with thin shafts and, even before they give birth to the first arches, pinnacles and little decorative roofs. Those things which should finish the line of the building against the sky are applied to the surface partway up, so they are unable to play their normal role. For the next two hundred and fifty or even three hundred years, piers, stairs, doorways, and buttresses would be covered with architectural motifs which were once useful elements in the building but which gradually degenerated into irrelevant complexities for their own sake.

The vaults collapsed in 1284. Yet the structural sizes were impeccable. The vaults collapsed because one of the central piers of the flying buttress was not seated properly over the aisle pier underneath. The wind buffeting the roof of the choir cracked the pier at about the level of the ambulatory roof. Forty years of repairs and alterations followed, which included inserting new piers between the original ones even though the problem could have been solved without them.

The original interior was more graceful and open than today's, for there were only half as many piers along the straight bays, and they were covered with wide and generous four-part vaults, looking like spinnakers. The inserted piers and the ribs over them turned the vaults into the old-fashioned six-part type. The restorers kept the height but lost the original openness of the interior.

THE TRANSEPTS (1500–1548)

As in so many French buildings, little was constructed during the two hundred years that followed the end of the boom. Repairs were made in the fifteenth century, but it was not until 1499 that Martin Chambiges was asked to draw up plans for the transepts. As a canny inducement, citizens who donated funds were allowed to eat cheese and butter during Lent. The canons contributed part of their salaries, and King François I gave a large sum for the later work, commemorated by the appearance of his symbols on the buttresses—salamanders, chimeras, dolphins, ermines. You will enjoy looking for these fabulous creatures through your binoculars, and you will discover much else besides.

Center of southern rose, Beauvais cathedral.

The Flamboyant is more at home on this tall Rayonnant structure than in Gothic Senlis. The lacelike surface harmonizes with the elongated and decorated forms of the earlier chevet. But where the choir is concerned with drama and space, the transepts were quite obviously preoccupied with surface and the patterns that could be spread across it.

The façade is covered with many levels of tracery that swirls and curls over and upon itself. Wherever we move across the façade, we tend to flutter finally toward the center of the rose, where there are minuscule projections to push our eye outward again, to return once more in an endless tidelike rhythm. This restlessness is framed by the buttresses and the gable, both of which are covered in more traditional Gothic moldings, as if to imply that none of this energy would stay in place without the support of the older system.

The crossing tower was begun a few years later, though we might wish the builders had directed their efforts to the nave. It should be remembered that the people of Beauvais knew theirs was the tallest church in Christendom. When they heard that the new Saint Peter's in Rome would be higher, they determined they would not be outdone, and they constructed the tallest tower in Europe, with a wooden flèche that brought the whole to an astounding 512 feet (156 meters), which was 40 feet (12 meters) higher than the dome of Saint Peter's.

The moment it was finished the townspeople became anxious for their safety, and before preventative measures could be taken, the tower collapsed. Miraculously, the building was empty at the time; the clergy and congregation had left the church in the procession of the Ascension. Parts of the tower remained teetering menacingly overhead. No one would approach for fear of impending disaster until a condemned prisoner agreed to demolish the unstable ruins in return for his freedom.

The ruined vaults were rebuilt.

Compare the little chapel on the west side of the south transept with the choir to see the difference between 1200 and 1500. The piers have lost the sharpness of their outline, and instead all the decoration and intrigue have shifted into the vaults. Where Romanesque vaults seem protective and Gothic vaults elevating, these are merely playful. Devoid of structural meaning, they demonstrate the inventiveness of the architect and the superlative skill of his men. If heaven is reflected here, then heaven is going to be a riot. Swirling, restless, meandering—there is little to still the soul or transcend the everyday. Like some elemental galactic formation, the ribs expend themselves in a tumult of energy. It is an architecture of baroque superlatives and little meaning.

BOURGES, Cathedral of Saint-Étienne

Department of the Cher, 106 km (66 miles) south of Orléans; Michelin map reference 69/1.

1130s	The doorways of the transepts added onto an earlier church.
1190	Fire compelled a total rebuilding, save for the lateral porches which were incorporated into the new building. Work began in the crypt and the eastern end of the building. The western porches carved around the 1260s and the whole dedicated in 1324.
1400s	Chapels added around the outside of the nave.
1506	The north tower collapsed and was thirty-two years rebuilding. The cathedral damaged by fire and pillaged by the Huguenots a few years later. The canons removed the rood screen and much of the glass in the next century.

THE LATERAL DOORWAYS (1130s)

The north and south portals are related to those at Chartres and Étampes: the familiar long column figures are dressed in tightly fitted garments, and the shafts are decorated with similar patterns and foliage. Yet here the doorways seem a little flatter, the figures less vital, and the vitality spare compared to the Chartres Royal Portal. The same sculptors worked in both places, but here they had not yet been animated by the fervor developing to the north.

To the left of the north door the two women with halos may represent the Queen of Sheba and a sibyl. There are traces of green paint in the crevices. The Virgin in Majesty dominates its tympanum, and in an arrangement that may have been used at Chartres before the tympana were recarved, the three Magi adore the newborn infant. The annunciation to the shepherds (in the right corner) was added in the sixteenth century.

The south door is richer than the north. The tympanum depicts Christ surrounded by the four evangelists, above the twelve apostles. In the archivaults the Virgin holds a branch of her genealogical tree, representing the prophecy of Isaiah that a Messiah would come from the family of Jesse, the father of David. The tree suggests a play on words because of the similarity between *virga*, a shoot, and *virgo*, a virgin.

THE REBUILDING (1190s–1324)

The rebuilt cathedral is one of the most extraordinary creations of the Middle Ages. Nothing like it has ever been built.

The flying buttresses are unique, for they are very steeply pitched and follow the three tiers of roofs. As a result the clerestory does not appear to be suspended on the tips of the buttress arches, as at Chartres. Instead one feels that the building is rooted like a banyan tree or stretched like a great tent out of the earth. It is an extremely logical and economical solution.

Bourges cathedral.

Though the region was part of the Royal Domain, this is more of a southern building, and it lacks that sense of mystic striving found in the Paris Basin. One senses that these people just enjoyed living.

The huge crypt supports the upper church where the hill falls away. The inner chamber is very simple. It looks ancient, as if it were part of an earlier building around which the outer aisles had been wrapped at some later date. But this is not so; they were built together.

People seem to have believed there was something primeval about the crypt, something so ancient that only the most austere forms could express it. For reasons given in our discussion of crypts, this may have been the last one built in France.

The upstairs nave of Bourges is the ultimate in multidimensional space. As we move we become aware of layers that expand beyond our vision. Where Romanesque space is defined, the Gothic interior implies other spaces beyond itself which cannot be grasped at a glance or even in a long peregrination through the building. Without transept, crossing, or lantern, everything is concentrated on the one central volume. The nave is certainly awesome, soaring high above us, yet it is not separate as at Beauvais but has been eased down to our scale because of the intermediate aisle. The volumes are graduated from the humane on the outside to the colossal at the center, and they entice the worshipper toward the middle, so we are always conscious of the vaults above us. They do not appear to hang from above but mount like a staircase to the middle.

The triforium and the shafts up the piers are very thin, creating a pattern across the surface rather than any sense of bulk. The effect is to broaden our angle of vision to encompass the whole rather than concentrate on the structural elements, to skim across the surface rather than focus on the parts. Similarly, the six-part vaults are less like ribbed and weighty structures than a sequence of delicate domes. As a result the elements are felt as subdivisions within one space, not the other way round as in Toulouse, where the whole is the sum of many parts.

The middle aisle is itself like a small church, with its own triforium and clerestory which, with the outer aisles, would have made a perfect building. Indeed, the small cathedral of Senlis was originally about the size of these two outer aisles.

But the central nave at Bourges that lies within that has its own clerestory and triforium. Looked at from the eastern ambulatory, the topmost floors are like another church floating over the "real" one in the aisles.

One feels at home here in spite of the scale, exposed yet exhilarated. It is a place to shout and dance in. The stained glass windows in the outer aisles are only just above your head, so you can see all the details of each tiny picture. Much of it is thirteenth century, and the patterns of the armatures (the metal frames that hold the glass) are different in each one.

The occasional painted pillars in rich blues and gold give a royal and cheerful feeling to the place, making it worldly if not a little frivolous. The paintwork is quite different from that of the frescoes at Vic nearby. Here it is sumptuous, reminiscent of wealth, power, and authority, where at Vic it is mystic and minatory. The one makes us feel princely, the other demands repentance.

The two rich bourgeois figures flanking the eastern chapel are clearly of this world. At first they seem a little out of place. They are larger than life, smug and self-important; they and their friends paid the indulgences that helped to build the cathedral. Confidently expecting their reward in the hereafter, they have nothing in common with the wealthy being led to hell at La Chaise-Dieu or with the rich man Dives at Moissac.

BRAINE, Church of Notre-Dame
Once the Premonstratensian Abbey of Saint-Yved

Department of the Aisne, 18 km (11 miles) east of Soissons; Michelin map reference 56/4

1175–1195	Choir and nave built, though western parts of the nave may have been a little later. The lantern in place by 1200 and dedicated in 1216, possibly when the westwork was complete.
1832	Western bays demolished and the sculpture scattered (as being cheaper than repairing the roof).

If you have time for only one abbey in France, visit Braine. With its exciting diagonally planned chapels, it is one of the gems of the Middle Ages. The plan is worth drawing to understand its vitality and simplicity. But its real importance was that the elevation was so harmoniously organized, and each of its parts so clearly enunciated, that it became the model for a generation of larger and better known works, including Chartres, Soissons, and Reims, for it was here that the classic Gothic elevation was worked out for the first time.

There is a middle story between the clerestory and the aisles which occupies the full width of the bay between the vaulting shafts. In this region around Soissons there are almost no churches built before Braine that have a middle story of any type, not even a gallery which may have encouraged some love for open upper spaces (except for four-story Laon or Soissons south transept).

Elsewhere in the Paris Basin the triforium was never extended across the entire bay without some walling being left between it and the shafts supporting the vaults. There are a few continuous triforia beyond the Basin, as at Saint-Benoît-sur-Loire or La Trinité in Caen, but they are more like decorative friezes and do not have the sense of spaciousness found at Braine.

Before this, the most common solution had been to enclose the gallery arcade with an arched frame, as at Mantes or Paris. This frame divided the interior into vertical compartments from floor to vault, encouraging little horizontal movement between the bays, apart from the rhythm produced by repetition.

In the Basin, Laon may be the first example of a continuous triforium from the mid-1160s. But its triforium is dwarfed by the gallery underneath, so it is more like a frieze than a story in its own right. At Braine—and this seems to be its particular contribution to the history of medieval architecture—the triforium was made an independent centralizing motif. It created a new canon that, within a few years, was to influence every major architectural undertaking for the next century. Over fifty buildings with continuous triforia were to be started in the Paris Basin alone in the next half-century.

The effect of leaving off the encasing arch is to make the arcade look like a continuous story passing behind the pier shafts. It is an articulated hollow threading through the verticals of the bay structure, annihilating the old compartmentalized interior and replacing it with a more unified and rhythmic arrangement.

A six-part vaulting system would have denied the unity brought by the triforium, so it was abandoned along with the alternating supports. The interior had been simplified,

Braine choir seen from the lantern.

and the journey begun toward a unified space. Designers were still consciously expressing the structure at Braine, but the process had begun that was to lead to the Rayonnant architecture of surface, where pattern and line would be more important than structure. The Saint-Denis nave and Carcassonne are examples.

When you visit Notre-Dame in Dijon, remember Braine. In the latter the apparent function of the vaulting shafts is maintained, while the triforium still appears to pass behind them. But in Dijon the illusion was made real, so that the triforium shafts actually pass *behind* the vaulting shafts, making the latter unstructural and the former unsupportive. The result is somewhat disturbing.

In between, the invention of the double clerestory window, tracery, and the tall clerestory was still needed to finalize the Braine solution into the classical format.

CAEN, Churches of Saint-Étienne and La Très-Sainte-Trinité
Once Benedictine abbeys

Department of Calvados, 124 km (77 miles) east of Rouen; Michelin map reference 55/11,12

1062	Abbaye aux Hommes and Abbaye aux Dames founded (the former may have been started a little earlier). The uncompleted nunnery consecrated in 1066, and both substantially finished during the 1080s. The naves vaulted about 1125.
1200s	Apse of Saint-Étienne replaced by a Gothic choir.
1560s	Both churches pillaged during the religious wars, as they had been toward the end of the Hundred Years War. In the eighteenth century the west front of the nunnery was badly restored; the monastery spires are recent.

The two abbeys, situated a mile apart on each side of the old town, need to be seen as a pair; one was for men, the other a nunnery for noble ladies. They were founded by William the Conqueror and his wife Matilda, Duchess of Normandy, as atonements for their sin in marrying in spite of being first cousins.

In Roman times the limits of marriage were established by counting seven generations, four steps up the tree to the great-great-grandparent and then four steps down. But the Church changed this and counted seven backward in time and then seven forward. Within the confined numbers of medieval nobility this rule limited choices considerably. Demands for dispensation were frequent and were usually granted.

The abbeys reflect the male and female aspects of their

times. Where the monastery is assertive, the nunnery is enfolding and soft. We stride through Saint-Étienne, ten feet tall and clanking in armor with the long rhythm of a canter, while one feels that La Trinité is textured like damask.

As you visit the monastery, think of Jumièges and Nevers, of Conques and Cahors, and recall the same masculinity and certainty of their plain walls and solid construction. As you walk through the nunnery, remember Laon, Longpont, and the other shrines of the Virgin. The design of the elevation of La Trinité leads directly to Chartres and the High Gothic, as if a century before Braine the masters in Normandy had intuitively foreseen that the appropriate architecture for these virgin nuns would also suit the Virgin. Properly, the nunnery has a crypt while the men's choir has none.

It is recommended that you visit Saint-Étienne first, and then drive across town to the nunnery; we discuss them in this order.

SAINT-ÉTIENNE (begun 1062, choir 13th century)

The stark no-frills façade ranks among the most monumental statements of the Romanesque era. It impressed Abbot Suger during a long stay in Normandy, and it may have inspired the arrangement at Saint-Denis which became the source of most Gothic façades. Suger wanted three doors, one for each section of the church, but the single doorway here is somehow more intriguing. Saint-Étienne does not throw itself open to pilgrim but bars his way, demanding allegiance if not vassalage if he is to pass through that single portal.

At the other end of the church, in surprising contrast, is an early thirteenth-century choir. It follows the three-story form of the nave but is much lighter, and it shows the effects of thinning the members and pointing the arches. The nave is stable and anchored, and one round arch leads us easily to the next. The choir seems to vibrate in the vertical plane: each thin shaft activates our eye so that the solidity and weight of the stone is transformed into movement. The snowflakelike openings above the arcades appear as some dazzling reward.

Instead of rewards, the nave offers an earthly certainty. The western galleries are simple, the arches wide and generous, so we concentrate on the space within the gallery rather than on the wall or its arches. It is not unlike Conques or Toulouse, where we catch a beckoning glimpse of paradise within the galleries.

The eastern openings are narrower, and the embellished jambs catch our attention, so the frame and adjacent wall are more noticeable. In the nave we are attracted by the void, in the choir by the surface. We have met this comparison elsewhere, in Bourges and Saint-Denis.

The patterning in the choir and the snowflakes divert us

somewhat from the architecture. Although it was believed that God was within the church, the decoration tends to bring us to the surface rather than into the essence of the stonework. It is superficiality versus depth, not only in appearance but philosophically. It is less intense, less demanding, and equally less passionate.

The choir energizes us so that we flow lightly and effortlessly over every surface. It takes us flying into some higher space. The natural music for the nave is the chant, where all sing together, repeating the age-old proven formulas. But polyphony is the music of the choir, many voices adding a rich texture as they fall over one another while being part of the whole.

LA TRÈS-SAINTE-TRINITÉ (begun 1062)

The nunnery is a soft building. It feels as sure as Saint-Étienne but with less power than the men's church. It has modesty and discretion, though it was built many decades before the cult of the Virgin came to dominate penance.

Instead of the tall gallery of Saint-Étienne, the nave has a blind triforium. The narrower aisles, the smaller bays, and the decoration emphasize the middle and upper zones rather than the pavement, so the effect is lighter and more feminine. Like embroidery, lively patterns of billets (checks) and hollow rosettes cover arches and capitals.

The delicate triforium raises our attention upward to the six-part vaults. They are among the earliest ribbed high vaults in France, following the arrangement first devised in northern England a few years before. With similar flat arches, as the transverse arches are circular, the ribs, which cover a longer span, are flattened. As a result they look like a lid fixed low over the nave. They are also unstable. A similar vault over the Durham choir had to be replaced shortly after it was erected.

Six-part vaults center our attention where four-part vaults would guide us along the direction of the ridgeline. Like a dome, the six-part returns us to wherever we are. In a low building it is an extremely satisfactory and embalming form; only in very tall spaces, such as Notre-Dame in Paris, do we feel any conflict between the vaults and the verticality of the building.

Because the vaults are low and the aisle windows unadorned and bland, the side walls tend to fade from sight, and we are conscious only of the central vessel, as if we were in a Norman longboat. There is no lantern tower to interrupt the eastward flow.

It is worthwhile sitting in the senior nuns' stalls in the choir in order to experience the feeling of the captain of a ship observing the congregation in the nave rowing their ark to God. The vaults above resemble well-filled sails.

Compare this to Saint-Étienne, where the aisles are wider and have windows that are decorated with shafts that hold our attention and so bring the center of gravity downward. The lower spaces seem to form a pyramidical footing for the upper, so it feels immovable. On the other hand, the Trinité interior eases you eastward—without the security given by the monastic nave yet with complete certainty. It is 269 feet (82 meters) long, which is twice as large as Conques, though not as high in spite of having a clerestory.

The weighty apse, not rebuilt in the Gothic period, has the darkness of the womb. It is mysterious, and the modern glass reinforces the uncertainty, but the uncertainty is not based on an illusion as it is at Saint-Urbain. The massive shafts supporting the screen in front of the apse windows frame each opening like an ambulatory arcade. They do not form a separate pattern but enhance the existing arrangement. In this La Trinité has the same assuredness as Saint-Étienne. Both were, after all, the gift of two of the most powerful people in Europe.

The screen resembles a gallery and suggests a heavenly world beyond it. As in Aulnay and Saint-Benoît, one looks horizontally toward a paradise beyond the windows.

The transformation of this architecture into Gothic occurred as a natural process, for everything is in the sizes and the detailing. Although Gothic changed the forms used in the Romanesque, it need not have, for the new style could have been (and in some places was) created merely by adjusting the detailing. Braine, for example, is not very different from La Trinité. Raise the vaults and make them four-part, thin the details and point the arches, and this nave would no longer be a tunnel leading to the womb but a space in its own right. Lighten the shafts and increase their number, and we would be carried upward instead of resting at their base.

When you move to the crossing, you will notice that the arcades in the transepts and the triforium could easily be modified into the Braine type, as could the tall clerestory. The differences between this transept and an elevation of 1200 are more in the way the elements are handled than in the elements themselves. This only highlights the three major and related inventions that transformed architecture—the flying buttress, tracery, and the window-wall.

CAEN, Parish Church of Saint-Pierre

Department of Calvados, 124 km (77 miles) east of Rouen; Michelin map reference 55/11, 12

1308	Western spire and first five bays of nave begun. The interior changed in the fourteenth century and the great vaults built between 1535 and 1550. The western rose is fifteenth-century Flamboyant.
1490	The chevet begun, the chapels and ambulatory added about 1518, and the east completed in 1545.

1944 Heavily damaged in World War II, the tower and some vaults had to be rebuilt. This work was finished in 1957.

You may want to read the discussion of Saint-Maclou in Rouen while examining the western Flamboyant part of this church.

The eastern Renaissance section of Saint-Pierre is the most interesting. The transition is startling but not discordant, for in the early years of the sixteenth century people were still sympathetic to the Gothic style.

The ambulatory was built over the edge of a canal that used to run outside the choir. Inside, it is like walking through the woods and seeing the branches and the hanging moss above. The detailing becomes richer as we look upward, and it is more complex in the chapels than in the aisles. There is a definite movement upward and outward.

The tracery under the supports of the figures is still Gothic while the windows are fully Renaissance. The vaults are ribbed and Gothic, but the superb stalactites are covered with fine Renaissance detailing. The arches are round and classical, the bases Flamboyant. It is a comfortable mixture.

Considerable skill is required to add successfully onto an earlier building. The rules would appear to be simple: design the detailing in the style of your own time without compromise, but keep to the forms of the older building. In this way you are true to yourself while keeping in step with your companion. These marriages usually last.

Here the forms were the height and shape of the enclosure, both in the aisles and in the nave, the window widths, the use of the pointed arch, and above all the materials. Great differences in style can live together happily when the materials are the same.

In the nave the triforium is not an arcade opening into a darker space but a continuous balcony. One could imagine Shakespearean figures looking over the railing or painted, Italian fashion, on the walls. Yet the eastern triforium is crochet work, an intricate clotted screen of lacy stone that resembles a thick tapestry. In the nave the Middle Ages is passing; in the choir it is just a memory.

These Renaissance sections seem full of the humanity of the Middle Ages, with a scale of detailing and love of nature that warms one's heart. There is an attraction here that is entirely lacking in the Baroque and in the authoritarian dryness of later centuries. Rococo and Art Nouveau recaptured this feeling to some extent, but the main trend in architecture in the last four hundred years has been to impress, even to impose, rather than to embolden and enchant.

CAHORS, Cathedral of Saint-Étienne

Department of the Lot, 111 km (69 miles) north of Toulouse; Michelin map reference 79/8

1091	Work began with the four huge piers of the central bay and the western piers. Around 1130 the north door carved with its projecting porch, originally part of the west façade.
1285–1316	Westwork added and the choir reworked afterward in a quasi-Gothic manner when Cahors became the financial center of the south. The painting in the dome was done about this time and later whitewashed, to be rediscovered in 1872.
1480–1504	Cloister and sacristy rebuilt.

One is hardly prepared for the vastness of this interior, 59 feet (18 meters) wide and 105 feet (32 meters) high to the keystone. It is a little hard to see what the original church would have looked like, it is now so full of extravagant additions. Although the Gothic choir is a curious mixture of provincialized forms and is covered with tasteless nineteenth-century paintwork, it helps to show how different the northern French architecture was from that of the west.

The two immense domes of the nave, one still displaying its fourteenth-century paintings, are typical of the region. Why domes were used in this part of France is a mystery, though nostalgia for the domed churches of the Holy Land may have had something to do with it. The feelings they engender are unmistakably different from those of the rib vaults over the choir.

The choir is vertical, moving our eye up into the thin ribs of the vaults until it disappears above the arch of the dome. It is an upwardly striving architecture. Both the supports and the thin glowing windows push us up. On the other hand, the dome lets us be where we are. It offers a view through a gigantic opening into the "sky," as at Souillac. Nothing much seems to be asked of us under a dome, for we are enclosed and in a sense stilled by its centrality.

Recall the great northern choirs of Reims or Essômes, where the many lines and thin shadows suggest we ought to get going, to concentrate our energies toward the goal. In this nave we feel the relaxed society of nearby Languedoc, which so tolerantly offered a home to the Albigensians, and which finally succumbed to the militaristic north.

On the west there is only one tower. The two small turrets flanking the central brick section are recent. Where two towers are placed on the west, as in most northern churches, they frame the doorway like gigantic pillars and stretch into the sky with the same injunction to do something that the northern choirs suggest. But the single west-work, with its very wide flat wall, is more like a castle keep that offers a haven.

In the end, people feel more at home in these southern buildings yet are more excited by those in the north. The cloister is typical. It has all the tenderness and delicacy of the fifteenth century. A spacious world of quietness, the vaults seem a protective tent or the overhanging foliage of a forest—not a forest of brigands or ogres or trolls, but of lovers and springtime. The tall complex bases support shafts with little holes for stone creatures to reside, and the capitals conceal people smiling at the world from their battlements.

There is a fairy-tale quality here that is epitomized in the small, mysterious staircase. The central newel supporting the treads is like the tail of the dragon, corkscrewing upward so you can stand at the bottom and look up the central hole to the top. The workmanship is exquisite. The frame of the little window emphasizes its spiral form. It is just the right size for Rapunzel to lean out and let down her hair.

The adjacent vault and the door into the choir are tenderly carved with pinnacles and ogee curves, like miniature stalactites. It is a sugar-icing creation, courtly and well-mannered, and it is worth comparing with the sculptured north door of the nave.

The north door, like so many of that time, shows Christ in glory, surrounded by angels and the apostles. The Christ here is unusually small compared to that of Moissac or Beaulieu nearby. He seems as far away and remote as the saints depicted on the dome inside. In one way it is rather peaceful to realize that He is not right on top of us.

Along the bottom of the tympanum there are ten apostles flanking Mary, with an eleventh pushing in from the left. The twelfth apostle, Judas, is missing, and the Virgin makes up the number. This question of eleven is discussed at Neuvy, and in connection with the labyrinth.

The same narrative material was reorganized at Chartres to create a new interpretation. On the left lintel are the ten apostles. The four cherubim flying above Christ at Saint-Étienne have been moved down at Chartres to occupy the second lintel. The Virgin has been promoted from the level of the apostles to the center of her own tympanum, where she became, as the hymns stated, the "Throne of the Almighty" to replace the mandorla.

CANIGOU, Benedictine Abbey of Saint-Martin

Department of the Pyrénées-Orientales, 49 km (30 miles) west of Perpignan; Michelin map reference 86/17, 18

1001 Lower church begun or refurbished, followed by the upper, which may have been consecrated in 1026.

1783 Site abandoned but restored after 1902.

After the fall of the Roman Empire, life became less bearable as society lost its respect for law. Monasticism grew out of the desire to withdraw from this terrible world. The first Benedictine monastery was founded in Italy about a century after the sack of Rome, on the top of a steep and inaccessible hill. Like it, the little monastery at Canigou was situated as far from the ordinary world as possible, where monks in their mountain fastness dedicated themselves to praying for God's help in securing the world for Christianity. Isolated from men, overlooking the inhospitable yet agonizingly beautiful crags of the Canigou, these men believed they were the guardians of the only path that would save mankind.

The Moors passed through these mountains but never settled here. The region remained stubbornly Christian and, during the enthusiastic days of the pilgrimages to Compostela, the money was found to rebuild many of the churches in the region. Few of the originals remain, like Canigou, as they were intended to be.

The modern tourist approaches the monastery along a somewhat easier way than its first inhabitants did. Even so,

Saint-Martin on the hills over Canigou, from the east.

it is a half-hour walk up a zigzag mountain road. The experience is exhilarating; we imagine the medieval path cut into the rock, no more than a track for the donkeys which toiled up it bearing food and wine, olives and wheat, the tribute of the valley. Donkeys also carried the stones from which it was built—a material so precious that after the monastery was abandoned in 1783, the people from the valley arduously carried much of it down again to use in building their houses and barns.

The two churches are Early Romanesque. The lower one is a simple, cellarlike, low-vaulted space; its rectangular piers sit solidly on the earth, with vaults that spring from near shoulder height. Few crypts are as elemental as this one. It may have been built long before the monastery was founded, in Carolingian times or earlier. It feels terribly ancient, hewn rather than assembled, as totally secure as the cave within the mountain. Appropriately, this crypt was dedicated to the Virgin Mary.

The church above has an arcade of slender, slightly bowed columns that support one of the earliest stone vaults. The decoration on the capitals is only on the surface and, like a painting, hardly disturbs the structural function of the capital. Yet the piers feel so lightweight that the tunnel vaults over them seem less heavy than they are. In contrast to the crypt, which appears strong enough to carry the mountain itself, the upper church floats over our heads.

Here, at the very start of the Middle Ages, is presaged in these simple forms one of the most important concepts of Gothic architecture: that of the canopy of Paradise. The vaults are made to appear lighter than they are by the thinness of the shafts, so we feel they are suspended above our heads. It is like the mountain outside the church, rising above us, remote, unpopulated, subject only to the moods of nature.

For some time this idea was submerged. Although it is lightly suggested at Jumièges, we do not find it in the active monasteries of the Cluniac order or in the domed churches of Souillac or Cahors, which are solid, earthbound retreats. When the concept returned, it was as reliquary rather than as the vault of heaven.

One of the capitals in the cloister depicts a procession of monks, probably with the founders of the monastery, Abbot Oliba and his brother. Do not be misled into believing that these capitals were the work of simple people, for they are no simpler than much modern art. They explain ideas with a directness which is powerful because it is childlike. They stem from dreams and fears of a thousand years ago that are not immediately relevant to us. But in this setting, isolated and far into the mountains, if we are quiet, something of their message will come through to us.

CARCASSONNE, Basilica of Saint-Nazaire

Department of the Aude, 92 km (57 miles) southeast of
Toulouse; Michelin map reference 83/11

1088   The nave being built, with a consecration noted
        in 1096.
1269   Choir begun and finished about 1320, when the
        rose windows were constructed.
1844   Church and town restored by Viollet-le-Duc.

The best time to visit is early morning, especially in summer. Despite the basilica's dedication to tourism, it is a very
special experience. We feel the power and privilege of those
who lived within its walls. It was a safe citadel with small
houses and rambling streets serviced as much by donkeys
as by vehicles. The view from the castle walls is immense,
and enemies would have been seen miles away. From the
surrounding fields you get a good idea of how a medieval
town must have looked in the thirteenth century.

The choir of the basilica shows us that the youthful stage
of Gothic was over, that all the elements of 1200 are here
but very differently organized and detailed.

The rose windows and the gorgeous blind tracery under
them are light and elegant, reflecting the new Court style
that dominated all of France. The pattern of tracery in the
stained glass windows has spread across the neighboring
wall areas, so the wall has become like tracery and the tracery another aspect of the wall. The divisions between the
chapels have been pierced with windows and filled with
more tracery so that they screen the real windows behind
them. The light is so broken up and the shadows so incho-
ate that it is exceptionally difficult to define the spaces
without moving around, or to say where the edges of the
structure are to be found.

The clarity of the earlier buildings has been hidden behind layers. God's light no longer transmutes the wall but
confuses it. Where the twelfth century separated the spiritual and temporal parts of the building and balanced them
against one another, Saint-Nazaire destroyed this clarity. It
gives an illusion of the spirit without the substance, like a
strong cognac on an empty stomach: exhilarating and
heady but after a while unsatisfying.

The carving skill is stupendous. The cusps are sharper
than ever before, the moldings more intricate, the lines
threading through one another without cease. The energy
is open, not latent. The excitement is palpable but without
bottom. The shaft bases are set at 45°, so their points
project, not their faces. The diamond, not the square, is the
form on plan, and the effect is to emphasize the corners
rather than the sides. If you were to hold a piece of paper

square and then turn it to form a diamond, you would feel the difference. Although both are the same figure, the position alters one's impression. The square presents us with four sides, and being straight, they are stable. It is the earthbound figure, solid, rocklike, and dependable as the sides themselves. The diamond presents the points, electric, full of energy, about to rotate; it is not stable but alive, in movement.

It is exactly this quality that the masons sought from here on. The detailing is crystalline and sharp-edged in the manner we call Rayonnant. The columns have fillets along the edges which cast shadows the eye will follow. These sharp-edged lines reduce the mass of the stonework. Compare it to Reims, where the members are stable and in proportion to their functions, and where the sense of immateriality comes from the light of the stained glass windows.

Here the stonework itself has become the illusion. The interior space of the building has been decomposed into a fantasy, all on the surface, so that one is more aware of the pyrotechnics than the sacred function. Flamboyant architecture grew out of this crystallinity made of innumerable surface patterns instead of clear functions. The thin arches and the diamond geometry were twisted and curved back on themselves to weave and wave like shimmering flames of pure energy, as in the porch of Albi.

LA CHAISE-DIEU, Church of Saint-Robert
Once a Benedictine abbey

Department of the Haute-Loire, 115 km (71 miles) southwest of Lyon; Michelin map reference 76/6

1342 Earlier eleventh-century abbey replaced, the apse and five bays almost finished by 1352, the western façade completed at the end of the century. A delay of eighteen years before construction began again.

This was one of the few churches to be started during the Hundred Years War, continued during the many recurrences of plague, and completed while hostilities still raged. It was some way from the war zone, yet the whole of France suffered from this conflict.

From afar it looks like a low-lying fortress, all wall and heavy buttressing and narrow windows. This impression is transformed on entry. The walls enfold a vast horizontal space in which one is rested, almost lulled under the flattened vaults that extend at the same level throughout. The ribs follow a curve more elliptical than circular, helping to amalgamate the nave with the aisles, which seem little more than the space beyond the intermediate pillars needed for the vaults. There are traces of paint on the ribs, indicating a once colorful interior. From within the aisles the vaults appear tall, especially as there are no capitals on the piers. This effect has been augmented by placing the string course very high up the wall and by thinning the windows. There is no sign of the Rayonnant here, yet it is thoroughly Gothic, the Gothic that might have been used all over France if the glass walls of the north had not been invented.

Our impression on entering from the west is one of a battlemented inner keep, strutting outward toward the doorway. It encloses the sanctuary temple, now a fortress within the castle-church. It is paradoxical to be well defended within these walls while feeling so relaxed and secure under the vaults. But this reflected the position of the monks compared with that of other members of the community. The monastery could be invaded and sacked or the monks could die of plague, but because they were monastic their reward after death would be greatest.

Their constant awareness of death is obvious on the north side of the stalls, where the *danse macabre* is painted. Bishops, kings, court fops, merchants, and peasants together are being led to the same end. The eastern panel shows the scratches the painter made on the plaster to block out the figure before starting to apply paint. The lines are free, made in large sweeping movements of his whole arm. We can almost see him doing it.

Inside the monks' enclosure, the inner temple, are well-preserved sixteenth-century tapestries. The stalls are not particularly intricate, but they are well carved. Sit in them and feel the enclosure and the safety they impart. While you are there, count them. Their total is twelve times twelve, the square of the fullness of all things, and in *gematria* representing *sedes sapientiae*, the gnostic phrase for total wisdom. There are seventy-two on each side, the number of wise men Moses chose to guide Israel, perhaps a reference to the role the monks chose for themselves.

It is also worth counting the number of seats in each bank. Along the walls are thirty-three, Christ's age and the sacred eleven times the Trinity. (For the meaning of eleven, see the discussion of labyrinth on page 74.) In front there are four banks of thirteen each. The thirteenth letter is M for Maria. It is the number of apostles plus Christ. It is also the number of the moon, there being thirteen months in the lunar year, and therefore the number of Mary.

Consider, too, the numbers in the building. There are nine bays in the nave and seven chapels. Both are Mary's numbers and are also used at Chartres. The total number of bays is thirty-five which is the sum of the letters BVM, the initials of the Blessed Virgin Mary.

Notice that the nave piers are octagonal, while those between the chapels are round. The pier at the junction between nave and choir is octagonal on one side and circular on the other. The circle represents the spirit and the all;

the octagon represents the resurrection. This reminded the monks that they in their stalls could look to the altars in the east and hope to be saved.

CHÂLONS-SUR-MARNE,
Parish Church of Notre-Dame-en-Vaux

Department of the Marne, 45 km (28 miles) south of Reims; Michelin map reference 56/17

1140s   Nave aisles and doors, with the lower stages of the eccentrically placed towers. The upper parts of the transepts completed in the next decade.

1175   Ambulatory around the choir and gallery added, with the upper vaults around 1195. About the same time the nave gallery and clerestory were built over the earlier aisles, and the western rose and towers.

1793   Sculpture of the south door mutilated and the two western spires pulled down. They had been replaced by 1870.

The sculpture around the entry door on the south side of the nave was systematically obliterated during the French Revolution. You may feel such sorrow that you want to turn away from the remnants. But look at it closely, for there are still traces enough to show what may have been here, and it could have been of a very high quality, perhaps as fine as the Chartres west portal.

In the center of the tympanum is a mandorla framing Christ, and around Him the vestiges of the four evangelists. The three magi were on the lintel, and perhaps a tumbling city on the left. The embrasure figures were tall and narrow as at Chartres, and we can still follow the folds of cloth, the patches of decorative edging, swords, and halos. Were they the twelve apostles? Or (as at Chartres) the prophets of the Old Testament?

Even the little animals around the bases of the columns were eliminated, leaving only the foliage on the capitals, as though all traces of any living thing had to be hacked out. People's anger against the Church was boundless.

Inside there is a curious anomaly: the towers were not placed on the same centers as the nave. The north tower was placed to the north of the ambulatory aisle, the south on top of the aisle, forcing it to detour outside it. Although the towers were begun a little before the nave, it was planned like this from the start. Some say that earlier foundations dictated the layout.

As the towers and the apse of the original choir were going up, the builders were also working on the nave. The capitals are quite magnificent; stylistically, they rest somewhere between the Saint-Denis narthex and Senlis. The

*Châlons-sur-Marne
from the east.*

piers alternate, but not noticeably, for the intermediate piers are not drums, but are just like the main ones. The only differences are in the dimensions.

There are capitals just above the gallery string course, intended for a church with a gallery, but no clerestory like Conques, in which the illumination would have come indirectly through the gallery windows. Because the capitals over the major piers were carved at the same time as the aisles, while the smaller ones were carved when work resumed in the 1180s, the vault may have been designed to be six-part, with the support under the central rib placed somewhat higher than the others. This suggests that the first stage of the work seems to have stopped just above the capitals over the larger piers.

With these vaults the nave would have been very low indeed, presumably as low as the first apse, and as low as the gallery on the eastern side of the transepts, also with capitals dating from the 1150s. When you stand in the south arm, the rose window in the north shows you how high the vault (or perhaps the wooden roof) would have been.

Thirty years later it was decided that this would not be tall enough, and the nave was raised at the same time that the new choir was being built. This shows how the view of height had changed during one generation, from a long, low building such as Senlis to a much taller one with more articulation and much lighter members.

The lightness reminds us of Saint-Remi in Reims, as does

the connected triforium and clerestory. Perhaps a model had been made for the Reims abbey and was shipped here to be used at Châlons. The plan of the chapels and the interior elevation are like Saint-Remi, though the scale is much smaller and the profiles quite different. Therefore we can say that the builder of Châlons did not work at Saint-Remi but went there to copy the arrangement, then returned home to prepare his own templates for the detailing.

The lightness makes the church seem tall and generous for such a small building, well lit and tranquil. It is worthwhile studying the ambulatory to see how cleverly they adapted the new work to fit around the older towers. Start with the vaults and notice how clearly all the junctions are arranged over the small spaces, especially over the screening columns to the chapels. Then notice how the wall arcades disguise the bulk of the older towers, and follow the way the gallery covers up the face of the southern tower so you would hardly notice it.

Masterly and very elegant.

CHARLIEU,
Ruins of the Cluniac Abbey of Saint-Fortunat

Department of the Loire, 77 km (48 miles) southwest of Mâcon; Michelin map reference 73/8

1048   The choir completed, followed by the nave to about 1100. The sanctuary consecrated in 1094.
1150   Narthex and sculpture.
1795   Sold as a quarry and demolished.

The abbey of Charlieu was founded by the Benedictines in 872 and came to a peaceful end before the Revolution. In 1792 the locals burned the manuscripts in the library and sold the church for its building materials. The early eleventh-century choir and nave were razed to the foundations.

Miraculously, the narthex survived, and with it some unusual and deeply moving sculpture. The tympanum on the west façade shows Christ in Majesty and the four evangelists. On the lintel is the Madonna with angels and the twelve apostles. On the right jamb Bishop Ratbertus holds a model of the church, and on the left jamb Duke Boso, the first donor, holds another model which looks like the choir that was demolished.

One purpose of sculpture was to instruct the faithful and help them avoid heresy. The most serious current challenge to Church doctrine was the argument that the Eucharist was irrelevant to salvation. For this reason the Last Supper was carved over the side door, for it reminded people that Christ first enunciated this central mystery at the Last Supper. On the lintel the animals offered in the sacrifices of the Old Testament are shown being led to slaughter: a calf,

Charlieu narthex, tympanum on west façade with the mandorla.

a ram, and a goat. The Lamb of God stands alone at the altar, again symbolizing the mystery of the Eucharist. Peter the Venerable, Abbot of Cluny, wrote, "The ox, the calf, the ram, the goat soaked with their blood the altars of the Jews; only the Lamb of God, which cleanses the sins of the world, stands on the altars of the Christians."

One wonders what terrible passions or uncertainties motivated the unstable energy of this sculpture. It has a *fin de siècle* feeling to it, a baroque frenzy in which sobriety was exploded in a chaotic energy. These wild ecstatic figures with their exuberant gestures and ardent expressions, found in many Burgundian buildings, seem akin to Saint-Gilles in the south. Sculpture was already changing, to be replaced with the monumental serenity of Chartres.

CHARTRES, Cathedral of the Assumption

Department of the Eure-et-Loir, 88 km (55 miles) southwest of Paris; Michelin map reference 60/7,8
(See also pages 69–77)

1020   Fire destroyed the church of 858, and the present crypt was built around the remains.

1134   Fire damaged the town; the north tower was started immediately afterward, along with the subterranean parts of the southern tower. When the north had reached the third story the south tower was continued and the sculpture of the Royal Portal installed, probably just before 1140. Both towers were completed fairly quickly and the glass in the three lancets over the portal made about 1150. The south spire, 339 feet (103 meters) high, was completed in 1165.

1194   After a third and more disastrous fire, the choir and nave had to be rebuilt. The south porch was installed by 1206, and by 1215 the north porch had been completed and the western rose installed. The high vaults were laid up in the 1220s, and the transept roses over the next two decades, with a dedication in 1260.

1316   The chapter house and chapel of Saint Piat were added, followed by the small Vendôme chapel after 1415. In 1506 lightning destroyed the north spire, which was rebuilt 371 feet (113 meters) high. This was followed by the choir screen and a new organ in the nave.

1757   The jubé (the screen which once enclosed the western face of the inner choir from the nave) was torn down and the present stalls built. The roof was burnt out in 1836.

So many great cathedrals and churches have been mutilated by war and fire. Sculptures have been deliberately hacked and glass wantonly destroyed; anger, calamity, and stupidity have taken too great a toll. We are fortunate to have at Chartres an almost untouched thirteenth-century

Corner buttress between the nave and north transept, Chartres cathedral.

cathedral, with the most marvelous assembly of images in Europe, a collection of stained glass without equal in the world—in all, an enduring encyclopedia of Christian thought.

Its preservation has been one of the miracles of modern times. During the Revolution it was threatened with extinction and was saved only by chance. The lead roof had been removed to make bullets, and the weather had begun to attack the vaults. The district administrator complained about the high cost of keeping the church repaired and suggested it be blown up. The proposal was seriously considered until an architect warned that the debris from the explosion would make the surrounding streets impassable to traffic.

Elsewhere the story was the same. The Sainte-Chapelle became a flour warehouse, Saint-Germain-des-Prés a saltpeter factory. Notre-Dame was put up for sale and might have been pulled down for a quarry, like Longpont and a hundred other famous abbeys, but for a legal squabble. Moissac was put up for sale but found no buyers at 6,000 livres. The great abbey church of Cluny, for centuries Christendom's largest edifice, was systematically demolished: a big hole was made in the nave to allow room for a market, then the towers were blown up and the vaults with them, and thereafter the great mound of rubble served as a quarry until it was bought privately in 1823. A thousand other abbeys and churches met similar fates.

The wealth and prestige of Chartres was based on one relic, the silken veil or *camissa* considered to have been worn by the Virgin. It had been given to the cathedral by Charles the Bold in 876. Three generations earlier, Charlemagne had received it from the emperor of Byzantium.

Three major fires affected the building. The first in 1020 destroyed the older church, which was then entirely rebuilt. A second in 1134 damaged the town more than the cathedral and led to the construction of the western towers and the Royal Portal. The third, sixty years later, destroyed most of the upper church, which was then rebuilt.

The cathedral built following the first fire was almost as large as the present building and was at that time the second largest church in Europe after Saint Peter's in Rome. Remnants still embedded in the towers suggest that it was three stories high with a middle gallery and that it reached almost to the rose windows in today's clerestory—an immense building indeed. The crypt from this epoch still exists.

THE CRYPT (begun 1020)

The architecture of the crypt is so spare that there is little to say about it, and this is how it was meant to be. It is form at its simplest, expressing the same elemental message as Le

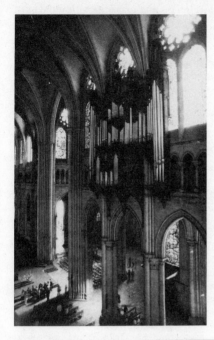

Chartres cathedral, interior from the nave.

Thoronet or Fontenay. The clergy claimed that the crypt had become the "Virgin's most preferred residence on earth."

The long, tunnel-like passage, low and without decoration, is the largest vaulted structure surviving from this period. Entering through the north tower, it seems to take us an endless time to walk to the chapels. (Today they can be entered only from the eastern end of the building.)

The chapels and ambulatory are like a cave. Without glass, the windows were merely barred openings to the outside, instanced in Abbot Suger's account of the pilgrims packed into Saint-Denis, where the monks "were *often* obliged to escape through the windows."

With no decoration, the curved planes of the architecture stimulate no thoughts or memories. It is a space for worship only, though the paintings, one of which may still be seen in a recess on the south side, may have distracted pilgrim. Stay awhile; do not move about. Accept that nothing is happening. Treat it as a silent meditation and let your thoughts fade without your doing anything at all. Aspire for a while to total stillness and see what happens.

A deep happiness may slowly rise in you, like a stream of water, supplanting all anxiety. You will feel enfolded and pleasantly timeless. When you come to leave, you may feel light and sharply aware of everything around you. You will then have been beyond your normal boundaries to a level of consciousness and awareness that may stay with you a long time; you will have glimpsed sainthood. This was the essential purpose of these simple buildings from the Romanesque.

On the north side of the crypt is a sacred well into which were thrown the first Christian martyrs of Chartres. To look into its murky blackness and be unable to see the water 130 feet (40 meters) below only reinforces the miraculous notions that have grown up around it.

THE WESTERN DOORS AND TOWERS (after 1135)

The three portals are probably the first to reveal the integration and unity which mark the mature Gothic style. The factors that made it possible seem to have had much to do with the new humanism and the growing cult of the Virgin.

The sculptures depict the fundamental spiritual and political truths of the times; they state what pilgrim had to believe to be a Christian. On the right is the birth of Christ and on the left His ascension. The latter was proof that He was God, that His birth was divine, and that the Last Judgment depicted over the central door would come to pass. Hence the left tympanum verifies the truth of the others and at the same time establishes Mary's crucial position. Church scholars devoted their lives, with every bit as much passion and intelligence as may be found among our scientists today, to unraveling the precious threads which bound the universe together and to discovering how to present them in one marvelous and numinous unity.

The sculptures imply much more than we can describe here, for they present many overlapping meanings. For example, each door represents one person of the Trinity: the second on the right as the Son, God the Father in the middle, and the Holy Ghost on the left as the dove descending from the center.

Similarly, the Ascension portal on the left shows Christ's physical body being assumed. It is framed by the signs of the zodiac and the labors of the months, thereby joining the physical Christ with the earthly activities of the year. It is the people's road to salvation through work.

On the right the Incarnation portal is surrounded by the Seven Liberal Arts and the scholars who propounded them. This is proper, as both knowledge and the Son came from God. This is the wise man's Way and, by implication, that of the Church. The Church, called the Bride of Christ, associated itself with the feminine aspect represented by Mary. Mary was also the patron of the Liberal Arts. Thus Mary in the center of the tympanum is the focus for all the other meanings.

The figures do not strive, they simply are. Compare them with Vézelay, carved only about ten years earlier. Where Vézelay is emotionally charged and intense, Chartres is serene and hieratic. The Chartres figures are more humane,

their stance self-contained. The drapery is set not to elec-
trify but to clarify. There is no drama. The movement and
ecstatic tension of Charlieu and Saint-Gilles have relaxed
into a meditative calm.

This is especially so in the embrasure figures, which
serve political as well as religious purposes, as was being
encouraged by Suger. They represent not only Old Testament prophets but also the ancestors of the kings of France.
Following the divisiveness of the Investiture Conflict, and
the growing threats from heresy, it suited the Church to
ally itself with the Crown, while the Crown relied on the
Church to reinforce the sacredness of its position. The
Church obtained secular support while the Capetian monarchs used the sanctity their position acquired from the
Church to prevail over the independent barons. Thus the
figures also symbolize the prerogatives of the Church and
the powers of the kings, representing the current treaty between the spiritual and lay leaders of France just when the
country was about to take over the leadership of Western
Christianity.

Tall figures had been used before, as at Bourges, where
they are so bulky that they appear to be buried in the wall.
At Chartres the figures have been attenuated and elongated
so that they are like the columns which support them. The
faces in earlier buildings are often remote, but at Chartres
they have an inner life that animates the stone. As columns
they are architecture, while at the same time they are
saints—the duality emphasized that their spirit had entered
into the building itself.

These figures, with their soft features and gentle smiles,
mystically conjoin the humane with the divine beings they
represent. For the first time the world of matter and the
world of meaning became one. As Saint Bernard wrote, this
reflects the natural unity "whereby soul and body are one
man."

Two of the knottiest problems in Christian theology were
resolved here, not for all time, for the discussion came up
again and again, but to the satisfaction of the twelfth century. One was Christ's dual nature as both God and man:
having been born of woman, He was a man; having been
conceived by God, He was also God Himself. The placement
of Gemini, the twins, to the left of the lintels expressed this
mystic dualism. The other was the sacrament, in which
Christ's body and blood atone for the sins of others. At first
this was symbolized in the Last Supper, as at Charlieu, but
heresy forced the Church to make these beliefs more compelling.

The orthodox saw the world as God's creation, while
some heretics believed it the creation of the devil, and
therefore that altars and churches were useless, being
themselves part of the devil's world. In 1139 the Lateran
Council condemned these theories, and the Church hur-
ried to advertise the sacrificial aspect of Christ's presence

on earth. Hence Christ is presented three times over the right door as the sacrifice, as if it had been His intention from the day of His birth.

The manger in the lower lintel became an altar with Christ laid on top, placed centrally as a sacrifice. He is also the sacrifice in the upper lintel, for in the presentation to Simeon He stands on another altar, calmly and frontally expressing this symbolic meaning, and thirdly on Mary's lap in the tympanum.

Thus the scholars squeezed the utmost symbolic significance from every figure to enrich the façade. No longer would a different story occupy each door, but by repetition and analogy a host of related ideas could be incorporated into the one work. As was happening in architecture, the Romanesque additive system was being replaced by the holistic Gothic view.

These portals were sculpted by a number of teams, one working after the other and each contributing something to the whole. The unity of the result, in spite of the varied inputs, is a credit to their sensitivity and to the skillful iconographic scheme of the clergy.

For example, the capitals with the little figures in them were introduced by a team which had worked at Étampes, not far to the east. At Chartres they carved only some of the capitals around the Virgin's door, along with the large capital on the inside with palm leaves carved on it.

We may have the name of the master of this team, for above the uppermost sculpture at the outermost edge of the jamb between the central and the right door is inscribed "Rogerus." This crew also did the tall embrasure figures on the left, then departed the site. The men who replaced them continued to carve the same type of capitals around the Ascension door on the left. The arrangement of the figures and the drapery show them to have come from a different part of France, and they were to move on almost immediately to Notre-Dame in Paris.

The present side tympana are not the ones originally carved for here. There is evidence in the archivaults that the originals were scrapped and replaced just before their erection by the Incarnation and the Ascension. It is possible that these tympana, like the side ones at Vézelay, contained an adoration of the Magi, the one subject that is conspicuously lacking at Chartres. In this case the ruling of the Lateran Council in 1139 condemning those who denied the sacrifice symbolized in the eucharist may have brought about the change. The date is appropriate, for Chartres was then in the process of being carved.

ASTROLOGY AND THE ZODIAC

It seems strange that, after the crucifixion and the nativity, the astrological signs should be the most common theme in the cathedral. After the fifth century astrology was condemned for being in conflict with free will, and the signs were seldom seen in churches until the crusaders brought back the texts from Islamic Spain. The texts argued that the zodiac was not a tool for discovering the future but the key to understanding the condition of man.

The scholars at the School of Chartres agreed that God had created the celestial bodies to be an indication of things "past, present, and future," and thus they used astrology to represent the three stages of God's purpose: the creation from Aries to Cancer, man's realization of self from Leo to Scorpio, and his return to God in the last four stages.

So it is surprising at first to notice that the signs around the Ascension door have not been arranged chronologically. Virgo (the seventh) faces Capricorn (the tenth) at the top of the left door, Cancer starts the sequence at the bottom left, and Pisces and Gemini have been placed on the right door. However, as we might expect, this seeming eccentricity hides deep meanings.

The two misplaced signs were moved onto the Incarnation door as reminders of what His birth meant. Both are double signs. One represents the new age inaugurated by Christ, which coincides with the commencement of the age of Pisces, just as we now are entering the age of Aquarius. The other, Gemini, the twins, represents Christ as both man and God, and because Gemini is also the entry point into heaven, it reminds us that with Christ's death man can be saved and enter into paradise. Rightly, both are placed in the nativity door, which celebrates the birth of Christ.

For each sign there is a companion panel for the appropriate labor of the month, and the labors have also been arranged for their inner meaning. In the upper outer stones of the Ascension portal, September treads the grapes. On the right, December shows two people resting after the year's labor, a loaf of bread on the table. Thus the bread and the wine have been placed at the top of the arch, symbolic of the Eucharist. The dove between them, badly damaged but still recognizable, represents not only the Holy Ghost welcoming the risen Christ in the tympanum but the Spirit transforming the bread and wine into the body and blood. Alongside the dove the inner topmost labors are June's scything and March's pruning, in which cutting back becomes an image of death. Thus through the death of Christ may the spirit ascend.

The inner arches represent the paths of creation and salvation in the first and last signs. On the left Cancer, Leo, and Virgo refer to the creation of all things and, by implication, the mother principle. On the right lie the signs for humanity, from Libra (the essence of man) through Scorpio (his predicament) to Sagittarius (his soul). In essence, the right refers to the Man and the left to His mother.

Every part of the portal forms a complex system of overlapping meanings which set out the Church's view of the world and man's place in it, if we have the eyes to read it.

And in this the signs are arranged to exemplify and enrich our understanding of this relationship.

THE ARCHITECTURE (1194–1260)

From a distance the cathedral looks stupendous, with its two jutting spires visible above the wheatfields from a dozen kilometers away. Like the Royal Portal, the architecture just is. It does not force you along the Way like Conques, nor does it surround you with a field of energy like Saint-Maclou in Rouen. On the one hand, it is a very simple building, its parts and detailing finished with as little adornment as possible; on the other, it was intended to be the greatest and most dramatic expression of mystic yearning ever contemplated.

The impact of Chartres on the people of its time was enormous. More than any other building, it represented an ideal. It achieved the status of an icon. It partook of the divine.

Like medieval philosophers, the architects of the cathedrals aimed above all at totality, so that each design would encapsulate all the elements of a perfect final solution. That there was not, in the end, one generally agreed solution to the cathedral form, in spite of the intense search for finality, may be due to the individuality fostered by the Scholastic disputes. The ground-plan geometry (see page 70) illustrates one of these interpretations.

Chartres is the most perfect of all the Gothic cathedrals. In a totally balanced way it employs, or was planned to employ, all the most important sacred concepts that are discussed in this book. In it Romanesque ideas are merged with Gothic, mingling the past with the future. It is larger and taller, and its nave was wider than any other French cathedral at that time, and though all the motifs of the period were enlarged to suit it, none has lost its essential meaning or humanity.

There is a beautiful balance between the lower walls of the nave and the upper zone of the clerestory. The external walls are plain and unadorned, and the triple rebates around the windows show off its fortresslike strength. The enormous weight of the buttresses anchors the walls to the ground as at no other church. The large projecting buds, called crockets, set under the cornice at the top of the wall, seem to weigh the wall down while at the same time providing a platform for the relatively light arches and windows in the clerestory and the lifting action of the flyers.

Internally, every shaft has a singular task and with the minimum of decoration proceeds to do it. One important detail, which is almost impossible to see in the dark, is that the shafts supporting the high vaults have been separated from the walls and laid *en délit*. They do not look as though they are part of the wall, as the shadow between the wall and the shaft would have been strong enough in normal light to have made them independent of the structure. Thus they would have appeared to be hanging from the vaults rather than supporting them, sustaining the illusion that the vaults were the tabernacle.

The *pilier cantonné* may have been used here for the first time. It is a partial amalgam of the drum and the compound pier, with one column to a side, each supporting a part of the structure, unlike drum piers. Because the attached shafts throw shadows, we are aware of the piers as part of the structure. Again there is balance, this time between the material solidity of the interior and the suspended weight-lessness of the vaults.

Chartres is architecturally straightforward. There is virtually no decoration other than the string-courses, the capitals, and the torus molds. There are only columns and arches, and between them there are plain walls or space and little else. Whether we look at the aisle arcades, the triforium and clerestory, or the vaults themselves, all we find are variations on the same theme: arches supported on shafts.

In the north spire, or in Saint-Maclou at Rouen, we have to make an effort to follow the connections between shafts and arches and to find our way among the tracery and the complexities of the vaults. But here everything is clear. There is a strict delineation of the parts that makes this enclosure immensely satisfactory. The piers and vaults are carved with such simplicity that they do not pretend to be anything but stone. Compared to such later buildings as Saint-Pierre in Caen, where the stone is so finely carved that it has the delicacy of ice crystals, everything here is in proportion to its function.

At Braine the middle story has become a genuine intermediate zone. At Chartres the relationship is particularly clear because it is written into the geometry (Figure 7). The height from the pavement to the floor of the triforium is identical to the height from the clerestory to the roof cornice. These can both be drawn as squares, and if the diagonal of one square is swung around, it will exactly meet the side of the other. The triforium thus occupies the distance left between the side of the square and its diagonal. The builders were not able to calculate the length of the diagonal, which is irrational, and so this length without a number would seem to have represented the intangible boundary that separated pilgrim from the spirit.

Yet even as this classic culmination to the Gothic style was being devised at Chartres, ideas were changing. When the triforium at Orbais was joined to the clerestory, it stopped being an intermediate zone and was absorbed into the Heavenly Jerusalem. As in the Saint-Denis nave and in Beauvais, this moved heaven out of reach.

Chartres was designed to have a lantern over the crossing which would have brought light into the very middle, illuminating the altar like the fingers of the Holy Spirit. In

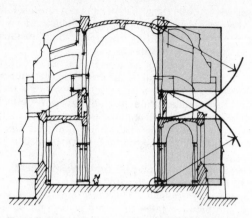

Figure 7. Section through the nave of Chartres cathedral, showing the geometry used to create the intermediate zone (triforium), separating the mundane (the aisles) from the heavenly (the clerestory).

1222 the chapter decided not to proceed with it, and the crossing was vaulted at the same height as the other vaults. This sealed the interior so Paradise would not be allowed inside.

The huge vault over the crossing seems to gather everything to the center, while the rose windows stare insistently through the surrounding darkness. The energy and vitality pulsating within the roses bespeaks a world beyond this world. Through them God looks down on pilgrim, who may observe Him too, but at a distance. Without the lantern pilgrim cannot share His light; it may be viewed only from within this darkness.

There is compensation in the many smaller roses of the clerestory, which may represent heaven glowing like a crown above our heads. The crown is so brilliant that the lantern, if it had been built, might have appeared superfluous, for why would we need a glimpse of heaven through the lantern when it was pulsing through the upper windows?

Stand in the crossing and observe the west and south roses. They hang suspended in the blackness, quite apart from the lancets, and they seem to pulsate in and out, as though moving toward us and away from us at the same time. Imploding and exploding simultaneously, they dominate the space as the spirit dominates its purpose. They are our pathway out of the enclosure and God's view into it.

Now turn and examine the northern rose. With the filling of the space between the rose and the lancets with additional windows, the separation has been lost; the rose has been absorbed by the windows. Without isolation, it no longer feels like God's eye. It has been demoted. Yet it is full of energy, and it foreshadows the increasingly spectacular roses of later years.

The dates of these roses are significant: the western rose was carved in 1215 and the south rose was begun in 1224; the north rose was carved a decade later, in the 1230s.

This was the moment of transition, when the older views so beautifully expressed at Laon were being altered. During one decade the lantern was eliminated along with the low roof, the isolated rose was absorbed into the transept lancets on the north in the 1230s, and all work was suspended on the apsidal towers. It was a while before they stopped building the remaining transept towers, but we can see that the key decisions had been taken by the early 1220s. This date marks the crucial transformation, when the immanental beliefs that had first shown themselves eighty years before in the Royal Portal again turned transcendental.

There were to have been nine towers and spires, the central one higher than the others, thrusting and sawing heavenward to a size and scale never attempted before. Such a mass of towers appears arrogant, like a prickly hedgehog, where the present tall roofline gives the giant some touch of modesty, a light capping of simplicity that restores the humanity of this great cathedral that may have been lost in soaring ambition.

It was as if Chartres were the medieval Tower of Babel, reaching ambitiously upward to touch the heavens when, like its Old Testament counterpart, it had a change of tempo during construction. The ambition dried up, the yearning dissipated, and the thrusting towers were abandoned unbuilt. Did heaven sigh with relief, saved from an immanent and irresistible invader?

One of the choir flying buttresses, Chartres cathedral.

THE SUPPORT OF THE TOWN

The townsfolk, especially the merchants, had good reason for being attached to the cathedral. As such things were usually arranged in the Middle Ages, the four key fairs coincided with the festivals of their patron saint. Souvenirs—tiny lead images of the Virgin and copies of her chemise—comprised the bulk of all goods sold.

Relations between the merchants and the chapter were excellent, largely because the canons had, shortly before the fire, brought the wealthiest townsfolk into their meetings. The favored burghers also benefited from this special relationship, for they could trade within the church's precinct and so avoid the heavier exactions of the local count. They also gained in social status, and in time their guilds were recognized. As a result they gave so much money that forty-two of the lancets were given by the guilds, when none of the windows in the earlier church had been donated by townsmen.

THE TRANSEPT PORTAL SCULPTURE

The range of sculpture at Chartres is vast. There are over two thousand figures—more than is to be found in any other medieval building. The subject matter is enormously varied. The most important scene is the Last Judgment over the central door of the south transept; its minatory message, spread across the greatest portals of France, warned of the fate awaiting all men of whatever station or fortune. Everybody believed in its terrifying portent, in the great leviathan with gaping mouth spurting flame and sulphur, in its rabble of devils stridently arguing over the risen souls and joyfully inflicting those unspeakable tortures which so terrified the faithful. No amount of wealth or power could protect one on that day. On this thought was based the power of the Church, on the equality of all before the Judge at that fateful reckoning. Every Judgment shows crowned heads and peasants, miters and gowns, kings and merchants. It was a democracy of the damned.

On the other side of the lintel we see the same inexorable impartiality in what might equally be called the democracy of the saved. Though there are a few wealthy persons among them, the majority are lowly peasants, pilgrims, and the poorer monks. It implied that each person's ultimate destiny was beyond the partisan views of the living. It offered a hope to the poor that their time would come, that in eternity they might gain the safety and recognition that was denied to them on earth.

What is so impressive and magical about the sculpture of Chartres is the perfect blending of the sacred with the humane. The embrasure figures are taller than we are by almost fifty percent; they represent what is larger than man, yet they are still individuals. The confessors in the right doorway are saintly priests but also strong-charactered churchmen who will brook no disobedience. On the north side each figure idealizes a principle of faith. Abraham may have been prepared to harden his heart against his love for his dearest son, but when the moment is on him and the angel swirls out of the adjoining capital to save the boy, we realize from the sculpture that Abraham is also God, prepared to sacrifice His Son for our souls.

If these figures were in museums, each set on its own pedestal so that we could walk around it, many would be as famous as the most exquisite creations of all times. Donatello and Michelangelo are on all our bookshelves because their names were not lost and each of their works can be studied and photographed in isolation. We must never forget that the best French sculpture is as superb as anything created in fifteenth-century Italy. It is just a little more difficult for us to see them. We have to concentrate on the pieces one at a time, often using binoculars, if we are to appreciate them fully.

THE WESTERN TOWERS
(south finished 1165, north begun 1506)

The north tower was the last medieval spire built in France until the nineteenth-century Gothic Revival spires, such as Saint-Maclou in Rouen. It is the tallest extant, though the crossing spire of Beauvais, at 512 feet (156 meters), held that distinction for a short time.

It is the tower of the sun, as depicted on its metal flèche, while the shorter spire on the left is the tower of the moon. These symbols represent all things that are, as encompassed by day and night, and the fundamental divisions of male and female, active and passive. It has even been suggested that the tower of the sun is taller because the solar year is longer than the lunar year by eleven days. Yet in design the north tower is too feminine to represent the robust energy of the sun. Examine the middle part with binoculars, just where the pinnacles rise out of the eight gables. The traditional purpose of the gable is to cover the end of the roof, like the one over the western rose. But these gables are perforated like fretwork and cover nothing, for the wind blows behind them. From the pinnacles run short flying buttresses to strengthen the tower. These too are pierced, with sharp-edged moldings to make them more insubstantial. Where each pair of flyer arches meet the tower, they are joined by upward-curving "arches" which turn *away from* the tower, denying the function of the buttresses they come from. It is as if the architect was ashamed of having to build anything as functional as a buttress, and good manners made him pretend it was only decoration.

The lightness and elegance of the tower are more sophisticated and in one sense more intellectual than the rest of the cathedral. It is closer to Rococo and the furniture of Louis XVI than it is to Philippe-Auguste.

Compare the two towers to see the inexorable changes of three centuries. The north is agitated and staccato, the south is peaceful and its direction clear. Both have rows of gables; on the south they structurally support the spire, on the north they deny themselves that function, leaving the spire hanging, as it were, in the air. Like the Royal Portal, the south spire expresses the calm faith of twelfth century. It is matter thrusting itself into heaven, eager to join the Virgin whose assumption it celebrates, while the north is a gossamer artifice that is neither of our world nor of God's. Where the earlier work is eternal and secure, the later is immaterial and refined. The solidity of 1200 has turned into papier-mâché. One moves our feelings, the other stimulates our mind.

CHARTRES, Church of Saint-André

Department of the Eure-et-Loir, 88 km (55 miles) southwest of Paris; Michelin map reference 60/7,8

1140	Nave, transepts, and western sculpture added onto an earlier choir, following the fire of 1134. Only the crypt remains from before the fire.
1500s	Chapel north of the nave, followed by the choir constructed on a bridge over the Eure.
1805	Apse began to collapse and was demolished in 1827. The rest was used as a storehouse until the fire of 1861.

Although the cathedral on the hill is relatively unadorned, Saint-André is quite austere. It illustrates the contemplative side of the period. Fire destroyed the smooth surfaces of the walls and in a way increased its simplicity: there is nothing here but stone and glass. The string course under the clerestory is just a half-round molding that divides the upper region from the lower.

The timber roof would have been painted and the windows filled with stained glass. Their color and intricacy would have contrasted with the plainness of the architecture, which seems to be anchored into the earth (as at Jumièges), an impression that is reinforced by the massive sloping plinths along the base of the walls.

The circular piers are like sentinels flanking a procession, or caryatids supporting the heavy walls above them. Burnt as they are, the ruined capitals seem like heads offering some note of emotion, just as our faces can betray our feelings to those around us.

This is one of the first naves to have been built with drum piers, with their unique quality of softening the barriers between the spaces of the nave and the aisles so that our attention flows easily from one to the other. But notice in this building how our eyes rest on the firmer boundaries of the walls of the aisles and clerestory. The lower space between the aisle walls flows past the piers, so our moving eye senses them but glides onward. The piers relate more to the upper boundaries of the clerestory than to the lower ones around the aisles. The effect is clear: the piers appear to have been inserted between the lower walls, perhaps from above, as if a giant toymaker had attached them under the clerestory walls, like the legs of a table, and lowered them into the church. In other words, the piers associate not with the lower parts of the nave but with the upper.

To feel this effect, go into the little fifteenth-century chapel on the north and look into the nave. Notice how the tracery and the refined complex vaults agitate the space and keep our attention on the architectural action. Compare this effect with the rest of the building where the architecture encourages quiet and contemplation. Then return to the chapel and notice how the column is integral to the vaults, the ribs coinciding with the facets of the column, and how the complexity of the base anchors it onto the paving. This space is an envelope, self-contained between floor and ceiling. The nave, as you will immediately recognize as you walk back into it, is almost boundless, and the piers for all their weight give the impression that they could lift off to some other place independently.

CLERMONT-FERRAND, Cathedral of Notre-Dame

Department of the Puy-de-Dôme, 179 km (111 miles) west of Lyon; Michelin map reference 73/14

1248	Lower walls of radiating chapels built to just over the windowsills. Then work proceeded slowly until the choir and crossing were completed by 1292, along with parts of the nave. Two more bays of the nave constructed over the next fifty years, a bit more in the next century.
1500s	The original high-pitched roof replaced with the present low one. The portal sculpture, the towers, and the interior fitments destroyed in the Revolution.
1866	Reconstruction of the towers and the façade.

The more typical architecture of provincial France up to the mid-thirteenth century can be seen at Notre-Dame-du-Port nearby. The revolution that the Gothic style caused when it was brought here can then be imagined. The cathedral was begun by a northern architect, Jean Deschamps, who was hired by the bishop in 1248 after working on the Sainte-Chapelle. In view of the small amount completed in the first campaign, he may have had to leave the site after the bishop died the following year. Only the external walls of the chapels seem to have been erected in the first campaign, and you may enjoy following the argument as if you too were an archaeologist.

The bases of the shafts around the walls are quite distinctive. They are made up of four courses with a splayed plinth, one intermediate projecting roll which continues along the wall between the piers, and above that, in one stone, both the torus mold and a small additional plinth. The torus is typical of the second quarter of the century, with a buckled upper roll and a squeezed-in scotia (see the discussion of column bases). The small plinth and the continuous roll mold are unusual; in the Paris Basin they are found only at the Sainte-Chapelle.

All the other bases in the building, including all the piers around the choir, would seem to be later because the gap between the torus molds has snapped shut. The minor plinth, which had been carved with the torus stone in the chapels, has now been carved from a different stone in a more traditional manner.

It would be argued from this evidence that there was a change in the templates from which the stones were cut—and therefore a change in the masters who designed them. We would then expect to find evidence of breaks in the construction, and this can be seen fairly clearly outside the chapels. On the north, in the first straight bay of the sanctuary, you will find the telltale breaks in coursing. They show that the first campaign continued to the second course above the sill in the chapels, stepped down to the second course below the sill along the straight wall, and then, to the east of the buttress, dropped down again to the plinth. How far the plinth was taken under the sacristy does not show, but it probably included the octagonal staircase (like the one at the Sainte-Chapelle) which was capped off, unused, at the sill.

There is a similar joint in the south, but you have probably seen enough now to follow how these arguments are compiled. As there are so few documents which tell us how these great buildings were put up, much of our understanding has to come from detailed observations and arguments.

We can see that the chapel walls were taken up high enough for the sills to be finished. This would have kept the water out of the rubble core of the walls when they had been capped with a couple of courses of the window jambs on which a roof could have been constructed. Light would have entered through the little windows, and the roof would have allowed altars to be set up in the chapels in 1250 or so.

Jean Deschamps may still have been in charge when work resumed many years later, though we know that his son Pierre continued the work.

CLUNY,
Ruins of the Abbey of Saint-Pierre et Saint-Paul

Department of the Saône-et-Loire, 25 km (15 miles) north-west of Mâcon; Michelin map reference 69/19

1088   Work begun in the choir, the apse consecrated in
       1095. Work proceeded steadily westward until the
       portal sculpture was installed about 1120 (the
       narthex was not completed until 1230). The main
       vaults looked in danger and were reinforced with
       flying buttresses in about 1200.
1470   Chapel of Jean de Bourbon set into the south
       transept.
1793   Sold and demolished until the present remains
       were bought in 1823.

The Cluniac empire was one of the great achievements in monastic history. It had the largest monastery with the largest monastic church ever built, so big that it could accommodate the monks from all 1450 dependent abbeys, were they ever to assemble. Its abbots were so powerful they were compared with kings. Thus men who had retired from life came to dominate it, filling the vacuum that followed the age of barbarism, for power naturally flows to those who are well organized.

This church, the third on the site, was at first financed from tribute paid by King Alfonso VI of Leon-Castille. But with Alfonso's death in 1109 and the consequent decline in Castilian power, the chief source of money failed. The slowing of construction work afterward reflected not only the death of a major patron but the decline of the order's influence and the economic problems that came with it.

The abbey had a huge nave with double aisles, 410 feet (125 meters) long, plus over a hundred feet more in the narthex and the chapels. It was covered with a slightly pointed barrel vault that, unlike Saint-Savin-sur-Gartempe or Saint-Benoît-sur-Loire, urged you forward just as the pointed arches of the aisles urged you upward. The nearby church of Paray-le-Monial is a pocket edition of Cluny.

If Paray looks big, then Cluny's two remaining bays are gargantuan. The vaults of the western major transept are almost 98 feet (29.5 meters) high, as high as Notre-Dame in Paris. They are so far above us that we seem dwarfed. Everything is large: the shafts of ashlar, the door in the side wall, the width of the windows, and above all the height of the aisle arcades, which are taller than those at Chartres. These monks were taller than giants, for how else can we explain the position of the triforium, thrust up into the vaults by the crown of these aisle arcades?

Walk away from the transept, then turn around and walk

The soaring height of the Cluny transept.

back in again to relive the shock of its size. It is not just tall but thin. The combination forces us upward. It is typical of Cluny that we are not left to worship in calm, as in the Chartres crypt, but are pushed and shoved on our way, just as the people were pushed to be pilgrims.

With double aisles on each side of the nave, the arrangement would have been a little like Bourges or Beauvais, where the outer aisles were lower than the inner ones so that the spaces became taller as pilgrim approached the center.

The major difference between the elevation of Cluny's nave and that of Paray is that the latter has only one window in the clerestory while Cluny had three. Without flying buttresses, and relying solely on the thickness of the walls for support, this continuous range of openings weakened the structure; cracks appeared, and the upper parts had to be strengthened with flying buttresses in the thirteenth century.

One of the chapels from the minor eastern transept remains, simple and huge, and next to it, in exquisite contrast, the tiny and delicious chapel of Jean de Bourbon, built in 1470. The wriggling curves of the little baldachins over the statue recesses and the flamelike leaves of the capitals make it a gay and happy place. No longer imposing or dominant, it is only thankful to be alive.

Today almost nothing remains of the church, which was sold during the Revolution for its building materials. All that is left are three bays of the south transept, bits of the smaller transept to the east, stumps of the western towers, and buried substructures. Some of the glorious capitals, dedicated to the tones of the Gregorian chant and their sacred meanings, are displayed in the old granary, along with a model of the abbey made in 1855 by a local clothier who in his youth had helped to pull it down.

The capitals show what a tragedy was perpetrated here. Their sculpture and the fragments from the west front come from the time that carving was reaching maturity. For the decades just before and after 1100, there was probably no comparable collection of exquisite foliage and figures as here.

As you leave, look again at the model in the entry to remind yourself how large the three remaining bays of the transepts are, and how small a part of the whole building they were. It was said that Cluny rivaled Saint Peter's in Rome until it was rebuilt in the sixteenth century—which was in fact true with regard to both its size and, for a while, its temporal power.

CONQUES, Benedictine Abbey of Sainte-Foy

Department of the Aveyron, 63 km (39 miles) east of Cahors; Michelin map reference 80/1,2

1031	Work begun in the east, completed by 1090.
1424	The abbey was secularized; in 1568 the Protestants set fire to it.
1860s	The west façade restored and the reliquary of Saint Foy discovered buried in one of the walls.

The abbey was one of the major stops on the way to the great pilgrimage shrine of Santiago de Compostela. On arriving, the pilgrims would have already traveled miles through hilly and thickly wooded country of few villages and even fewer travelers. They moved in convoy for protection from the wolves, bears, and robbers who inhabited the dense woods and inaccessible hills of the region. The pilgrims would set out early in the morning (travel by night was dangerous), and their joy in a safe arrival, their exuberance that this particularly perilous section had been successfully navigated, would remind them of the Way to God.

The architecture of the church exemplifies this and extols the virtues of the Way. For it is tall and beautiful, magically lit, with a solidity and comfort and sense of purpose in its tall galleries. It is like a citadel, a bulwark against animal and spiritual predators.

The Benedictines came to Conques in 819 and found life hard and the site isolated. Most of the monks would have defected to a more comfortable monastery if Saint Foy's relics had not been hijacked and brought here in 866 (the story is told on page 37).

Saint Foy was a little girl martyr who was roasted in 303. Her relics are still in the abbey, housed within a gold statue, which is extraordinary and somewhat barbaric. Covered in jewelry, sparkling under the candles, it would have transported pilgrim to another world. It survives as a solitary reminder of the enormous number of such reliquaries lost to war and theft.

Pilgrimages to Conques brought prosperity. In the eleventh century the abbey owned lands in most French dioceses from the Alps to the Rhineland and in Normandy, Spain, and Tuscany. These lands helped the abbey to survive in later years as the pilgrimage trade dropped off. By 1420 only twenty-nine monks lived at Conques. During the Revolution the remaining monks managed to hide the church treasure to save it from being melted down.

Conques is a typical pilgrimage church, with a complex east end and a nave without clerestory windows but with indirect lighting through the galleries. The interior is a narrow vertical space 68 feet (20.7 meters) high. It is built of red and yellow sandstone from nearby quarries, which gives it a warm feeling.

Stability is ensured by the thickness of the vaults and walls. The barrel vault over the nave is two feet thick. The side thrusts from it are secured by the half-vaults over the galleries which lean inward against the nave. It is a well-balanced structural system—as long as you do not wish to increase the amount of light. Once a clerestory is required, the upper wall has to be extended above the gallery vaults, as at Nevers.

The interior is lit in two ways. The traditional windows around the apse and in the central lantern are like spotlights and glare brightly. We are drawn toward them as to a theatre stage, as though the clergy were about to show off their prowess as intermediaries to God. At the eastern end salvation is presented as a great drama, as it was for those who were passing on the most important journey of their lives.

The nave gives a different impression from the choir. In the nave there are no clerestory windows, and light filters in from unseen openings in the flanking galleries. These galleries are placed high up under the main vaults, with their own half-barrels that seem to glow with light. Because there are no ribs or groins, our eye finds nothing to fix on in these vaults. The "sky" behind the gallery arches seems to dissolve into eternity, evoking the Heavenly Jerusalem itself.

Notice that the spiritual world is not in the parts we occupy. It may be in the galleries over our heads, or beyond the bright windows behind the altar, or above the central axis through the lantern tower, but it does not extend down to the pavement. He transcends our space.

At Conques we see one way of delivering this message—indirectly and austerely. The same format was followed at Toulouse. Another way was tried in Burgundian monasteries like Paray-le-Monial, and a third in the domed churches of the west, Souillac and Cahors. In all of them heaven was beyond the walls. Its glory shone through with that light so praised by Abbot Suger, but it was not physically present within the sanctuary.

Then, just a few years later in the north, this was to change: the theatre in the choir, the light from above, and the architecture were to fuse so that the church would become paradise itself.

DIJON, Church of Notre-Dame

Department of the Côte-d'Or, 229 km (142 miles) southeast of Paris; Michelin map reference 66/12

1190   Charter granted for the church and construction begun at the east. The triforium was being erected in the 1220s, the clerestory in the 1230s; the western façade completed around 1250.

1711   Small rose windows added to the choir. The sculpture destroyed in 1794 by a fanatical pharmacist known as the "Iron Axe." The lantern, the side chapels, and all the sculpture on the western front restored in the nineteenth century.

Approach Notre-Dame from the east, along the pedestrian way, and as you turn the corner to the west front, look up! These extraordinary apparitions, seething out from the bands of foliage, are nothing like the figures that people the Chartres Royal Portal or even Charlieu. There are no saints or didactic popes here, but animals, weird beasts, frogs on human bodies, and dancing leopards. True, there is a monk, and one of the violinists has wings; yet the scene is a grotesque circus, not a mystic vision. For authentic gargoyle hunters, there are a few original ones on the lateral faces of the north and south towers.

How times have changed, compared to Vézelay or Paris. Where now is the façade that daunts or terrifies, or is even helpful and emboldening? The sculpture has become a charade of mountebanks, reflecting the loss of spirituality that marks the thirteenth century.

It also shows in the porch. The capitals supporting the arches to the side portals are higher than those supporting the center, and the piers inside display a charmingly eccentric change in levels. The tympanum over the central door is protected by a wide vault that seems to diminish its importance, while the side doorways are accentuated by the taller spaces. Symbolically, how can the sides be more significant than the center? You can see why they did it, for if the center had been higher as well as wider, the top of the three porch vaults would not have been the same level and the lower register of façade sculptures would have had to be placed higher up. This only highlights the problem, for the natural order has been reversed in favor of a visually exciting but meretricious design solution.

*West front,
Notre-Dame,
Dijon.*

Notre-Dame is a mélange of Soissonnais motifs. It has the lantern tower and scale of Braine, an exterior like the Laon transept chapels, and so on. But fundamental modifications have been made to the interior that have turned it into something new.

The walls are made to look paper thin, as cleverly demonstrated in the thickness of the arches over the triforium and over the wall arcades and the adjacent windows in the east. Using a similar technique, the clerestory windows have been separated from the internal wall plane by placing a walkway in front of it so that the vaults appear to float.

All this gives the impression that the inside face of the wall is in fact no more than a thin skin that has separated itself slightly from the real mass. To emphasize this, each layer presents its own arrangement of openings, suggesting that there may be two buildings, one sleeved inside the other. In fact the house of God has been disengaged from its external protective shell.

This is not all, for the remaining sections of walling on the inside have also been detached from the shafts. From the nave you can see that where the wall over the arcade arches meets the crossing piers, a gap has been left between the shaft and the wall plane so that the wall appears to pass behind the shaft. Unattached to any structure, the last reminder of solidity has been detached from its supports, so it too appears to float.

Everything is in layers that shift across one another, or disappear just when we expect them to be most firmly anchored. A papier-mâché church has been inserted within the real structure and uncoupled by just a few centimeters. The temple has been peeled off the fortress.

It is a rarefied design, one with little passion—and yet it is contemporary with Chartres. Its model was Braine, whose triforium *appears* to weave behind the piers, but here it actually passes behind them. The illusion that the arcade might disembowel the vault supports has become an actuality. This is clear in the nave triforium, where the end columns are partly hidden behind the vaulting shafts.

You feel how unsettling it is to realize that the vaulting shafts really carry no load. The beauty of the Paris Basin buildings is that the apparent function of these shafts is not openly denied by the triforium, so the illusion of both is maintained. Here it is as if the lights had suddenly been turned up in the theatre to expose canvas castles and paper battlements.

And finally the crossing: look up! Fix your eye on the huge window at the top, then follow the corner shafts down past the clerestory capitals and the triforium, past the aisles and the chapel capitals to the floor. With one infinitely long "structure" as thin as string, the building seems to hang.

Some scholars have wanted to date this building to the 1230s, but the detailing will not support that. The base moldings, with the full-round upper torus roll, would be before 1200, and the simple crockets on the arcade capitals would not have been carved anywhere else after 1210. From the vaulting ribs to the window profiles, all elements bespeak the years around 1200. Therefore this master took the Braine scheme, finished at about the time Notre-Dame was begun, and etherealized it. The mannerisms he used to accomplish this became, thirty years later, the basis for the Rayonnant of Saint-Germain-en-Laye.

It is surprising to think that this is the Burgundy where Cluny and Tournus had been built less than a century before. Local Romanesque was vigorous and, as discussed at Paray-le-Monial, more materialistic than in other areas. One has the impression that this worldliness is still with us.

ESSÔMES-SUR-MARNE, Church of Saint-Feréol
Once a Benedictine abbey

Department of the Aisne, 97 km (60 miles) east of Paris; Michelin map reference 56/14

1210   Choir commenced, and a decade later the nave and the eastern triforium started. The choir clerestory, under way shortly afterward, may have been vaulted around 1240.

In a sense Essômes is not unlike Braine to the north, begun some thirty years later: it is Braine opened out and made much taller. Yet it is to its contemporary Chartres that Essômes should be compared.

Essômes is smaller than Chartres, minor elements such as the shafts and window colonnettes are much thinner, and the scale of the triforium and the windows is many times lighter. So the massive western crossing piers come as some surprise. On the eastern side the compound crossing piers move us upward with some delicacy. But on the west the gigantic *piliers cantonnés* explicitly divide the nave from the choir and transepts. We might compare this way of marking the end of the nave with the earlier arrangement at Nevers. Both call for the same response, though here it was being used for one of the last times, as the universal glass cage was about to take its place.

The lower half of the building feels thick and inert, an effect that is reinforced by the big splays to the apse windows and the size of the stones. In the nave, for example, the bases to the cylindrical piers are made from a single block and the courses above are over two feet thick, with one stone per course. The western crossing piers are just as enormous, carrying up into the high vaults like great gateposts.

Above the triforium string, as at Orbais, this immutability disintegrates. The slender members, the tall and narrow

Essômes from the east.

openings, and the light and elegant tracery aerate the upper parts. Essômes is both mammoth and marmoset, in a beautiful balance between massiveness and lightness which makes this abbey a diamond compared to the agate of Reims.

Rayonnant was derived more from Essômes than from Chartres, for here the master has both attenuated the members and replaced the wall with patterns of stone. And it was here that tracery was first conceived.

Observe the windows in the northern transept chapels on the left. If you have already visited Orbais, where the clerestory rose is placed some distance above the lancets (see page 232), you will notice that the roses in these chapels have been lowered so that their edges merge with the arches over the lancets. This isolates a small triangular space between them.

See how this triangle on the north has been treated, then move to the southern chapels, and in the eastern windows notice what has happened. The centers of the triangles have been hollowed out. The master recognized that this little junction could play a role of its own, and he became fascinated. So in the third step, in the last window on the southern wall of the chapel, he excavated further and cut the hole right through the wall. The triangle had become an opening to the outside, which the master filled with glass. It was at this moment that tracery was born.

The master had only to continue the outer shafts over the top of the rose, as in the nave aisles, and the fully traceried window of Reims was before us. At Essômes we are fortunate to be able to follow the process of invention step by step.

This little triangular piece of glass introduced something new to medieval architecture. Earlier the geometric form of every element, be it window, chapel, or porch, was determined from centers that lay *within the element.* In a rose or in the plan of a tower this is obvious: every part relates to one or more middle points. Windows were designed symmetrically around a central axis, and the centers of their arcs lay within the window opening. Buildings were an assemblage of such forms, and in one sense the wall was just infilling between them.

But this triangle is not a centralized form, for its shape was geometrically accidental, the result of other actions. With it came a new esthetic, one in which the indeterminate came to be as important as the determined. The multicurved and multifaceted decoration of Flamboyant, which was not conceivable in the twelfth century, was the flowering of this concept.

This master was one of the geniuses of Gothic. Starting in the clerestory of Orbais, he followed his ideas through at Essômes, and in the aisles of Reims he finalized the design for one of the fundamental motifs that was to dominate architecture for three centuries. Tracery was an impressive element in the building, for it helped to make the window more interesting than either the volumes or the surrounding wall. Thus in time the building became a frame for the tracery instead of the window's being merely a hole in the wall.

It created the means for the theatres of illusion at Saint-Urbain in Troyes and for the great transept façades of Paris and Beauvais. Older buildings were half-demolished (as in the transepts of Laon) to accommodate these extraordinary glazed screens.

ÉTAMPES, Church of Notre-Dame-du-Fort

Department of the Essonne, 50 km (31 miles) south of Paris; Michelin map reference 60/10

1046	Crypt constructed. Then nave aisles added, followed by the southern door around 1140. The many campaigns in the east culminated in the vaults being set up in the 1160s. The south side of the church was at one time a hospice, and the dead were thrown into a pit under the church.
1220	Western wall and doors added against the earlier tower, to close off the nave.

The sleepy town of Étampes has not always been so quiet. In the twelfth century it was the pivotal defensive bastion on the king's southern boundary. To capture Paris, one first had to capture Étampes.

Nothing remains of the eleventh-century church except the endearingly small crypt and the huge drum piers of the nave. The choir was begun around 1140, then there were five major changes of plan and even more changes in builders. The variety of capitals, the differing heights of the vaults, and the irregularities of the plan around the eastern end all indicate the difficulties of its history. The circumstances at Étampes have made these vagaries so complex that its detailed construction history has never been solved, and a number of historians have given up in despair.

The eastern crossing piers have enormously tall drums embedded in them, which finish in eleventh-century capitals. Partway up there are smaller capitals which once supported a low entry arch into the apse. Then shafts were added over the drums on the eastern side, with arches built below the level of the apse arch—traces are visible on the eastern side of the northern pier. Further shafts were added later (but to different templates on each pier) and carried up to the height of the drum capital, though these too were finished at different times, the ones over the original apse arch probably being the last—but how can we be sure?

The result of the many additions is the airiest church in

France. It seems to be much taller than it is because there are no low aisles in the east. As you can see when you stand in the choir, the multitude of piers disguises both the covering vaults and the walls. As the boundaries are blurred, the space appears endless. The enormous windows deny the traditional introverted darkness of most contemporary churches and instead increase the spaciousness even more. It is expansionist and exultant, like the monarchy itself at that time.

Everything is done in pairs. The narthex or entrance hall is made from two bays directly under the west tower. The short nave has only two bays and is flanked by two wide aisles. The transept has a double crossing, leading straightway into the chevet with two bays. The irregular double aisle surrounding the chevet terminates in paired chapels.

The south portal of 1140 was carved by men who also worked on the Royal Portal at Chartres and at Saint-Denis, though the ecstasy of the clothes of the figures and the manic movements of arms and heads suggest that the sculptors may have come from the south, where there is much similarly vital sculpture at Charlieu and Saint-Gilles. Were they heading north into territory that was becoming richer while their homelands had for some reason lost some of their prosperity?

The Church mistrusted the New Testament—rightly, as the Reformation was to show. It interpreted the unacceptable parts of the Gospels through the patriarchal bias of the Old Testament. This is why at Chartres the four evangelists are shown, in the lancets of the south transept windows, sitting on top of Old Testament prophets, "like pigmies astride giants" (in the words of John of Salisbury).

For this reason every Old Testament figure symbolizes something from the Gospels. Here Esther on the left prefigures the Virgin in her role of intercessor, Moses holds the tablets of the law to symbolize Christ as the new lawgiver, and Melchizedek, king and high priest of Jerusalem who blessed Abraham with bread and wine, evokes the Last Supper. On the right side, David represents Christ's descent from the kings of Israel, Bathsheba the Church, and Solomon, Christ the Judge. All is seen through the Old Testament.

The capitals with their miniature scenes protected by canopies and the embrasure figures under them were carved by men who also worked at Chartres. If you examine with care the little carving on the left return of these capitals you will see it has a tree on it, with a twisted trunk and symmetrical foliage. There are identical trees on a large capital on the *inside* wall of the Royal Portal at Chartres, only a course above a stone inscribed "Rogerus." Was this the name of the master from Étampes?

FONTENAY, Cistercian Abbey of Notre-Dame

Department of the Côte-d'Or, 81 km (50 miles) east of
Auxerre; Michelin map reference 65/8

1118   The monastery founded on instructions from Saint
        Bernard.
1139   The church constructed, and parts consecrated
        in 1147.
1793   Sold as a paper factory, and restored in 1906.

Fontenay is isolated in a peaceful, wooded Burgundian valley. It is the oldest surviving Cistercian abbey in France, a
typical example of the monks' functional planning. They
did not want towns or fairs to grow up around their monasteries, and they did not build near protective castles. For a
long time laymen were kept out, so there was no need for
didactic sculpture or an elaborate west portal. Not even the
capitals have the light touches of ornament found at Pontigny. The rules were scrupulously observed.

At Fontenay nothing was meant to distract from the contemplation of God. Its utopian ideal is somewhat hard for us
to visualize in the damp spaces we enter today, with their
lichen-covered walls and earthen floors. But people the
church with devout and serious men, add altars and candles, and fill the space with their chants and responses and
see how alive it becomes.

The plan is a simple cruciform with a small rectangular
choir. The western doorway was used by lay brothers who
could not come past the rood screen. Monks entered from

Fontenay cloister.

the cloister or at night descended the stairs from the dormitory on the right. The only door shared by the monks and the lay brothers was the little door in the north transept through which the dead were taken for burial.

The elevation has only two stories. It was not until Longpont in the 1180s that the triforium was added. The dualistic arrangement expressed the separation between the world the monk must inhabit during his period of waiting and preparation on earth, and the divine world to which he aspired.

Thus the small clerestory windows give a glimpse of heavenly light, Suger's *lux nova* in simplified garb, while the austere capitals and arcades reduced his world to its bare essentials. At Longpont and later Cistercian buildings this distinction was more or less retained, even where there were three stories, by increasing the height of the arcades and using circular drums as piers. This separated the lower part from the upper and the inner section from the outer, so that the vault and triforium seemed suspended above the church even while being perfectly supported.

The use of corbels under the high vault shafts seems to reinforce this idea. Corbels occur again and again in Cistercian churches, and though in the choir it may have made it easier to back the stalls up against the piers, such a pragmatic explanation will not do for the rest of the nave. Once again the reason would seem to have been theological and didactic.

The shafts and their corbels seem to slide over the face of the square piers. These piers are solid, as befits the structure, but the shafts seem to slide over the face of the piers as though they were more securely attached to the vault. The corbels are, if anything, more like knobs at the ends of the shafts than their supports. They pass over the rectangular piers and like interlocking fingers join the uppermost realm representing the heavens with the lower structure as mundane reality. The monk stretches up and clasps hands with God.

The church is covered with pointed barrel vaults. Those in the aisles do not run parallel to the nave vault but at right angles to it, to cope with the lateral thrusts, just like the gallery vaults at Conques. The Cistercians may have been remote from society, but their buildings were in the mainstream of the architectural experiments of the twelfth century.

In fact it has been argued that the Cistercians were responsible for many of the concepts which led to Gothic, such as the simplified elevation and the rose window. Simplicity is in itself a powerful force: it compels one to think about essentials. Normally we do not question our fundamentals but accept them and plow on with our daily lives, resolving problems as they come due.

Any builder employed by the Cistercians had to work things through from the beginning, for the abbots demanded total purity of form. This required an effort akin to cooking a complex meal with only a wood fire or having to wear clothes of only one color. When we have the ability, we find restrictions inspiring, and we begin to question old habits. Thus the Cistercians had a profound influence on the new generation of architects.

They showed that the forms were more important than what was carved into them, and that structure was something to be displayed rather than hidden. They also insisted on meaning and purpose in their designs. In the Paris Basin these ideas fell on fertile ground.

GERMIGNY-DES-PRÉS, Church of la Sainte-Trinité

Department of the Loiret, 30 km (19 miles) east of Orléans; Michelin map reference 64/10

806	The eastern part of the building finished.
1060	The nave added, and rebuilt in the fifteenth century.
1869	Massively restored, with hardly an original stone left.

This is one of the oldest stone churches in France. It was built by Bishop Theodulf, one of Charlemagne's counselors and the abbot of Saint-Benoît-sur-Loire nearby, as his private chapel.

The most important concepts of the Romanesque exterior were present in the first Christian churches, even as early as the fourth century. The plan is simple and appropriate, for it is an assembly of cylinders and cubes in a cosmic marriage of the circle and the square. There being almost no embellishment, the beautiful effects inside and out result from the distinctive qualities of the forms rather than from decoration.

In plan there is a square central space, originally surrounded by four semicircular apses, one of which was demolished when the nave was added. The square symbolizes matter, the circle the spirit; the four apses represent the four directions, the four winds, and the four gates of paradise. Thus the chapel encapsulates paradise on earth.

A distinct Moslem flavor in the building comes from the horseshoe arches that remind one of Cordova and Africa. Only a hundred years earlier the Arabs had conquered most of Spain and were on the verge of the greatest cultural advance in their history. The growing trade between Europe and the Arab world, had the bad times of the following two centuries not occurred, might have led to this type of arch becoming as popular in the north as it was on the other side of the Pyrenees.

However, Europe adopted the stilted arch, in which the curved voussoirs rest on a number of vertical courses, lifting the arch above the capitals. Visually, one or another of these techniques is needed to give life to the arch; otherwise it seems to lie heavily on the capitals (see page 126).

The cubic form of the outer walls encases an inner square which reaches through the cube to support the central lantern tower. This creates an ambulatory all round the building, which is quite dark while the central space under the tower is brilliantly illuminated. As was to become a feature in the twelfth century, the light of heaven flows through the interior from this hidden source, infusing the square tower with the spirit of paradise.

Another important twelfth-century motif was used in this center: partway up there is a middle zone that is neither of the aisles and their arcades nor of the top lights with their intimations of heaven, a zone that would develop into the gallery and in time into the triforium. The effect is quite magical.

The lower part of the apse, with its three slot windows, is domestic in scale. The upper section with its mosaic-covered blind arcade and semidome is ethereal. The arcade shares something from both zones that flank it, combining earthly motifs in the arcade and heavenly in the mosaics. Similarly, in palaces it was usual to adorn the upper floors with loggias and arcades where, well protected by the solid lower walls, the nobility could parade, both to be seen and to look down on the masses below. The arrangement signified the wealth and security of those who dwelt therein, and the envy and longing among the people down below. But instead of seeing the sky between the pillars of this arcade as we would in a palace, we see mosaics which, like those in the semidome, represent paradise. So the arcade stirs both feelings: as worshippers we devoutly wish to be in that paradise, and as noblemen we know how good it is going to be if we can only get there.

The major mosaic in the semidome is like the oratory, ninth century, and is exquisite. Containing over 130,000 tiny cubes of pure color—blue, yellow and red, white and black—it was buried under plaster in the eighteenth century, then providentially rediscovered in about 1820 and restored a generation later.

It depicts the ark of the covenant as a sign of the first covenant between God and the chosen people. It symbolizes the second covenant, made at the death of Christ, and the inscription asks us to pray for the soul of Theodulf, who commissioned it. The ideal is united with the private. Even though the new contract is for all men without favor, the bishop remains uncertain and needs our prayers. He reminds us not to forget him. It is his insurance.

JUMIÈGES,
Ruins of the Benedictine Abbey of Notre-Dame

Department of the Seine-Maritime, 28 km (17 miles) west of Rouen; Michelin map reference 55/5

1037	The choir begun, followed by the nave and westwork between 1052 and 1066; the dedication postponed for a year while Duke William, an honored guest at the ceremony, was away on business in England.
1270s	Work begun on a new choir and continued for fifty years.
1358	Abandoned during the war; sacked in 1562; sold as a quarry in 1795; the remains bought for preservation in 1852.

The two great towers, 170 feet (52 meters) high, are formidably male. The plain walls and sharp-edged windows make no compromises. One senses that the people who built this church were united in their purposes. The elaboration at the top of the towers takes your eye up and, in a breakneck way, holds it there. Unlike any of the later abbeys in this guide, there is no frivolity anywhere, just the relentless face of smooth stonework. It rises straight out of the ground without preparation, as though the rock had been extruded to this great height by some giant cataclysm of willpower.

Rightly, the consecration was delayed so that William the Conqueror could be there, for this building reflects the Normans' dedication to the relentless pursuit of power. At the same time this abbey combines a magnificence and generosity in its scale, an unostentatious and almost naive simplicity. A genuine spirituality entwines the severity.

The twin towers flanking the central projection suggest an armored knight with his weapons raised—or an enthroned power flanked by impregnable henchmen. Architecturally these towers framing a main entry door established a canon that was to lead in time to the great portals of Chartres and Reims.

One wonders where this gargantuan sense came from. Before the turn of the century Norman churches were made of wood, perhaps in the style and tradition of the *stavekirke* in Scandinavia. They were small wooden structures, delicately detailed; what could have happened to instigate the greater size?

Once inside, we find the height awesome, raising us ten feet tall. The great lantern tower that had once capped the crossing would have added further to this extraordinary sense of height. Much larger than Nevers, it is almost as tall as Cluny even though it was built two generations earlier.

Jumièges had a wooden roof like an upturned ship,

The nave of Jumièges seen through the ruins.

painted in a glory of colors. The continuous string course under the gallery, and the huge clerestory windows, are one of the first essays in separating the upper heavens from the base earth. The vaulting shafts which break through this string course were added when the nave was vaulted.

The clerestory windows, not to be made as large in any other region for another century, and initially without stained glass, would have let in lots of light, making everything visible and clear. If you think there was to have been stained glass, examine the window jambs and determine how it would have been held in place.

The square bases to the piers are stamped into the ground, making the nave into a hall of giants. Because the shafts alternate, each second pier being circular, pilgrim is forced to pause on his way down the nave; he is allowed to advance only by measured stages to the altar.

The groin vaults over the aisles are among the first, and they help to turn it into a tunnel leading eastward. You never feel you are in a separate space taking you eastward, for you remain part of the greater central one. The aisles share both the divisions of the nave and the way to the altar.

The original choir was probably like Nevers or Tournus, for you can see the same type of projecting tables under the bases at the eastern end of the nave. If so, the choir would have "floated" while the nave was "anchored." The older apse was replaced with a Rayonnant choir with enormous traceried windows in each chapel. It is instructive to compare these chapels with the nave: the many thin shafts against the smooth surfaces of the west, the delicate base profiles against the earlier monumental pads, the jeweled capitals in the chapels, and the purely practical cushions in the nave that brook no nonsense. Where the west is spartan, the east is sybaritic—the two are strange companions in the one building.

In less than three centuries the warrior has become a courtier.

LAON, Cathedral of Notre-Dame

Department of the Aisne, 37 km (23 miles) northeast of Soissons; Michelin map reference 56/5

1150s	An ambulatory choir erected with the eastern walls of the transepts to the top of the triforium; the building gradually extended westward in the next decade.
1180s	The ambulatory torn down and a square eastern end built; the west front begun with the triforium in the eastern bays of the nave. The east and west rose windows followed in the 1190s, the vaulting and the crossing lantern around 1200. Work on the towers abandoned around 1225.
1300s	Southern picture window added.
1845	Heavy restoration, especially in the west and the towers.

In 1112 the city of Laon was the scene of an extremely bloody uprising by the citizens against their lord bishop, Gaudri. The townsmen beheaded Gaudri, who was found hiding in a barrel, and set fire to the cathedral. Half the town had burned before the fire could be put out.

In time, as the townsmen won the right to conduct their own affairs—a situation that made them extremely wealthy—relations between the city and the chapter improved. As at Chartres, the goodwill made it easier to raise the enormous funds needed for the rebuilding.

The choir was built in the later 1150s, though it was not flat-ended as we see it today. The original apse had three bays and a semicircular ambulatory as in Notre-Dame, Paris, without chapels opening off it.

The whole of the apse and the eastern walls of the transepts were erected at the one time, story by story, until they reached the sills of the clerestory windows. They did not proceed to the main vaults but roofed the choir at this low level. The choir could then be used while, in a more leisurely way, the rest of the transepts and nave were added.

As the work progressed westward, the nave was built in steps rather than in full-height bays, as many have been taught. The fourth bay in the nave, for example, was erected at the same time as the third bay of the gallery and the second bay of the triforium. In this way each story buttressed the lateral thrusts from the one above. Seeing it finished, we forget that it took time to construct, that at the end of each day the parts that were finished would have been supported only by what was already in place.

We do not know why, but in the 1180s the ambulatory was torn down and extended eastward seven bays. The square end wall of the choir is unusual in French cathedrals, though it is the commonest way to terminate the smaller churches of the region.

This was less than twenty years after the first stage had been completed, and even before the westernmost piers of the nave had been begun or the nave triforium more than just commenced. The site was still covered in scaffolding, the surrounding streets with building yards and cranes, and the roads leading to the town were daily clogged with bullock carts delivering stone. Yet it was decided to delay the completion of what had partly been built in order to pull the most important section down and extend it further. They did this quickly, for the work was completed up to the triforium within a decade. Though some of the old materials were reused, the cost of the extension was prodigious.

Many of the piers and capitals of the old ambulatory can be seen when you stand in the choir underneath the north wall and look up at the fourth or fifth bay. The curved outer faces of the imposts over the capitals, and the sides, which

The gallery of Laon cathedral.

are not parallel but splay outward as though cut from the rim of a circle, show they were once around the ambulatory.

The square end horizontalizes rather than verticalizes the building. It directs the eye along the axis toward the great eastern windows. Though the lantern over the crossing pulls us upward, the eastern rose, especially when the morning sun blasts through it, is like an apotheosis, a dramatic theatre proscenium beyond which lay the heavenly drama itself.

The flat ends are in keeping with the lowness of Laon. It feels down-to-earth, reflecting the practical issues of the prosperous *vignerons* of the region. It is unlike its contemporary in Paris which, at a height of 98 feet (29.5 meters), was the tallest church in France at the time, presumably reflecting the enormous ambitions of the monarchy.

Laon's interior elevation was the most unified that had been achieved at that time. It had four stories, not unlike Paris, but with a triforium instead of the blank roses. The alternating arrangement of columns used in so many earlier buildings, including Sens and Senlis, was diluted. Nearly all the columns are single drums, and the alternation required by the high vaults is only lightly sketched in the clusters of shafts.

THE LANTERN

The central lantern profoundly affects the scale of the building. It opens up the crossing and fills it with an intense light that reduces the importance of all the other spaces. It is a little like being in an elevator shaft, with all potential movement directed vertically. Just stand under the lantern to feel the effect of the light pouring onto you. The arms of choir and transept appear to expand outward from the crossing, and if the stained glass were still in place, the surrounding darkness would turn you outward toward the rose windows. The ecstasy lies both in you, from the lantern, and beyond you, through the wheels of glass. In this sense Laon is the archetypical mystic church, in which we stand immanent in the light of God while expanding outward in each of the four directions.

To compare the effects, consider the vaulted closed-in crossings of Chartres and Reims, where we no longer share in or stand absorbed by God's light; we may view it only from our own darkness. The light transcends our world. When begun, crossing lanterns were intended in both cathedrals, and at Chartres we can precisely date the decision to omit it and vault it over. This was in 1222, which marks the beginning of that crucial transformation of the beliefs which had first shown themselves eighty years before in the Royal Portal. It was at the same time that the long roof replaced the tall towers and tracery began its beguiling history.

THE EXTERIOR

The foundations for the western front were put down just after the eastern extension, and the sculpture was in place by 1200. This was a few years before the Chartres transept porches, and it was the first place where the doorways were integrated with the rest of the façade. The projecting portals reduced the importance of the buttresses that would normally have divided the front, as in the transepts. Instead the buttresses have been elevated so that they start above the porch. Using them to frame the rose enlarges the porches as far as the roof and forms a second platform from which spring the towers. The façade is a series of jumping-off places, a staircase to the heavens.

The towers turn this very horizontal building into a vertical one, leaping in stages from story to story, as the forms work their way past the layers and recesses of the façade toward the sky. Like the hill on which it is built, Laon clambers upward in short steps, each lighter than the last, the upthrust of the towers even more effective for being tied to such a dachshund of a building.

There were to have been seven towers, two at each arm and one over the crossing. The lantern was built but not the spire over it, though the staircase for that spire does exist, jutting above the roof like some mad conjurer leaping into space. The completed silhouette would have been extraordinary. The long building on the butte would have had six fingers stretching into the heavens, set around one incredible spire as the *axis mundi*. Just as the forest is something different, in feeling and character, to the individual tree or to the ordered avenue, so the massed towers would have been different to a small grouping.

Like the flying buttresses, the towers fracture the silhouette into prismatic fingers that vigorously uplift the whole structure. Restless, straining at their earthly moorings, filled with nervous ecstasy, they reflect exactly the mystical longings of the twelfth century. It is a pity none of these turreted buildings were completed, attitudes having changed since the inception. Reims was to have had seven towers, Chartres nine, and Amiens six. Only Laon displays a part of what may have been possible.

The roof pitch was kept low, as the tall roofs of Reims and Chartres would have obscured part of the central tower and forced them to build it even higher if it was to have any impact at all. The low roof with many towers delivers an entirely different message from that of a church with a dominant roof. The latter had been used at Senlis, Paris, and Mantes, but during the 1220s it became the standard French solution, by which time Laon had managed to raise only parts of five towers and then decided there was no point in continuing.

The topmost stage of the western towers has four pairs of

oxen, their hoofs on the very edge of the precipice, peering down on the visitors. They commemorate a miracle: at a critical moment a team of oxen appeared from nowhere to drag the stones from the quarry, then disappeared when the job was done. The oxen also honor labor—a new notion for the times, as there had been nothing in the slave societies of antiquity to encourage the idea that work was noble. In a penitential age this respect naturally became "redemption through work," a concept that is more familiar to us.

LONGPONT,
Ruins of the Cistercian Abbey of Notre-Dame

Department of the Aisne, 16 km (10 miles) southwest of Soissons; Michelin map reference 56/3,4

1180s	Choir begun, possibly vaulted around 1195; the western walls begun shortly after the choir, and the whole consecrated in 1227.
1795	Sold for demolition; the remains bought privately in 1830. Further damage in 1918.

Ruins are always magical, with their overtones of romantic novels, of Keats and Poussin. These ruins still tower over the tiny houses in the village, and the gigantic hole of the broken rose window stares accusingly outward.

Like Cluny and Jumièges, it was sold to a local builder who blew it up for the stone. Little of the choir remains, yet there is enough to show that it was started by the same genius who began Chartres, but about a decade earlier, before the invention of the *pilier cantonné* (which is why all the piers are round).

The nave of Longpont from the north.

With Braine, Longpont has the earliest three-story elevation in the area. The remnants of the triforium can be seen
against the western wall. It does not have a passage behind
the shafts to create a dark and mysterious space but is applied straight against the wall. As in all human endeavor,
the early stages of great ideas are full of experiments, not all
of which succeed. The blind arcade of Longpont was not as
acceptable as the open arrangement at Braine. The experiment failed to attract adherents.

The aisle arcades may seem too tall for the clerestory
above, but they have a specific effect on us. As the aisles are
almost twice as high as the clerestory, they seem to thrust
the top stories upward. The drums are so thin they make
the upper zone appear weightless, so the main vaults appear to hover, as at Soissons. But this effect is contradicted
somewhat as the triforium is more like a wall than an open
passage, which makes the upper zone appear weightier
than at Braine. It was the church of Paradise floating above
the monks. The Cistercians had created a building that, in a
way, appeared to float off the ground.

MANTES-LA-JOLIE, Collegiate of Notre-Dame

Department of the Yvelines, 60 km (37 miles) west of Paris;
Michelin map reference 55/18

1140–1150	Central and north doors on the west built and the foundations laid. The choir continued in the 1160s, the gallery with the nave walls in the 1170s, the clerestory in the 1180s, and in a separate campaign the westwork and western rose after 1190. The towers finished in 1265.
1285	Southern door on the west and the radiating chapels added.
1844	Heavy restorations in the west; one tower replaced.

Mantes is a quiet, subtle building in which we feel extremely secure under the observant rose windows at the
back of the gallery. The walls are thinner than usual. To
emphasize this, the glass in the clerestory and the gallery
has been placed as close as possible to the inner face of the
wall. Further, the shafts under the vaults are clearly inadequate for what they purport to do. Compare them with Sens
or Senlis, where they are thicker and protrude more into
the nave to accentuate the mass.

Here the walls deny mass, so the eye easily follows the
surfaces upward and discovers that the wall seems to be
thinner at each level. In the aisle arcade there are two rows
of arches with four roll molds at their corners. In the gallery

there is one arch with only two rolls, and the lightest possible arch encases each bay. In the clerestory above there are no rolls at all, and the wall is almost flush with the glass. As a result the interior seems encased in paper. It contrasts with the very thick walls and deeply recessed windows of the aisles, which are best observed in the unaltered western bays.

The effect is twofold. First, the apparent vertical movement of the shafts creates a vortex or a lateral spatial flow *through* the wall. This sideways motion is no longer contained, and so liberates us from a sense of enclosure. Instead we are free to move inward and outward as well as up and down.

Second, where Jumièges and Tournus were bounded and limited and thus safe and predictable, the lightness of the Mantes wall and shafts has achieved what the flying buttress and stained glass succeeded in establishing at about the same time: the apparent elimination of mass and the dematerialization of hard stone. There may also have been economic reasons, for if the builders could resolve the technical problems of lightweight construction, then the costs would have been less.

The verticality is emphasized by the stilting to the apse arches which, like Nevers, throw our glance upward. Unlike Nevers, the string course under the gallery is unobtrusive, and instead of there being another horizontal band under the clerestory, the pointed arches over the gallery send us even further upward, like firing the second stage of a rocket. It is further accented by the six-part vaults which seem to hold us suspended a few feet off the ground, almost level with the roses at the back of the galleries.

One feels so secure here that the verticality combines with the thin walls and our knowledge that *this is Paradise* to suggest that the barrier between us and it has almost disappeared. Contemporary with Saint-Remi and Laon, Mantes was built at just the time that people seem to have been most sure of God's presence among them.

One only has to turn around and observe the relatively weighty western spaces, their deep-set windows, and the hooded centripetal rose, to see how massiveness was returning in the 1190s. This rose is contemporary with the choir and nave roses at Laon, and like them it represents the "eyes of God."

MOISSAC, Church of Saint-Pierre
Once a Cluniac abbey

Department of the Tarn-et-Garonne, 66 km (41 miles) northwest of Toulouse; Michelin map reference 79/16,17

1100	Cloisters carved, according to a dated plaque; the arcade above is somewhat later.

1120–1125	Porch-tower and sculpture built onto an earlier structure. The nave and main portal added in about 1150.
1431	Choir and lateral chapels rebuilt after the ravages of the war and dedicated in 1483.
1628	Secularized, then suppressed altogether in 1793.

Moissac was affiliated with Cluny in 1047, an association that brought prosperity, as at Vézelay. (One consequence of the greed this encouraged will be found in our discussion of Toulouse.) An important station on the pilgrimage route, it housed several hundred monks.

The sculpture in the portal is spectacular. It is set deep within the tower and illustrates the choices of good and evil. The tympanum depicts the Last Judgment with Christ in Majesty. It is a literal transcription of the apocalypse. On the central trumeau three superbly sensuous lionesses are interlaced, each standing on the one below, roaring and stretching to heaven itself. Saint Paul and the prophet Jeremiah occupy the side trumeau. Panels on the inner left side of the porch portray gluttony, lust, and avarice. The annunciation, visitation, and adoration of the Magi are on the right. The stone was originally painted in rich color, traces of which can still be seen.

The cloister is the most famous in southwest France, for the delicacy of its carved capitals and its great sense of composure. Red-brick arches, each brick shaped as if it were made of stone, rest on beautifully carved impost blocks. Hieratic and somewhat somber figures, watchful and remote, are carved onto the corner piers. The whole atmosphere is contemplative and sacred, yet many of the capitals are covered with elaborate foliage and amazing beasts

The Moissac cloister.

or figures that have no religious significance whatever. We should never forget that the people of the Middle Ages did not separate themselves from nature as we do. The berries and thistles on the capitals, the entwining birds and stilled animals were intimates of daily life. Though Saint Bernard may have railed against irrelevant decoration, these superb carvings were not distractions but reminders that the spirit is to be found everywhere.

MONT-SAINT-MICHEL,
Benedictine Abbey of Saint-Michel
Also known as Saint Michael in Peril of the Sea

Department of La Manche, 80 km (50 miles) southwest of Caen; Michelin map reference 59/7

1017	Original choir begun over a Carolingian crypt and completed in 1048. The nave finished in 1090, the lantern tower around 1135.
1203	Abbey buildings burnt by the French. Rebuilt by 1228, including the cloister, which has always gloried in the impressive name of La Merveille. Choir collapsed in 1421, rebuilt between 1446 and 1521 over a new crypt.
1780	West front and adjoining three bays of the nave collapsed and were demolished. Ten years later the monastery turned into a state prison, which it remained until 1863. Thirty years later the west front replaced and a new belfry constructed.

At the time that Mont-Saint-Michel was founded in 708, monks, like everyone else, had to defend themselves. It was a natural strong point, and one easily defended. After Louis IX added to its fortifications in 1254 it was impregnable, even during the Hundred Years War.

The structure grows out of a humped block of granite surrounded by ocean and quicksand. The tides rise and fall an enormous 45 feet (14 meters) in this part of the channel, cutting the monastery off from the land for much of the day. The causeway is recent. The best time to visit is thirty-six hours after the full moon or the new moon, when the tide is in.

The mountain has been hollowed into crypts and crowned with high ramparts and towers; piled upon one another are lilac-tinted halls, chambers, shrines, and cloisters. Here is quite clearly expressed the hierarchy of the medieval abbey. It was a large household, in a sense like a royal palace with a church at the center.

As at Canigou, the rock forced the builders to place the church where it belonged, dominating the monastic buildings below, which themselves stood stories above the mundane if essential defensive walls. And among the rooms of

La Merveille the cloister for contemplation was planned above the refectory, which lay over the lowest stratum of all, the kitchens and stores—just as the head is higher than the stomach. Thus the levels of function reflect their importance in the order of things.

On the top of the tower, wings outspread and sword raised, stands Saint Michael. The devil crawls beneath him, and the cock perches on his foot. The cock is the symbol of eternal vigilance, which may be why he crowns the spire of nearly every French church today. Henry Adams wrote:

> Saint Michael held a place on his own in heaven and on earth which seems, in the eleventh century, to leave hardly any room for the Virgin of Chartres, still less for the Beau Christ of the thirteenth century. The Archangel stands for Church and State, and both militant. He is the conqueror of Satan, the mightiest of all created spirits, the nearest to God. His place was where the danger was greatest. (*Mont Saint-Michel and Chartres*)

The monastery exemplifies the symbolism of the mountain and the cave, which is nowhere expressed as clearly as here. The Mount is the fullest expression of the great citadel of God raised on the highest pinnacle. At Saint-Hilaire in Poitiers and at Saint-Denis the cave lies *within* the mountain, for the crypt lies almost at the nave floor level and thrusts the floor of the choir upward. But here the earth itself has thrust the entire assembly heavenward, so that the whole abbey is the mountain and the church's nave, choir, and crypt are the hollowed-out sanctuaries within it.

The abbey was subject to Cluny when the Norman Romanesque church was built, and it was one of the northern collection points for the endless stream of pilgrims moving southward from Britain and Scandinavia. When the Norman choir collapsed in 1421, it was a sign of the times that the monks had to wait almost thirty years for it to be rebuilt. And it is a sign of the unity of their religious ideals that the architecture of this elegant choir sits so well with the massive and relatively rough-hewn simplicity of the nave. Strength and grace join hands.

NEUVY-SAINT-SÉPULCHRE, Church of Saint-Étienne

Department of the Indre, 86 km (53 miles) southwest of Bourges; Michelin map reference 68/18,19

1045　Outer walls of rotunda begun; the plan changed toward the end of the century. Upper parts of the rotunda built between 1120 and 1130. The nave added in the eleventh century and vaulted at the end of the twelfth.

1524　Sacked, then much restored in the mid-nineteenth century.

This church was begun by the Lord of Deols after visiting the Holy Land about 1042—a pilgrimage undertaken before the first of the Crusades. There he would have seen the most important shrine in the world, the Holy Sepulchre. A circular building, it had twelve columns symbolic of the twelve apostles, and although it was immensely popular, few circular churches were built in France, perhaps because mass-in-the-round did not suit the Christian processional rituals.

As you walk around, you become aware of the irregularity of the vaults and the poorly organized junctions between the walls and the piers. The chapels vary in size, so that some vaults are spread-eagled while others are constricted. From this confusion some historians have concluded that the builder was incompetent, intending twelve piers but being unable to work it out properly. Yet the high quality of the capitals shows that the builder was no fool, for they are quite extraordinarily well carved for the period, with animals, monsters, and complex foliage.

The real reason for the confusion may be less disparaging to the builder. The three chapels on the northwest are larger than the other eight. The sizes of the eight are similar; if they had been continued around the building, it would have made a perimeter of twelve chapels. One has the impression that at the foundation level the eight chapels had been set out before the larger three, that there was then either a change in the plan or a pause in the construction. You may confirm this theory by taking a look at the bases of the two piers between the three largest chapels. They are sculptured with figures while the others have traditional torus moldings. Thus it was decided after work had commenced to alter the numbers of chapels in the perimeter wall so there would only be eleven.

Afterward the eleven circular piers were put up. The spacing between them does not vary, an indication that the builder could get the division into eleven parts quite accurately if he wanted to. (Try dividing a circle into eleven equal parts!)

Since the use of eleven seems to have been deliberate rather than a mistake, the meaning of eleven becomes important (see the discussion of labyrinths). There is only one axis in a circular building, the vertical. There is no progression on the material plane, only movement upward (or, unhappily, downward). As in the labyrinth, the number eleven implies a connection with the number one which should be added to it, lying in the center. The eleven piers are thus like the eleven true disciples ringing Christ.

NEVERS, Church of Saint-Étienne
Once a Cluniac abbey

Department of the Nièvre, 69 km (43 miles) east of
Bourges; Michelin map reference 69/4

1070s	Apse begun, followed by the nave; the building consecrated in 1097. A porch added at the end of the twelfth century.
1792	Crossing tower pulled down, along with the porch.

The choir is rounded in plan, with an ambulatory and three
chapels, while the nave is rectangular. This difference reflects the union of the Church and the material world, symbolized by the circles in the plan of the apse and its three
chapels, and the squares in the nave. The transept forms
the stabilizing cross axis, and two additional chapels open
off it, making five altogether. There are three windows in
each chapel set under five arches, and four between them
lighting the ambulatory. The seven arcade openings are
supported on six columns. These numbers seem to follow a
reasonable logic.

But vertically there are nine paired openings in the triforium and five in the clerestory, which do not coincide

The apse of Nevers.

with the seven openings in the arcade underneath. However, seven may have represented the Church as the essence of earthly creation and divine knowledge, and the five clerestory windows the light of Christ as the sanctified man (which is four, the mortal man, plus one, the spirit). Together they frame the altar, and hovering between them is nine, which may have represented the Trinity raised to the first power and thus the state of the first division into essences and substances. Medieval people would have had less difficulty in recognizing the symbols than we do.

The columns around the apse are cut from single blocks of stone. It would not have been easy to find suitable material for these huge monoliths, and it would have been even more difficult to transport them from the quarry and set them in place. Their "seamlessness" was considered a reflection of the perfect number six. Appropriately, these columns surrounded the altar like the six-petaled rose in the center of the labyrinth.

The narrowness of the shafts draws our eye upward, as do the tall stilted arches between them, so thrusting the upper two stories toward heaven. The string course under the triforium combines with the squat proportions and the visual shove from the arcade to separate the upper zone from the lower even more.

Here, in the later eleventh century, occurs the concept that was to play a major role throughout the Middle Ages: the illusion that the upper parts (here the triforium, the clerestory, and the semidome over it) were not really part of the building but the City of God hovering over the altar. Paradise may be revealed in all its glory, yet here it does not suffuse the entire building (as it will at Chartres) but transcends it.

There is an interesting detail, also found in the apses of Jumièges, Tournus, and Notre-Dame-du-Fort, which buoys up the choir. There are projecting plinths under all the shafts around the ambulatory walls that make it look as if this part is floating off the ground. If they had all been placed at the same height, they would have formed a continuous plinth that would have appeared to be holding all the parts up. But being broken into sections, the shafts seem to be floating without a particular foundation.

The nave, on the other hand, pretends no such separation; it is a single enclosure, the ark in which the congregation may be secure and protected. Its "down-to-earthness" is reflected in the aisles, which are not as tall as those in the ambulatory, and in the way the unbroken shafts link our plane on the pavement to the barrel vaults.

Over them the piers are straightforward and functional, not unlike a Romanesque version of the *pilier cantonné*, with a square central core and four shafts for each of the four elements it supports. These knit the foundations to the vaults bay by bay.

Each shaft has a specific function, so those continuing

up to the high vaults are not merged with those under the arcades. Each separately proclaims its purpose. For the next five centuries every medieval architect was to maintain this clarity, just as theologians and philosophers were to retain the same Scholastic principle that expressed in words what the masters were expressing in architecture.

The gallery has no practical function. We cannot stand in it and see the altar, and its stairs are too narrow for pilgrim to use for separate worship. It would seem to have had a purely symbolic role.

The void behind the gallery arches suggests that there is something beyond the world of our senses, a world—unseen but real—of the spiritual universe itself. At Conques and Toulouse, where the light of the church filters through these galleries, this interpretation is much clearer. Later, when the gallery structure was lightened and its windows made visible, as in Mantes or the Soissons south transept, this spiritual presence became more overt. Here the light does not enter through the galleries but comes in at the clerestory. As it is from higher up, we naturally feel that something is illuminating our lives from above—and in those days people believed that light, of all the things we can sense, was the closest to God.

The nave as the world and the choir as heaven are separated by the transept and the crossing, with a dome over the center so that the western vaults do not meet the dome over the apse. From the nave there is a spatial division to the sides and above, that separates our world from the Church's. If the vaults had been continued at the same level without a raised crossing, the nave vaults would have flowed naturally into the choir's. This separation was maintained until the 1220s.

The terminal walls of the nave and transepts are flat, with modest roses that would in time be expanded to occupy all the available space. Thus we see here most of the fundamental concepts from which Gothic would be created over the next two centuries. The arrangement of the details changed; ribs, flyers, and tracery were invented; yet most of the ideas found here are the same as at Sens a century later, as they are at Laon or Beauvais.

From the outside, the symbols used to differentiate the nave mundane from the choir celestial are very clear. The nave and transepts are assembled from rectangular blocks, the choir and all the projecting chapels are made from circles. The square (four) represents all the things of this world, and the circle, having neither beginning nor end, represents the infinite and the eternal.

Even the reuse of the triforium outside the apse, but placed above the clerestory windows and just under the roof, reinforces the concept that this was the palace of God and that He might appear as King on this "balcony," just as the emperor appeared before his subjects as *sol invictus*.

Walking around this exquisite building, one is aware of

both the security offered by the fortresslike walls of the
nave and the outward thrusting urgency of the choir. The
one provides the safety that the other requires if man's spiritual needs are to be met. Little of this changes at Reims or
Saint-Urbain.

NOUVION-LE-VINEUX, Church of Saint-Martin

Department of the Aisne, 10 km (6 miles) south of Laon;
Michelin map reference 56/5

1120	Southern tower begun; upper stages built in the 1130s, 1150s, and 1180s.
1155	Apse and transepts begun; the crossing lantern around 1170.
1180s	Two bays of the nave begun, with a temporary wall across the west which still remains. The porch was a little later.

The district around Nouvion is exceptional, for nearly every
village there has a church with something from this very
creative period. Yet this little church had been neglected for
such a long time that its stones were covered with a green
slime and its floors decayed. It is now about to be restored.

The church illustrates well the changes that occurred
during the twelfth century, from the blocky solidity of the
eastern end to the taller and lighter early Gothic nave. This
transition occurred during the decades from about 1160 to
the 1180s when the nave was begun.

There is a lantern tower like that at Laon, which opens
up the middle of the church. Notice that the arch under the
lantern on the western side is much higher than the other
three. It forms the middle of three graded steps between the
lower apse and the higher nave. Examine the impost over
the crossing capitals next to the nave. The one to look at is
on the eastern side of the north pier. The side of the stone
nearest the nave has been shaved off at 45°, as if something
was to have been added to it.

Then examine the capital higher up on the same pier,
under the arch into the nave. It has a similar shaved end,
slightly tucked into the pier, showing that it too would have
met another impost. What seems to have happened is that
this pier was being built after those on the eastern side (you
will see that the plan of the pier is different) but that the
south pier was a little less advanced than the north. Thus
the capital under the crossing on the north was reached before the south, and the imposts were carved for the one
level with the intention of continuing the western arch at
the same level as the others.

However, when the builders came to place the capitals on
the south pier a few years later, it was decided to raise this
arch in preparation for a tall nave. So the capitals were

*Nouvion from
the south.*

taken off the north pier and raised. The little splays on the imposts are the only indications of this change.

This occurred in the late 1160s, just at the time that northern builders were beginning to pursue height, as in Paris. Here the process is happening during construction, and we see how the design of these churches was being constantly modified as they were going up. In fact, we can probably say that most builders would keep their work as up-to-date as possible.

It is fascinating to look carefully at these capitals, perhaps even to draw them. The individuality of the carving, the magnificent animals all made with the utmost care are well preserved in spite of the general dilapidation. Grapevines curl up their faces, symbolic of the eucharist. Two lions claw at fruit. On the southwest crossing pier three figures share a book while a fourth holds a phylactery (a little leather box holding slips of paper on which are written scriptural passages). The exact meaning here has faded for the modern visitor, but the character of the figures remains rich and vivid.

ORBAIS-L'ABBAYE,
Church of Saint-Pierre et Saint-Paul
Once a Benedictine abbey

Department of the Marne, 49 km (30 miles) southwest of Reims; Michelin map reference 56/15

1150s	Ambulatory walls and chapels erected; a generation later, the arcade piers and ambulatory vaults, which were dedicated in 1180.
1200	The triforium begun; the clerestory windows and choir vaults finished before 1210. The upper parts of the nave were a little later.
1568	The Calvinists so damaged the abbey that in 1651 two bays of the nave had to be pulled down. In 1795 the abbey became a parish church.

It is a total surprise to find behind the rough-hewn and coarse-grained exterior of this old abbey one of the most elegant churches in France. The interior is extremely sophisticated yet spare. The white stone is a local chalk, while the coarse exterior is a local toffee-colored stone honeycombed with small holes.

It is an indication of how far inland the marauding Norsemen came that the earlier Carolingian abbey was destroyed by them in 963. The present church was begun around the middle of the twelfth century, but thirty years elapsed before more than the outer walls had been completed. Possibly the earlier apse was sitting where the arcade piers are now, and by erecting the outer walls the monks were able to greatly enlarge the perimeter space of the eastern end at minimum cost. The number of additional

The choir of Orbais.

altars may in time have attracted the funds needed for the builders to proceed with the rest of the work.

The vault over the altar is serene and smooth. The ribs are like fingers stretched between the cells, and the walls seem to merge with the glass as there are no wall arches over the roses to emphasize the junction. The difference these arches make can be seen at the top of the transept walls.

The small roses in the apse clerestory, with their six petals, seem to hang in space. Underneath, the window has a central shaft which continues into the triforium and divides it in two. The perspective seems inverted, for the smallest spaces precariously occupy the bottom row.

The shafts connecting the triforium with the clerestory, as at Saint-Remi and Essômes, have no string course between them, so the lancets are elongated downward into the triforium. The upper stories so interpenetrate that there are no divisions between the parts, and the whole of the upper zone registers as a single entity.

The vault capitals have been shifted upward above the windowsill. This may be the first Gothic example of the tall clerestory, though you will find it in the earlier La Trinité, Caen. At Braine (see page 165) the vault capitals were set below the windows and joined to the string course to separate the vaults visually from the lower stories. At Orbais the vaults are set within the windows, dematerialized and made more heavenly by being floated on a bed of light.

The double clerestory window was a crucial step in the evolution of the forms used at Chartres. Braine and Longpont both have single windows in the clerestory, and Chartres was probably planned to look like them, with single windows. Then there seems to have been a change to the Chartres elevation in 1211, not long after Orbais was finished, when the double window was introduced. Triple windows had been used before at Saint-Remi, and the central lancet was carried up a little higher than the others. Unlike the triple window, the double window asks to be capped with a rose, as here.

This idea was continued in the Soissons choir and Chartres, but unlike Orbais, they had an encasing arch under the vaults. As discussed at Essômes, the arch made it possible for the Orbais scheme to be translated into tracery, as the vault could be held up by the arch and the wall deleted altogether.

The clerestory at Orbais may be the first to have combined the double window and rose with the tall clerestory, around 1205. All the great High Gothic solutions are derived from this.

It followed from this solution that the lantern would have to be eliminated—one heavenly zone is enough in any church—and the decision to omit the central towers and lanterns at Chartres and Soissons in the 1220s seems to have been instigated here.

The stalls are medieval. The rare carvings of monks between the seats show such a diversity of beards and ways to attach the cloak (with buttons, clasps, wooden pegs, and tasselated cords) that they may have been portraits of those who sat here. The exception would be Death himself at the end. If you are careful, you may lift up the seats to examine the sculpture underneath, called misericords, which supported the monks when they stood at mass.

PARAY-LE-MONIAL, Basilica of le Sacré-Coeur
Once a Cluniac abbey

Department of the Saône-et-Loire, 68 km (42 miles) west of Mâcon; Michelin map reference 69/17

1109   The church begun in the east; the nave completed around 1230 in the style of the century before. The apse fresco dates from the fourteenth century.

1856   The crossing tower rebuilt; in 1935 the painting over the apse uncovered.

In 999 Cluny took charge of a tiny Benedictine monastery thirty miles west of the great abbey, with twenty or thirty monks, and transformed it. Since they were allowed to manage their affairs independently of the king or the nobility, the Cluniac monasteries became powerful and wealthy. They worked to benefit what they thought were the two greatest issues of their day: the pilgrimages and the growth of their order. They were somewhat like a modern big business (though on a medieval scale), but where they were very successful in the eleventh century, they found their pragmatic values and love of ceremony out of step with the more mystical religious feelings of the 1130s.

The church at Paray-le-Monial was built by some of the masons who had been working at the mother abbey of Cluny and is a smaller version of it. Compared to contemporary churches in Normandy and the west, something had been injected into Paray, something both strange and exciting. The thousands of pilgrims who tramped through Burgundy brought the whiff of adventure into these valleys, and their devotion brought foreign exchange into the abbey coffers. So there is a tallness, a hugeness to the buildings. Vastness in itself can induce ideas that are not available on an ordinary scale.

The apse shafts are incredibly thinner than at Nevers or Saint-Denis, so the structure over the vaults appears to float above the frothy edging of the arches. It is as if the altar were on a stage, with draperylike patterns around the ambulatory wall and a lightweight canopy over it. Apparently the Cluniac mass was a spectacular drama. This theatre-apse is lower than the vaults over the nave. As at Cluny, the apse is very tall for its width and makes the space feel

Paray-le-Monial from the northwest.

heady. Yet it is the space of the monks that is energized by the height, not the altar.

The airiness is emphasized by the uppermost string course under the clerestory windows, which is supported on consoles, or little brackets that project from the wall. This is not usually an internal motif but one that repeats the external supports for the cornice under the roof. By placing the clerestory above a "cornice," the builders implied that these windows and the light from them were the sky above the roof.

In later buildings the verticalizing forces lead to the altar; here they embolden the community itself to enthusiasm and action. This is not what such mystics as Saint Bernard had in mind: they sought contemplation and withdrawal rather than involvement. Fontenay is almost contemporary with Paray, yet spiritually it is on the other side of the universe.

This church does not have the unity of Fontenay; we tend to examine one bit, then another, each part demanding equal attention. For example, in most churches the shafts are the same size from floor to vaults, but at Paray the shape of the pilasters changes at every level. Above the arcade capitals of the nave they step out slightly, so that the space across the nave is narrower at the arches than it is at floor level. This supports the impression given by the cornice and gives the nave a top-heavy look. It also forces our attention onto the tactile fluting of the pilasters.

Where the shafts of Nevers extend unbroken to the ground to tie the whole space together, at Paray they are in short lengths. This makes each story distinct and the interior layered. The strings between the shafts break up its unity and emphasize the parts. Where at Chartres the horizontal strings seem to be weaving across the verticals, rather than forming distinct boundaries, here the stress is on substantiality and separation. The world of the monks is on earth, separated from the empyrean. Nevertheless, in the drama of the mass they are encouraged to aim for the distant Paradise.

Paray seems a materialistic building, somewhat earthy if not a little fussy, and we may miss the effect of the whole in our delight in the details. We are more aware of the tactility of the surfaces than the inner forms; like the use of gold and incense, it made the abbey appear wealthy, as indeed it was.

Sitting here, we understand Bernard's dislike of Cluniac pomp and worldliness. One doubts that Gothic could have evolved from these Burgundian monasteries, for they are too horizontal and layered, their detailing too distracting to allow much concentration on the architectural essentials that made the new style possible.

PARIS, Cathedral of Notre-Dame

First arrondissement; Michelin map reference 56/1,11

ca. 1150	External walls of the ambulatory built, with the tympanum and some archivaults now in the Saint Anne portal.
1160s–1182	The arcade piers of the choir, with gallery and clerestory. Shortly afterward the nave begun; the western doors laid out around 1200. The gallery of kings dates from about 1210, the nave vaults shortly after. The western towers completed before 1250.
1220	The clerestory windows enlarged into the triforium, and chapels added between the nave buttresses after 1240, followed by the chapels around the choir.
1246	The south transept begun, followed by the north in 1258. The south completed in 1285, the north early in the next century.
1771	The central portal removed so that a processional canopy could be carried through the door. In the 1790s, when it was turned into a Temple of Reason, the jamb sculpture removed and the western rose knocked out. Restored as a cathedral in 1795. Repairs, involving considerable alterations, begun in 1845.

THE CHOIR (ca. 1150–1182)

Paris lies at the center of France, with the wealth and prestige that came from being the home of the king and the permanent administrative center of the kingdom. As rulers did
in every other country, the French king once moved from
place to place according to a fixed timetable. After the
English seized his baggage train with all his records, Phill-
ipe-Auguste changed this, and thereafter the treasury was
stationed in Paris. Money breeds money, power produces
more power; thus Paris accumulated supremacy over all
other regions in France. No other town reached its size, not
even the famous cloth-making towns of Flanders.

Notre-Dame is appropriately huge. The aisles form twin
passages round the church, emulating Saint-Denis and the
old Saint Peter's in Rome and recalling an imperial grandeur that was intended to help the French kings in their ri-
valry with the German emperor.

Daily life in the cathedral was varied and interesting. The
records tell us that at Notre-Dame there was a permanent
choir of some sixty musicians and singers, probably working much longer than the forty-hour week we know. The
cathedral would have been saturated with their music at all
hours of the day. Because there were no office buildings in
Paris, lawyers and other professionals often met to conduct
business in the nave, and booksellers and money changers
placed their stalls in the porches. Amid all the bustle there
were daily and hourly masses, processions of pilgrims, con-
fessions, and crowds milling around the sick. We may not
enjoy the crush of tourists in the summer, but it probably
resembles more closely the typical medieval scene than the
emptiness of Essômes or Soissons.

Western rose window of Notre-Dame, Paris.

In the late 1140s men who had been working on the choirs of Saint-Denis erected the aisle walls of the apse and the chapels—and nothing above that. As the old apse remained, the new wall, with a lean-to roof over it, trebled the size of the choir at little cost.

At about the same time, perhaps contemporary with the Royal Portal at Chartres, a new tympanum was carved for the nave of the old church. It shows the Virgin in Majesty, flanked by angels as in the one over the Incarnation door at Chartres. When the Paris nave was demolished just after 1200, this tympanum was so loved that it was incorporated into the new right-hand doorway.

Nothing more was done for at least another twenty years. It may be that time was needed for the additional altars in the ambulatory to attract the donations that would make further work on the cathedral possible. Then, just after 1160, the remains of the earlier choir were demolished and work began on the daunting task of constructing the arcades and galleries.

Workmen dug through a Gallo-Roman wall to make the deep foundations that run beneath the entire perimeter of the monument, following its horseshoe shape. The wall widens as it descends in steps a yard tall. The size of the foundations suggests that from the beginning the plan was to push the vaults to record heights.

Cluny's barrel vaults reached 98 feet (29.5 meters) above the pavement. Paris was taller at 107 feet (32.6 meters). Nothing exceeded this until Chartres reached 118 feet (36 meters) in the early 1200s. The urge to build higher and higher, expressing itself even in such minor churches as Nouvion, was first expressed here in unmistakable, and for a time unbeatable, terms.

The elevation was once divided into four stages. The original third story consisted of circular windows, as can be seen in the bays alongside the crossing. Around 1220 the clerestory windows were lengthened by shifting the sills downward. In the nineteenth century traces of these roses were found in the walls, and some of them were reinstated to show what the original cathedral could have looked like before the windows were enlarged.

We have to imagine this four-story arrangement continuing around the church to the western end. The roses would have been like eyes looking inward. They were not glazed as they are today; they just opened into the darkness of the roof space over the gallery, in which there is a second row of roses illuminated from the outside. The arrangement is not very satisfactory, either spiritually or esthetically. The three-story scheme at Mantes has roses in the gallery, and there it seems to work perfectly well, so the problem here lies not in the gallery but in the third story.

To understand the symbolic problem, recall the arrangement at Saint-Remi. The two upper stories are like a little church floating over pilgrim's head, presumably identifiable with paradise itself. The gallery underneath has been left in limbo, so to speak, for it is no longer the Heavenly Jerusalem as it was at Caen or Conques, yet it cannot be included in the earthly plane. The meaning of the gallery thus became somewhat ambiguous in four-story churches—which may be why there were so few of them. At Notre-Dame the ambiguity is particularly unfortunate because roses were used. It was not right symbolically that the gallery eyes should be more bright than those of Paradise. Was this why the upper roses were eliminated so soon after they were completed?

Work on the nave proceeded slowly from about 1180, reaching the western doors in 1200. There are so many changes to the pier bases that one has the impression that after 1180 there was much less money, or less enthusiasm for raising it. Many builders were employed in rapid succession, each pursuing his own ideas on the small portion that he had funds for.

This is a good place to compare the six-part vaults over the nave with the four-part vaults over the aisles. Sit under the arcade arches where you can see both vaults. Choose a place where they are well illuminated, and then read the section on the vertical connection (see page 60).

THE TRANSEPTS (1246–1285)

The north façade is a splendid example of medieval design techniques. Normally the process is not so explicit, but here one may, perhaps with the aid of binoculars, follow some of the process.

It is a complex collation of gables, lancet windows, and railings, all surmounted by a giant rose. Yet everything derives from a limited range of forms: the circles, arcs, and straight lines are all obtained from the compass or ruler and intimately reflect the tools used by the master. The arcs and lines are combined into quatrefoils and trefoils, as in the rose and the windows under it. They are arranged in overlapping or diminishing series, as can be seen clearly in the gable over the door. The circular opening in the middle has sixfoil tracery within it, all designed with a compass. Each curve ends in a *fleur-de-lis,* made up of arcs, behind which one glimpses the railing to the walkway behind the gable. The openings in the railing have tracery just like that of the windows above, and between them tiny trefoils simulate those on the gable. Thus every detail reflects a small number of concepts, and the master rings the changes on them in every imaginable scale.

In the large and the small, from the gigantic rose window to the little incision on the railing, everything is assembled from the same limited range of elements. Could anything be closer to the *manifestatio* of the Scholastics? How well it exemplifies the tools of the master mason, and the sacred concept that all creation stems from a single word. An apple is always an apple, yet from the one tree comes such a fascinating variety of individual apples that no orchard is a dull place. This was the philosophy that created the transept façade.

PARIS, the Sainte-Chapelle
Once a royal chapel

First arrondissement; Michelin map reference 56/1,11

1239–1245	Both lower and upper chapels completed; the western rose replaced in 1485.
1841–1867	Restored, including interior paintwork and roof flèche.

The chapel is a kaleidoscopic jewel-box, covered in gold and magenta *fleurs-de-lis*, brilliant mosaics, and some of the finest stained glass in the country. It is the very essence of medieval royalty.

The thin buttresses finishing in finely hollowed-out gables make it soar out of the adjacent courtyard. We expect height as we enter, and so the minute scale of the lower chapel comes as a great surprise. Then we climb a narrow staircase, winding upward with only inches to spare, until we turn a corner to enter the astonishing upper chapel. Nothing can prepare us for the slimness and incred-

Dado arcade in the upper chapel of the Sainte-Chapelle.

ible feeling of height, the magical colors of the glass and walls, and the sheer ecstasy. Emerging from the dark and narrow stairs, we enter a fairy-tale world of sparkling jewels.

The building was a gigantic reliquary made to house some of the most precious relics in Christendom. All came from the passion; one was the crown of thorns, which the emperor of Constantinople had given to the Venetians as collateral for a loan. King Louis IX paid off the loan in exchange for the relic (and another just like it came up for sale a few years later). Within two years he had augmented his collection with a piece of the cross, one of the nails, the lance, and the sponge. When the relics were delivered to Paris, the king walked barefoot through the streets to greet them.

There is no sense of uncertainty, as at Saint-Urbain in Troyes, nor is the building arrogantly eternal, like Reims. The Sainte-Chapelle lies between the two. The members are thin but functional, and the usual illusion of weight-lessness is well expressed, for though each shaft has a purpose, the shafts are too fine to actually carry the vaults. At the same time, the chapel is a glass cage like the nave of Saint-Denis. It ushers in the full perfection of Rayonnant, with all the refinement and exquisite love of detail and line, of enameled surface and daring structure, which was to characterize later architecture. Though there would be changes in emphasis and detail in the centuries which followed, few essentials would be altered.

However unified the two chapels appear, the unity is largely the effect of the paintwork and the glass. Examined carefully, none of the details in the upper chapel appear to match those in the lower, neither the structural elements nor any of the capitals. Since the profiles would all have been carved from templates prepared by the master mason, the differences indicate that the lower chapel was detailed by one master and the upper by another.

At first it seems strange that two masters should be employed on such an important building. There was probably no shortage of money, as it was being paid for by the king. Yet the first master, whose work does not seem to have been unsatisfactory, was required to leave before he had finished the building. The reason for this seems to have been a technical one. Mortar was made of lime in those days, and lime took three months or more to harden. When an arch or a vault was being set up, the formwork under the stones had to be left in place until the mortar had set. If there was nothing else for the builder to do, he had no choice but to depart the site. This was standard practice; not even a wealthy client like Louis would have expected otherwise. The earlier builder would then have found himself another job, perhaps some distance from Paris, and he may not have been free when the time came to pull out the formwork.

What we find most surprising is that when the mortar had set, a new master would be selected. In some buildings the details change in each bay so that piers, capitals, and windows are all constantly altering. Few people would notice these changes unless they were pointed out; nevertheless the variations are pleasurable, for we are looking at a group of individuals rather than a uniform team.

Our esthetic expectations come from a later age—the Renaissance—and they condition us to expect that unity in architecture can come only from one person. The Sainte-Chapelle shows that the Middle Ages sought a different type of unity, one in which details and even major concepts could be altered without detracting from the work's artistic value. As a result, medieval buildings have a comely, unpretentious air, like a house that has been lovingly restored and added to by many owners. By comparison, Classical buildings are somewhat regimented and cerebral.

See the discussion of geometry (page 67) for the ways in which the masters maintained unity within this diversity.

POITIERS, Church of Saint-Hilaire-le-Grand

Department of the Vienne, 100 km (62 miles) south of Tours; Michelin map reference 68/13, 14

1025   Outer choir walls started; with a wooden roof, dedicated in 1049.

1130   Fire initiated rebuilding the inside of the nave, with the domes; probably finished around 1168.

1869   Western two bays restored after destruction during the wars of the sixteenth century, and it was used as a quarry after the Revolution.

The interior spaces are superb, the volumes varying from small to enormous and from broad to narrow. In some directions forests of columns block our view; in others we have glimpses of five, even six ranges of openings. The variety of spaces and solids is impressive. Yet most of the complexity comes from additions and rebuilding.

The upper part of the crypt is above the nave floor level, so the floor of the crossing is well above the congregation's eye level. The floor of the apse is set higher again. These floors form a series of planes that ascend toward the east to culminate in a huge eastern window which, as at Saint-Benoît-sur-Loire, draws the eye along the main axis toward the altar and the act of redemption enacted there in the mass. So pilgrim climbs to God, level by level, ledge by ledge, up the steep sides of the mountain. And under the mountain, secured by the giant pillars of the crossing, lies the cave/crypt.

Three images are joined together here. The building itself represents the impregnable citadel of the Church protecting its members from Satan. Within this fortress lies an elevated shrine, a kind of internalized Mont-Saint-Michel. And within the mountain is the original cave, the chthonic sanctuary in which are hidden the sacred vessels. Saint-Hilaire is more compelling than Saint-Denis, which lacks the massive crossing piers to protect the mountain.

In most cases the church itself is the mountain, to be seen from outside towering like a gray cliff over the small houses of the town. To enter the church is to enter the cave. But here pilgrim's journey lies within it, for he does not begin until he has entered.

Originally the nave would have given some sense of horizontal movement, but this effect was confused by the domes, which were inserted decades later. Their spaces are visually superb, but they have spoiled the original symbolism. The ascent would have been clearer if all the vaults were tunnel or groin, as in Saint-Savin-sur-Gartempe or Notre-Dame-la-Grande nearby.

Before the fire of 1130 the nave was a hall 50 feet (15 meters) wide with two aisle bays per main bay. The aisles were also wide, and all had wooden roofs which were susceptible to fire. The only protection against this recurrent nightmare was to cover the interior with stone vaults. The builders decided to use domes, but because the nave was too wide, an inner row of columns was added to make the spaces square. The aisles were subdivided so that they too could be vaulted. These additions illustrate the differences in designing for a timber roof and a stone roof.

Buildings with aisles as tall as the nave have a comparatively different impact from the more usual pyramidical arrangement (as at Étampes). The various impressions can be experienced here in one building. Low aisles define our space, the zone of our lives, and therefore represent manifested reality. The procession will first weave its way around the church through these aisles, and only at the end will it proceed up the axis of the main nave. The openings between the two, the arcade arches, are like glimpses from the mundane into the lofty empyrean of heaven. Stand in the aisle and walk toward the east, looking into the nave, and savor this feeling of enormity, half-hidden, its fullness only suggested.

When the aisles are as tall as the nave, as at Gartempe or Tournus, all space is dedicated to the one spiritual purpose, without distinction. When pilgrim enters, he is immediately as fully part of the spirit as he is capable. To share this feeling, move out of the aisle so that you stand just inside the tall shafts that support the domes, and look up into the nave vaults. The ancillary vaults seem like tall aisles next to the nave. By moving in the aisles and back again, you should feel the difference.

Also, look up at the groin vaults over the ancillary aisles and observe how the builder has handled the intersection of the longitudinal tunnel with two conditions: the two cross-barrel vaults over the outside windows and a single barrel over the interior arcade arch.

We are often taught that Romanesque spaces are simple

The nave vaults, Saint-Hilaire-le-Grand, Poitiers.

when compared with Gothic, and, as at Jumièges, this can be true. Again, we are taught that the use of light and large windows are exclusively Gothic qualities. However, these clerestory openings date from the half-century before the Gothic window was first invented. Here we can reassess some of the definitions we inherited, for they are often too simple, designed primarily for ease in teaching; they seldom reflect the individuality and originality of masters who were not limited by the definitions we have made for them.

PONTIGNY, Church of Notre-Dame
Once a Cistercian abbey

Department of the Yonne, 20 km (12 miles) northeast of Auxerre; Michelin map reference 65/5

1140s	A small choir and the transepts begun. Work extended westward in the 1150s.
1185	Original choir replaced, probably complete around 1212. The western porch is more or less contemporary.
1793	Abandoned in the Revolution. The crossing tower demolished, the monastic buildings became a quarry. Restored in the nineteenth century.

The abbey lies on gently sloping lands which are less hilly than Burgundy to the south or the Soissonnais to the north. Few other Cistercian churches remain, for they were situated in inaccessible or remote valleys and were thus far distant from the towns that could have kept them as parish churches. When the order was disbanded in the Revolution, most of the churches were sold for the value of their materials.

Like all Cistercian monasteries, Pontigny grew quickly. Its growth was chronicled: "The holy life of the monks of Pontigny scattered its fragrance over the whole earth, seducing persons of remarkable grace, high descent, of great learning and worth from every quarter." Thomas à Becket received his monastic habit at Pontigny in 1164 and remained there in exile for two years. Two other archbishops from Canterbury found shelter here, and one still lies in the church. Stephen Langton, with some of the chapter of Canterbury, took refuge here from King John in 1207. Tradition assigns to Langton the division of the modern Bible into chapters and verses, work that was probably done while he was at Pontigny. The third archbishop of Canterbury to take refuge in the abbey was Edmund, who died there in 1239. His remains were placed in the chevet behind the high altar in 1244 by Saint Louis (IX) and Queen Blanche.

These simply arranged churches with their rectangular piers, barrel vaults, and regular spacing suit the slow rhythms of the countryside. Like the Cistercian abbeys, monastic life was uncomplicated. As shown in the labors of the months, the round of work was repeated each year for the whole of most men's lives. It was unchanging, yet life in the monasteries was not unstimulating, for they read, sang, and enjoyed a community life that was richer than anything outside.

In 1140 the church was rebuilt at the expense of Theobald, Count of Champagne. In length and breadth it is almost as large as Notre-Dame in Paris. There used to be a small, square-ended apse, not unlike Fontenay, probably

Pontigny from the north.

with a small rose window. It was simpler and less ornate than the present Gothic choir, for it was just a room for communion.

Surfaces and relationships are stated clearly. The nave capitals are typically Cistercian in their simplicity. Pontigny was the first Cistercian church with rib vaults, supported by flying buttresses, which some think may be the first in France.

In the second building campaign the rectangular apse was torn down and the present choir built. The eleven radiating chapels are enclosed by a continuous curved outside wall, so there is no external ostentation. The capitals are so simple and the forms so straightforward that for a long time the choir was thought to be of the same date as the nave; though it is simple for the period, its structure and capitals are unmistakably Gothic.

REIMS, Cathedral of Notre-Dame

Department of the Marne, 143 km (89 miles) northeast of Paris; Michelin map reference 56/6,16

1210   After a fire, work commenced on a new apse the following year. The choir reached the ambulatory vaults by 1220, when the northern doors were in place. The whole choir finished by 1241 and stained glass installed.

1255   Western end of the nave laid out and doors begun (some of the sculpture prepared many years earlier). The towers finished in the mid-fifteenth century.

1918   Heavily bombarded.

It is easy to romanticize the construction of great works such as Reims by a dedicated clergy and their supportive congregation, but the reality, like all human endeavor, is filled with political antagonisms and agreements, hope and despair.

The area around Reims was less rich than the Soissonnais to the west, and the funds raised by the bishop and chapter, even though aided by the pope, proved inadequate. Extraordinary pressure was put on the townsmen to fill the gap. In 1233 the burghers negotiated a large loan to the commune of Auxerre. Sensing his opportunity, the bishop demanded one-tenth of the funds, which the merchants refused to pay. The bishop then ordered the burghers not to leave their parishes, and the result was a riot.

The burghers stormed the palace, killed the bishop's marshal, and erected barricades with stones that had been cut for the cathedral. In the end, however, the town lost, the bishop was reinstated by force, and heavy penalties were imposed on the merchants. The bishop won the politi-

*One of the angels
set above the
choir chapels,
Reims cathedral.*

cal battle, but his cathedral lost the war: it was finished in
spite of the townspeople, not with them.

Significantly, none of the windows were donated by the
guilds but by the nobility or the clergy themselves. The
spirit of cooperation at Chartres, where forty-two windows
were donated by the burghers, is totally absent at Reims.

And one feels the difference: Chartres has a warmth and,
for all its size, a humanity that is missing at Reims. The coronation cathedral is immensely overpowering in the scale of
its details. It emanates a mood of authority, as though every
builder was affected by the self-righteous covetousness of
the bishop and expressed it in his work. The western walls
spread an air of immense and impervious solidity. In no
other building are the stones so large, the builders' stairs so
wide, the statues so massive.

The chapter and the bishop built the cathedral themselves, in anger as well as in pride. The defeated town could
do nothing but suffer it to be done. It may be no accident
that Reims was a prominent center of heresy, while few
cases are reported from Chartres or Amiens.

THE ARCHITECTURE (begun 1210)

Reims follows the three-story, cruciform model established
at Chartres, with *pilier cantonné* and sculptured portals,
but there are important differences. At Chartres the aisles

and clerestory are equal in height, and the triforium forms a thin band between them. Here the aisle is very tall—much taller than the clerestory—and the triforium is not only proportionally taller than Chartres, its shafts and arches are much more massive. So it plays a more dominant role, acting as a lid on the spaces below.

The elaborately and skillfully carved capitals are so large that they impress like a glimpse into the Garden of Eden itself. Theologically this is a nice possibility, that the capital represents that twilight zone between the chaos of manifest reality and the order of the spirit. In most buildings it is the only point where natural foliage enters into architecture.

Everywhere we are aware of the hugeness of things, the enormous blocks of the pier bases and the size of the courses. Even the flying buttresses are enormous, and the pinnacles are full of vitality.

Bar tracery was employed for the first time in the ambulatory chapels: a web of thin stone mullions which separate the lancets from the rose, with little triangular spandrels of glass in between. (The origin is discussed at Essômes.)

The stained glass at the western end of the aisles enlivens the entire building and makes the interior quite exciting. On returning from the apse we get the best view, for the aisle vaults receding into the distance are quite magical. It is like walking through some great forest; no wonder it was thought that the inspiration for Gothic came from their overhanging branches.

The western wall is like Notre-Dame at Poitiers turned inside out. The interior is covered with exquisite sculpture set into arched niches like little theatres, emphasized by the stone drapery along the bottom. The tympana have been replaced with stained glass, bringing the Last Judgment inside. These reversals dominate the nave as though the Church wanted to spread the message *into God's space* as well as outside in man's. It seems to fit the bishop's attitude toward the town congregation.

THE SCULPTURE

To some extent the north porch reflects the feelings of the town. The broad-shouldered apostles Saints Paul, James, and John plant their feet firmly on their bases. These stocky figures need to be securely supported. The canopies over them are enormous, emphasizing by their weight the support they give to the vaults above. The statues are individualized works of great power that stand beyond their frames and present themselves to any direction. More antique than feudal, they are impregnable in their certainty.

Similarly in the west, the overpowering weightiness of the embrasure sculptures was mitigated by setting pointed gables over them. It is a simple architectural motif that enlivens the façade and diminishes the importance of the capital. It has the effect of a strip of lights over the modern cinema; perhaps more to the point, it was then a popular device over the glazed triforia which were coming to represent the City in silhouette under the *lux nova* of the clerestory.

The figures are elegant and worldly, with heavy drapery. They are the product of a new, purely visual sensibility rather than of archetypes. Surface patterns coagulate into solid and void, forming a luxurious envelope without contrasting plain surfaces. What tracery is to the window, the new drapery is to the statue: a pattern within the form that in time came to dominate it.

The west façade is one of the most richly carved structures in medieval architecture. The gallery of kings was not placed between the doors and the rose, as at Chartres or Paris, but as befits the coronation cathedral, it was raised to the skyline. There, huge and confident, it dominates the façade.

We are lucky the cathedral still exists. In the last months of World War I it was bombarded with over three thousand high-explosive shells; while the statues had been sandbagged for protection, much of the rest was pitifully damaged by German artillery. Amazingly, no tower or wall collapsed under the bombardment—a testimony to the incredible strength of the building.

REIMS, Basilica of Saint-Remi
Once a Benedictine abbey

Department of the Marne, 143 km (89 miles) northeast of Paris; Michelin map reference 56/6,16

1005	First building campaign, with remains in the north transept. Twelve bays in the nave date from 1036–1049.
1160s	Western façade begun, and the choir ambulatory. The nave raised and vaulted in the 1170s, along with the gallery arcade. Gallery external walls, triforium, and clerestory all date from the 1190s.
1506	South façade rebuilt; the northern rose in 1602. Heavy restorations after 1829 and after the enormous destruction of World War I.

On entering, we sense the superb generosity of this space, wide and welcoming like few others. The importance of geometry can be gauged by the seven-sided bases under some of the western piers and, on the outside as you enter from the west, the sympathetic repetition of the heptagon around the small window to the right tower. This is one of the most difficult figures to use; it is almost impossible to set it out perfectly.

Pierre de Celles became abbot in 1162 and began to re-

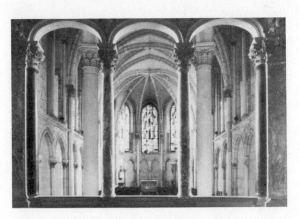

Eastern chapel from the choir of Saint-Remi, Reims.

build the choir and the western façade. The arrangement and the lightness of the members recalls Notre-Dame in Paris, but here the spaces are more complex, particularly around the ambulatory.

The chapels are superb, screened from the ambulatory by tall shafts. Stand in one of the chapels and bring your eyes down from the complexities of the vaults to the floor. Notice that the circle of the outer walls, if continued inward, would meet the curve of the ambulatory. In plan the chapels would look like a string of pearls around a neck. But instead of the chapels becoming smaller toward the inside, the inner parts of the curves have been opened outward, as though on hinges, so that at the ambulatory the walls between the chapels are as thin as possible. They open out like flowers from the aisle.

Saint-Remi offers a good example of the complex way in which medieval buildings were put up and altered. From the crossing, imagine the church of 1050, with three small chapels on each side of the half-domed apse. Two of these chapels, the outermost ones, can still be seen in the transepts. They are small, and they give us some sense of the scale of the earlier building, which was long and low.

When the choir was begun in the 1160s, the two smaller chapels on each side were demolished to gain access into the ambulatory, and the original central apse was left in place so that services could continue. The new work up to the aisle vaults was wrapped around the old. At this stage the work was taken no further, presumably because the funds were not forthcoming. Building only the chapels, while leaving the apse, was an economical way to add more altars to attract the gifts that were essential to completing the work. Around 1180 the apse was torn down and the last two arcade columns next to the crossing were inserted.

With all the arcade arches in place, the internal arches of the gallery could be erected but not its external wall. Thus the maximum space and effect were provided for the funds available, and pilgrim could now see the aisles and the internal wall of the gallery with a roof over it. The outer walls of the gallery and the clerestory were not begun for another decade, so for more than a generation the monks worshipped beneath a temporary roof.

The upper level of the choir is like Orbais, where the shafts of the triforium rise to the clerestory, but it is not as tall, as both stories had to be fitted within the height of the nave vaults erected twenty years before. The nave may have been tall enough then, but it was too short by the 1190s. In fact the smallness of the clerestory hints that at first the builders may have intended only three stories, without the triforium.

The effect of joining the triforium to the clerestory may not be easy to see here as the interior is dark—Orbais is the place for that—but what we do see in the darkness is closer to what would have been experienced originally.

Hugh of Saint Victor wrote in *Arca Noë Moralis,* "There are doctors who affirm that the windows of the ark are placed between the second and third stories so that its light and the base of the third story will be contiguous." He is writing about the gallery as the second story and the clerestory as the third; he says that the ark, as the ship of God, floats between the gallery and the clerestory, and that it will appear to illuminate the church through these windows. This triforium seems to be a replica of that ark. It is just like a chapel, with windows and dado arcades connected as in a screen, forming a complete unit floating on the windows at the back of the gallery.

At Chartres and in the cathedral nave nearby, the triforium is an independent zone lying between the aisles and the clerestory, separating the region of light from that of darkness, heaven from earth. But here it is linked to the windows, and so it becomes a part of Paradise, a stage supporting the figures in the stained glass. The effect is particularly striking when we stand in one of the chapels.

This new work, light, playful, and elegant, is typical of the 1160s and early 1170s. One wonders why a later generation returned to the massive regularity of Chartres.

ROUEN, Church of Saint-Maclou

Department of the Seine-Maritime, 139 km (86 miles) northwest of Paris; Michelin map reference 55/6

1436   Building commenced in the east; consecrated in 1521. Cloister added between 1526 and 1533.
1868   Spire added.

Saint-Maclou is the most important Flamboyant building described in this book. Because the pier bases are very tall, they meet us eye to eye instead of being a couple of courses above the floor. Take time to examine them, even to draw them! At first they may seem impossibly complicated, but with care and patience you will find a sustaining logic in every part. These shapes have not been produced by free-hand doodling; they are the most careful expression of the structural and decorative function of each element.

Notice how every rib and arch in the nave merges into one of the shafts in such a way that each is implied from the ground up. In detail this connection can be quite complex, as in the arch of the main arcade between the nave and the aisle. This arch has a sharp-edged molding on the inside, next to the cell of the aisle vault. (You need to stand in the aisle to see this.) The leading edge of the arch has its own shaft, tucked in behind another dedicated to supporting one of the diagonal ribs. (Stand close to the stonework and peer behind the rib shaft to see this little one.) At the top the two can clearly be seen weaving independently through each other, like two distinct waves on a lake that approach one another, each one continuing as though the other had not been there, each unchanged by their meeting. It was an important principle in all medieval buildings that every molding have a function, with a source and an end; no matter how one may temporarily occupy the space of another, it was never submerged in the other if it could be made visible.

Notice how the bases coalesce at different levels which

Base to one of the piers at Saint-Maclou, Rouen.

relate to the function of each. The upper row of bases connects to the decorative projections on the arches, while the lower bases, which shelter behind the upper so that they are only glimpsed, relate to the structural core of the arch behind the decoration. In the lowest courses these manifold forms have been rationalized. It is like the bole of a tree below the lowest branches where the trunk is rounded off, yet it still has facets and projections which indicate the miscellany of branches above.

In more robust buildings, such as those of 1200, the movement of our eye across the surface is impeded by the size of the parts. The huge piers and thick walls are obviously there to support the roof. But at Saint-Maclou the piers and their fascicles of shafts, like the tracery, form a multitude of pathways across which our eye roams easily. This delights the eye but misleads the mind, for the structural functions have been concealed behind the plethora of sharp edges and flowing curves. Saint-Maclou is less of a building with a purpose than a space to delight in.

This is illustrated in the windows. The tracery undulates as it rises, quite unlike the classic tracery of Reims or even that of Saint-Urbain. There the tracery leads the eye upward to the circles at the top of the window, which then hold us. Flamboyant tracery does not slow the movement of our eye as it rises up the mullion but speeds it up. This is especially clear in the aisle windows, where the outlines of the tracery sway from side to side like tadpoles urging themselves upward and outward. The window frame gives the tracery some coherence, yet there is so much energy in the shapes that we seem to be at the center of the cyclone. All its energy is moving around us, impelling us upward and out. It makes us passive. The window supplies the activity. Pilgrim does not move voluntarily toward the spirit but is being moved. The active penitent of 1200 has become the passive worshipper of 1500, no longer controlling destiny but accelerated by it. The hypersensitive emotionalism of the times is reflected in these windows, as the melancholia and pessimism is in its passivity. The building does not ask pilgrim to move within it; the building moves instead.

The vaults are similarly energized, for there are no capitals to impede the upward movement within the interior. In 1200 the capital defined the zones of the building as well as the structural functions. There was no need to merge the zone of heaven with that of earth, for people felt comfortable believing that God was as much present in their world as in the other. Later, as God was firmly removed from this world, a vacuum was left. In the prosperous times that followed the Hundred Years War this vacuum was filled with energy.

To carry the congregation aloft was a major preoccupation of all Gothic builders. At Chartres or Reims pilgrim feels elevated into a tranquil world where he is enfolded by the Almighty with serenity and security; at Saint-Maclou the vaults and their supports are too thin to be supportive, while the shapes are too energetic to be secure. This building is post-war and post-plague; the worst has already happened, yet one feels that the future still cannot be trusted.

The apse looks excessively thin and boxed-in, for there is no central bay. Instead of the usual opening—and beyond that a window that leads us onward and outward—there is an eye-catching central member which thrusts us upward into the vaults and allows pilgrim no exit in that direction. Nor, for that matter, is there any way for God to come in, as at Saint-Benoît-sur-Loire.

The western porch was a theatre stage, and here the mystery plays based on the stories of the gospels were presented to the people standing in the square, which was called the parvis. (The word stems from the ritualized exclamations of the audience who felt that they were sharing in Paradise.)

The church was lovingly restored after the destruction during the last war, unlike what happened following World War I, when some sixty partially destroyed Gothic churches in the Laon area alone were replaced with modern ones and the remains wantonly discarded.

SAINT-BENOÎT-SUR-LOIRE,
Benedictine Abbey of Saint-Benoît

Department of the Loiret, 35 km (22 miles) east of Orléans; Michelin map reference 64/10

1067	Choir begun after a fire in 1026; transepts and lower western porch probably completed by the consecration in 1108.
1160	Nave walls and north door, followed by the nave vaults around 1200; consecrated in 1218. Choir stalls made in 1413.
1836	Restored and crossing tower replaced. Benedictine monks returned in 1944.

The abbey is situated in a beautiful and tranquil spot on the edge of the Loire, next to a small village that has not grown much over the centuries. It is still occupied by black-robed Benedictine monks who sing mass in the Gregorian mode of centuries ago: deeply toned, sonorous, unaccented, it delivers the spirit up to heaven. To hear it is to enter the chant of faith; the self is offered unconditionally.

The spirituality of medieval times was not like ours. No matter how deep our faith, we are too educated, our lives too sheltered. Death is not our ever-present companion, nor is law simply a whim of our rulers. Our safety does not lie within walls whose strong gates must be closed every night. In those days there was only faith. Therefore the church was an enclosure, the barrel-vaulted ceiling turning over-

Triforium in the choir of Saint-Benoît-sur-Loire.

head to enfold all mankind within its warm cloak. The thick walls and stalwart columns would never bend, even under the weight of the devil himself. The church was an affirmation of certainty.

The Middle Ages was a time of great ignorance and many faiths, a time when only half the population practiced Christianity. The Classical gods and Celtic shamans were still present. Travel was rare and full of uncertainty, and people knew little of distant places. Yet on entering the church, we of a different time feel immediately at home and are drawn toward the apse. The central opening between the eastern piers really is a little wider than the others. The window opposite in the outer ambulatory wall is as large as any in the apse of Saint-Denis, famous for its light-filled windows said to enhance the mystic role of the church. This window in the eastern wall, just above eye level, conjures up the possibility of hope—muted yet apparent. It suggests a way past the altar to the beyond, and in the early morning the sunlight pours onto the congregation like a finger of God.

From the nave you can see that this window is set a little to the left of the arcade piers. The central axis through the ambulatory is bent slightly to the north of the axis through the choir so that the left-hand window jamb is slightly hidden behind the pier. The bent axis imposes a pause, almost a veil, between the promise and its fulfillment. The window is here only because there are two chapels instead of the usual three. With three chapels there is no room for a window of hope; one more altar takes its place.

A stately calm prevails in the side arcades of the apse. Small in scale, they form a colonnade without pomp. It is a modest work, not in scale, in workmanship, or in cost, but in effect. In some buildings the aisles are so grandiose, so megalomaniac in their bulk, that we are shortchanged. Saint-Benoît is quiet and comforting. The thick walls and the delicate indenting of the triforium arcades suggest safety. The plain walls and simple window openings offer stillness. The quick rhythms of the small-scale arches instill desire to put away the petty concerns of everyday and dedicate oneself to the greater goal.

Going into the crypt is like entering into the earth itself and traveling far back in time. It feels eons older than the choir above. One hardly needs the notice for silence. It is squat, easing you downward, utterly peaceful within its overly huge columns.

There the choir reflects the here and now, the nave already shows the changing times and the broader views of the later twelfth century. Compare the eastern vaults with the western. The simple barrel vault of the choir is reinforced with arches which ensure that we do not forget its circular form. Our eye rises up the wall and, on meeting the vault, glides across the choir to descend on the opposite side. The vault ties the two walls together, and by returning our glance to the floor it binds the whole structure to the earth. It is an earthbound enclosure. Horizontally the effect is also to enclose and to return us to base, for the half-dome of the apse grips our attention and swings us back to the center. Our world is emphasized; we know it is dangerous, and the calm of the building helps us to live with it. God is outside and beyond the substantial, though not far, on the other side of the eastern windows.

By contrast, the vaults of the nave, with their pointed junctions and steep profiles, lead the eye up and out of the building. To bring our gaze back again after reaching the apex requires an effort. The vaults reinforce not the earthiness of God's place but its ethereality. God's presence is clearer, and therefore intercession is possible. The concept is audacious; it would have been incomprehensible in the eleventh century when the choir was built.

The western porch is not like the double towers and triumphal gates of Saint-Denis and afterward. Superbly strong and solid, it is a portico version of Cahors, a shelter covered from the storm of life. Open on three sides, its massive piers divide the porch into nine bays. As if to compete with the scale of the open fields of this flat landscape and the fast-flowing Loire, the capitals are enormous, overscaled to retain some potency against the infinity of the endless floodplain.

Examine the second pier from the left on the western

outside face. On the top of the right-hand capital is faintly inscribed, under a row of three staring animals, "Unbertus me fecit," or "Unbertus made me."

Startling and beautiful, placed on the southern crossing pier, is a lone wooden statue of the trumpeter calling to prayer. This angel is the only Renaissance ornament in an otherwise utterly medieval building.

SAINT-DENIS, Basilica of Saint-Denis
Once a Benedictine abbey

Department of the Seine-Saint-Denis, 10 km (6 miles) north of Paris; Michelin map reference 56/11

1130–1140	Narthex built, the upper parts and towers about a decade later. The crypt rebuilt immediately afterward; ambulatory chapels dedicated in 1144.
1231	Inner apse piers replaced with larger ones in preparation for the new clerestory. Transepts extended and nave begun during 1240s.
1771	Western sculpture restored and mosaic removed. The jamb figures destroyed in the Revolution.
1839	Entry level raised and the remaining sculpture again restored. North tower demolished.

The first bishop of Paris, Saint Denis, was tortured and beheaded on Montmartre in the third century, after which he is said to have walked to the site of Saint-Denis with his head in his hands. He is also supposed to have brought Christianity to France. Knowing how Abbot Suger manipulated the legends, we find it hard to credit any of these stories.

The reconstruction of the abbey after the 1130s gave Abbot Suger the opportunity to initiate architectural concepts which were to enjoy an enormous popularity during the next three centuries. He had traveled widely and collected ideas from many places. The monumental west front with twin towers may have come from Saint-Étienne in Caen, but it is embellished to resemble a Roman triumphal archway; the layout for the doorways was inspired by the sumptuously carved Burgundian and Italian churches he visited on his many trips to Rome; and the double ambulatory recalls those Roman churches of the days of imperial grandeur, especially old Saint Peter's itself.

As there had been no monumental carving in the Paris basin before the narthex was built, and very little masonry building, Suger had to assemble craftsmen from many lands. The abbey became the foremost artistic marketplace of its time, and appropriately it was at the royal abbey where the kings were buried that France's first truly national style was conceived.

It is probably fortunate that in the struggle between himself and Bernard of Clairvaux, Suger's views triumphed. Cistercian architecture was simple, pure, austere; in its own way it was exceedingly beautiful, as Fontenay shows. And though Cistercian demands for pure architecture had an enormous influence on the masters, the Gothic of Chartres would have been inconceivable through Bernard. It was through Suger that architecture became resplendent and as richly varied as his gem-encrusted chalices and embroidered copes.

THE NARTHEX (mainly 1130s to 1150)

The west front and narthex was designed to welcome the crowds of pilgrims that streamed into every major sanctuary. It was the symbolic gateway to heaven (see the discussion of the doorway) and the first in which the sculpture was integrated with the architecture. It marked a new epoch.

The façade has three doors, matching the nave, and two aisles inside; the doorways are shorter because the pavement has been raised about 5 feet (1.5 meters). The splayed jambs were once covered with column figures, as at Chartres. There were also two towers which were as high above the rose as the rose was above the pavement so that the rose became the fulcrum of the façade. This may have been the first time a rose was used as a pivot.

One must compare Saint-Denis to Jumièges, Charlieu, or Aulnay to appreciate how integrated the architecture is— and to justify the dramatic claim that Saint-Denis is the birthplace of Gothic. Earlier portals contained a curious mixture of local stories, unconnected biblical tales, and arguments against transient heresies, but Saint-Denis before its destruction dealt with the basic theological truths of Christianity. As Chartres retains most of its sculpture, this new cohesion should be examined there.

THE CHOIR (1140–1144)

The fortress mentality of the façade is abandoned in the transparency of the choir, the castle replaced by a crown of light. The choir combines in one place characteristics which had up to then been found only singly, and it does so in such a convincing way that the assembly became a prototype. This refers, of course, to the ambulatory around the choir, which was the only part completed by Suger; the triforium and clerestory were added in the next century.

You feel like a bird in the choir, as if you could take wing and fly from bay to bay in an ecstasy of freedom. The double ambulatory allowed the clergy to move between the altars even when the outer ambulatory was crowded with pilgrims: the inner ambulatory was the fast lane, the outer was for slow traffic.

By using two rows of thin columns (we must imagine the inner row being as thin as the middle one, for it was replaced in the 1230s) rather than the usual compound piers, the builders for the first time made the space more important than the structure. This decision had vital consequences.

The undulating walls of the shallow chapels do not force us into any one compartment but encourage us to flutter from one to the other. A similar flow is maintained in the vaults, for the separateness of each cell, as was usual in the Romanesque, has been mitigated by keeping the ridges level. This has been achieved by pointing the transverse arches and rounding the ribs so that both reach the same height. We are not constrained under each vault but can move fluidly between them.

Ultimately it is the glass that makes the choir so spacious. Wherever you stand you will see many windows. They are not hidden in separate compartments, as in the Senlis chapels, but are everywhere. Every direction is appealing, so the main axis has in a way been exploded.

Saint-Denis was not the first building to use wide windows. The side windows in the choir of La Trinité and the eastern window at Saint-Benoît are wider, but we are more aware of the Saint-Denis windows because the setting was so appropriate and because Suger had described them. However, the real impact comes not from the width of the windows but from the position of the sill.

The sill is about waist height in the apse, and even lower in the crypt, so that the priest would be silhouetted against the glass. His arms upraised with the host, set against the Technicolor splendor of the windows, must indeed have

An apostle on the altar of Saint-Denis, carved about 1145.

been something to behold. Can we see the hand of Suger in this also? It is curious that the low sill was not used elsewhere, for it is the novel feature of these windows, and it ensures that the brilliance is at our level. Perhaps that explains it; one effect of placing the sill over our heads is to remove the brilliance from our zone and establish it above the earthly plane. Light emanated directly from paradise, Suger wrote, and lowering the sill could let us infer that we were already there.

Work on the nave was suspended after Suger's death, for his successors did not want their abbey to remain at the center of French politics, with its hassles and tension, but wished to return to their interrupted spiritual disciplines. They heeded Bernard's words:

> This place had been distinguished and of royal dignity from ancient times; it used to serve for the legal business of the Court and for the soldiery of the king; without hesitation or deceit there were rendered unto Caesar the things which are his, but there were not delivered with equal fidelity to God the things which were God's.

THE NAVE AND THE UPPER PARTS
OF THE CHOIR (after 1240)

After the invention of tracery—which turned windows into focal centers—the master of Saint-Denis went one step further and separated us from the radiance of the glass and reintroduced the compound pier. It is a delicate and homogenized cage from which we gaze at a distant splendor. Robert Branner called it the Court style for its fragility, its reserve, and above all its formality.

Just as the choir made space flow with light, so a century later the nave made the material form more important than the spaces around it. Our eyes sweep magisterially over the enclosure without lingering on the details. The piers are compound and not circular, covered in shafts that are so thin and so multiplied that the piers disintegrate into a collection of indecipherable shadows and edges.

The compound piers should be compared to the circular drums in the east. The shafts and the encasing frames of the compound pier cast shadows that attract the eye, while our glance easily slips around the drum. The surface is more important than the space. Also the compound pier links the ground with the vaults, while the drum divides the building into a lower zone (up to the capitals) and an upper zone. This gives the building a weightless quality that seems indifferent to the normal laws of gravity.

Thus the introduction of the drum signaled the preeminence of space over structure in the 1140s. The last time the drum was used was in the 1230s; its popularity had coincided with the most creative period of Gothic. As Rayonnant became the dominant style, space became less important than the elements. The nave of Saint-Denis is much more integrated than Paris or Reims, for the entire interior is perceived as one concentrated streaming band. The traditional distinctions have been lost and blurred. The shafts are like a decorative patina, texturing every surface without emphasizing any.

The shafts begin at the bases of the compound piers and are augmented at the triforium until the upper stories consist of nothing but vertical edges. The shafts added above the triforium string course seem to push the wall back from the nave so it hovers independently of the vaulting.

The triforium has been raised into the clerestory, as at Essômes and Orbais, by continuing its shafts upward. But the process has been continued here, the clerestory having been lowered into the triforium by glazing the rear wall. The triforium, which at Chartres was an intermediate zone, has been absorbed into the glazed church in the sky. The boundary between heaven and earth has been moved further out of reach. Where at Laon or Fontenay tentacles from the upper zone almost brush against our heads, here they have been elevated far above us, as at Beauvais.

In the aisles, the passageway over the dado arcade separates the windows from the vaults, and as the arch under the vault is very large, the interior structure has been kept independent of the windows. If anything, the windows seem to have been detached from the wall, rather than the other way round, leaving the shafts under the aisle vaults to get on with their business. There is a similar gap behind the dado arches, so they too are detached from the wall and become a screen. The end shafts sit just behind the pier supporting the vaults, so this screen is also detached from the vault structure. Thus the dado divides the vault from the wall.

The aisles are an exercise in disintegration, for the windows no longer hang between the shafts, the wall floats somewhere far behind the dado arcade, and the vaults with their supports sit like a bower in between. The symbolism is exquisite. In the aisles the round arches of the dado arcades are like the waves of the sea supporting the ark of God in the windows, just as the nave (which comes from the Latin word for "ship") is the ark which protects the congregation. In the triforium above, the little gables resemble the pointed roofs of the City silhouetted against the skylike windows of the heavenly paradise.

Thus both window stories, the aisles, and the clerestory have been disemboweled from the rest of the structure. While the multitude of shafts draw our attention away from the space lit by the windows, the windows draw themselves away from our realm. In a sense we have been shortchanged, for the freewheeling joy in great spaces that was promised in the choir has been replaced with a surface decorativeness that shuts us off from any deeper penetration, while the windows have retreated from us. There is a sense of being abandoned in the nave.

The world of the spirit has been removed beyond the enclosure. It is ironic that in the abbey where Suger's great windows ensured that the choir would be "*pervaded* by the new light" of Christ Himself, and where he intended that "the middle part will be brightened by the bright light," a later generation should send this luminescence into exile.

SAINT-GERMAIN-EN-LAYE
Once the Royal Chapel of Saint-Germain

Department of the Yvelines, 21 km (13 miles) west of Paris; Michelin map reference 55/19,20

1238–1243   Built.
1800s   Severely restored and turned into museum.

Saint-Germain-en-Laye was one of King Louis IX's favorite hunting lodges. He had this small chapel built just before the Sainte-Chapelle, and it is the first Rayonnant building.

The whole of the exterior, between the plain lower walls and the cornice, is filled with glass—even to the upper edges, so the spandrels above the arch over the window are also glazed, and the window frame is rectangular. This was done by slicing the wall in two and separating the window plane from the piers supporting the vaults. These piers carry an arch which supports the vault cells on one side, and a flat ceiling on the other which covers the space between the vault and the window tracery. The windows are rectangular because they continue to the underside of this ceiling. Thus from outside the vaults do not show, while from inside the vaults appear to float within a glass cage, separated from the enclosure. They have become insubstantial.

The space between the window and the vaults begins at the windowsills, with a narrow walkway that had first been used twenty years earlier at Essômes. It detaches the window plane from the interior and thereby distances the glowing radiance of the glass from the observer. As the glass symbolizes the heavenly light, His world has been removed one step from ours.

Underneath this walkway there is a dado arcade, with trefoil arches which are detached from the wall so that they are more like a tracery screen than a part of the enclosure. The fortresslike walls of earlier churches have been concealed, and the image of the temple *within* the citadel has been replaced. In the new image the fortress has been turned into a gilded cage, beautifully decorated and cunningly worked, like palace furniture or a reliquary. The chapel suggests an open loggia with a canvas roof on light poles, set up for some courtly ritual or extravaganza. Meanwhile the glass, which at Chartres is the radiance of paradise, has been relegated to some distant zone beyond us.

Where the Sainte-Chapelle lies at the end of the classical period epitomized by Chartres, Saint-Germain-en-Laye marks the beginning of another. At the Sainte-Chapelle the detailing, the clear expression of each function, and the separation of all the elements is in the tradition of Chartres and Reims, though more refined. Here the windows have been detached from the vaulting, the dado arcade from the wall, and nearly every plain surface has been screened or disguised. It is just like the illusionism of the Saint-Denis nave.

These two little buildings, almost contemporaries, represent the end of one theme and the start of another. Though we might call the former Rayonnant from the quantity of glass, it uses none of the illusionist techniques found here. Perhaps they first appeared at Notre-Dame in Dijon in the 1190s, but it is here that they were first fully expressed. This led in time to the uncertainty of Carcassonne and Saint-Urbain in Troyes.

SAINT-GILLES-DU-GARD, Church of Saint-Gilles
Once a Benedictine abbey

Department of the Gard, 17 km (11 miles) west of Arles; Michelin map reference 83/9

1121–1125	Construction began in the crypt; the upper church and west front carved in the 1140s and early 1150s.
1562	Fire caused the vaults to collapse. The original apse demolished in the nineteenth century.

Saint-Gilles lies on a small rise in the flat, almost arid country alongside the Camargue. The area, the first territory Rome acquired outside Italy, was called "The Province," whence the Provence of today. In the Middle Ages the town lay on one of the most frequented routes to Santiago from Italy, which brought it considerable wealth.

The monks decided to build a most ambitious church. The eastern end must have been impressive, with massive columns and heavy vaults not unlike those in the crypt.

Although all the architecture of the period is called Romanesque, it is here that it is most Roman. There is a blunt solidity to it, the figures impregnable within their frames. The niches and the squared bases, as at Arles, make the architecture appear rigid and authoritarian, perhaps reflecting those harsh and unyielding policies that fomented discontent and led to many of the conflicts between the abbey and the local people.

One of the most dramatic conflicts occurred in 1208 when a papal legate, Pierre de Castlenan, was assassinated. Count Raymond of Toulouse was blamed. The affair was

Lion from the porch of Saint-Gilles.

the Sarajevo of the Albigensian Crusade. Raymond was excommunicated and forced to stand naked in the square in front of the church to swear his obedience to the pope before being beaten by the monks. One wonders if our prison system offers a better way; in those days sin was dealt with at once and finished with.

No other tympanum in France has a crucifixion carved on it. The subject may have been chosen to counteract the local cross-burning insurrection of Pierre de Bruys. Notice the two angelic figures over the cross carrying the sun and the moon; the sun is on the left, which is Christ's right. Notice also the superbly drilled dress of the swaying figure to the left.

On the left tympanum Mary is adored by the wise men while an angel tells Joseph to flee the coming persecution of Herod. This, like one of the side tympana at Vézelay, shows mortals paying homage to Mary; at Chartres all contact with ordinary people has been eliminated, so Mary is flanked only by heavenly courtiers. The work was not finished. The statues were never placed on the columns flanking the central door, and the towers and the upper parts of the nave were left incomplete. Heresy may have undermined the enthusiasm for the donations that would have completed it. For five hundred years the upper church remained empty while services continued in the crypt. The flat rib vaults make it more of a subterranean cavern than most, and it feels immensely protective.

By the early fifteenth century the roof had partly collapsed, the bell tower was only half completed, and civil war and a succession of savage epidemics had driven pilgrims from the roads. The population of the town had fallen to eighteen taxable families and the number of monks to twenty-six. The abbey's income, which had once been 4000 livres a year, was now so small the monks could not buy food or winter clothes.

The basilica was used as a fortress during the religious wars. When the Protestants were forced to abandon it in 1622, they tried to blow it up but were forestalled by the timely arrival of the royal troops. The façade had already been mutilated by musket fire. The miracle of Saint-Gilles is not that something remains but that despite so much damage to the rest of the church, the grandiose ambition on the west shows so clearly. The remnants of the façade still give a feeling of stupendous power.

SAINT-MAXIMIN-LA-SAINTE-BAUME,
Basilica of Sainte-Madeleine
Once a Dominican abbey

Department of the Var, 43 km (27 miles) east of Aix; Michelin map reference 84/4,5

1296 Church begun over a fourth-century crypt; by
       1316 only the eastern end completed. Between
       1404 and 1412 the crypt demolished and the
       paving laid.
1508 Western end with the doors; the vaults completed
       in 1513. The lateral western portals followed, and
       the west completed in 1532.
1860 Altar and screen replaced; the crypt renovated in
       1884.

While northern France was working in Rayonnant, the south, even under the patronage of members of the royal family, continued to build in the massive wall tradition of the region, with little use of the skeletal frame developed in the north. Like contemporary Albi, Saint-Maximin is a stolid, earthbound work. There is virtually no decoration; the exterior walling is quite plain except for one rounded string course and occasional gargoyles from the last campaign. Inside only the vaults are finely detailed. There is no carving on the capitals.

The piers, like the *pilier cantonné* from the north, have four shafts set around a central core. This core is more or less octagonal and feels more like a wall than a column. The bases sit heavily on the floor and are large for the span they have to support. Even the liverish gray color of the stone adds to the immobile and dour character of the building. The roof is hidden behind the parapet, making the building a low form seen from afar, as if it were only a walled fortress. Perhaps not inappropriately; for the Dominicans, the inquisitors of the Middle Ages, were installed here.

There is no hint here of the illusionism of the north, as at Saint-Germain-en-Laye. Only the tracery is playful, and this is restricted to small, narrow openings unaccented with capitals. The small windows allow the wall to dominate, especially in the clerestory, adding further to the feeling of immobility. It is a tall building, almost as tall as Cluny, though it does not feel tall because the columns are so stout.

Only the vaults appear light (because of the unexpected delicacy of their moldings), but they are not integrated with the shafts. Where the vaults of the north seem to hang from heaven, with shafts trailing from them, these vaults sit on top of the undecorated capitals like a lid. It is worth comparing this with the almost contemporary high vaults at Beauvais.

The inner sanctuary of beautifully carved Renaissance stalls sits within the church with the same solidity as the piers. It is not a reliquary protected by a strong fortress but a nest in the cave.

One has to remember that the Crusades against the south and marriage brought in alien overlords—though Provence, like Burgundy, still owed allegiance to the Holy Roman Emperor. The Hundred Years War began as the first campaign ended. The second campaign, started during a lull in the war, only continued the ideas begun in the first, as if imagination had deserted the builders. In fact this is one of the few works to have been built anywhere in France during this century; like the Vendôme Chapel at Chartres, it added nothing new to the architectural formulas developed 150 years earlier.

The third campaign only marginally reflected the burgeoning influence of the Renaissance and the scintillating extravagance of northern Flamboyant. Compare it with the transept façades of Sens, the porch at Albi, or the pier bases at Rouen. These comparisons are important as an indication of how creative the northern architects were in their search for the grand illusion. Even after wars and pestilence their architecture is magical. Something very deep in northern society encouraged this up to the time of the Reformation, and only after Gothic ideals had been replaced by Classical was this restless and curious spirit replaced by the orderliness and seriousness of Louis XIV's classicism. In fact that seriousness was nearly always present in the Provençal south, as in Saint-Gilles. It appears authoritarian and humorless, in sad contrast to the natural gaiety and warmth of the people who live in this balmy and beautiful landscape.

SAINT-SAVIN-SUR-GARTEMPE,
Church of Saint-Savin
Once a Benedictine abbey

Department of the Vienne, 41 km (25 miles) east of Poitiers; Michelin map reference 66/15

1075–1085   The western nave, followed by the choir in the 1190s. The middle portion of the nave with the paintings erected 1095–1115, tower in the twelfth century, and the spire in the thirteenth.

1562   Gutted by the Protestants, and in 1574 by the Royalist troops.

The impact on entering the church is quite extraordinary. Because the floor of the western tower is well above the nave, we seem to be floating, almost gliding into the tall columnar hall. The columns are large and set close together, so we see little of the aisles, which extend full height into the vaults, as at Tournus. The unexpected richness of the capitals seems to elevate the vaults; they are poised like a canopy from another world.

The central barrel vault is covered with the finest medieval paintings in France, spectacular frescoes called the Bible of Saint Savin. They depict Old Testament scenes that prepared pilgrim for the New Testament frescoes which originally decorated the transept, ambulatory, and chapels. The paintings are complemented by the marbling of the piers. Marble was rare in France (compared with its superabundance in Italy), and it was sought after whenever a church had enough money to import it. When not, as here, the monks painted the columns in imitation, with an extravagant if somewhat bilious effect.

We often blame our nineteenth-century grandparents for covering churches in garish or somber colors. We are used to the simple beauty of unadorned stonework, like that of the Parthenon and Chartres, which are remembered for the pure colors of their limestone. But contemporaries never saw these buildings as we do. Most of their sculpture and much of the walls and ceilings were painted. In the natural darkness of the medieval interior, with light flickering only from the innumerable candles, the effect was very rich indeed.

The choir is in some ways even more startling than the nave. The ambulatory is incredibly narrow, with scarcely room for two to walk abreast, as though it had been designed for the priest to use on his own. The circular piers are almost as high as those in the nave, so the feeling is one of being within an ascending tunnel. Typically for the period, it is not you, the viewer, who ascends, but the church which rises around you.

The capitals are enormous, a choir of rampant lions and intricate foliage holding court high above your head. They were carved by the same men who worked on the Saint-Benoît-sur-Loire porch and on the choir of Notre-Dame-la-Grande at Poitiers—but less imaginatively.

The local Protestants in the late sixteenth century, obedient to Luther's call to "destroy their nests, for then the storks do not return," demolished the conventual buildings, burnt the choir stalls, and threw the relics into the river. It is beyond comprehension why they spared the frescoes. For a while the ruined abbey became the headquarters of the brigand Baron des Francs, who scandalously married the abbot's sister. When returned to the Benedictines, the church was so decrepit that repair hardly seemed worthwhile. The monks were too poor to do anything but whitewash the interior and add little edges of flowers.

It was probably the whitewash that saved the frescoes from the bigots of the Revolution, for the decree of October 23, 1793, proclaimed that it was everyone's duty to "obliterate all monuments that could feed religious prejudice and which recall the hated memory of the kings."

There is some argument about whether the western tower was before or after the nave, and the argument provides a nice exercise in following the intricacies of stone junctions. It is just the sort of exercise that architectural historians love. There is a joint in the wall, near the second buttress from the west on the south side, just where the tower finishes. It runs vertically from the ground to the cornice. Examine it and decide whether the eastern or the western side was first. Hint: Examine the lower stones which are laid level, especially the one with the projecting corner, and the junction of the western nib of the adjacent buttress where it meets the top of the cornice. (Answer below.)

The question is important for historians because the style of the tower would seem to be simpler and more archaic than that of the nave. It demonstrates that people could and did build simply at all times, and that simplicity is not in itself a sign of greater age.

SENLIS, Cathedral of the Assumption

Department of the Oise, 51 km (32 miles) north of Paris; Michelin map reference 56/111,12

1153   Work commenced in the choir and proceeded
         westward. The western sculpture in place by 1160,

Answer: Once a stone was in place, it would not be touched when another stone was placed against it, for to hit it with a hammer would dislodge the weak lime mortar. Therefore the stones cut over others would have been laid later than the ones they were cut over. The stones on the west are not laid to level courses where they meet the work on the right. This would have happened only if the masons were trying to match up with coursing already in place. The nib is thicker on the western side of the buttress, as can be seen at the top of the window. Therefore the extension to this nib was intended to be flush with the western wall, not to be part of any construction to the west.

the consecration in 1191. The southern spire
followed in the early thirteenth century.

1504   After a fire in the roof, the clerestory and high
vaults rebuilt and the transept façades added. The
south completed in 1538, the north in 1560.

1848   Axial chapel added in the Gothic style.

THE TWELFTH-CENTURY CATHEDRAL (1153–1160s)

Senlis appears light and airy, with a pleasant scale, as we
walk around the ambulatory, but we should imagine the
cathedral without the well-lit transepts or the tall clerestory.
To do this, sit near the crossing and look westward. The low
arch and vault over the organ loft show the original height
of the vaults before the fire of 1504. It was a small,
low building, the smallest cathedral in France; like Mantes
and Bourges, it was a single space from the organ to the
altar.

With vaults as low as this, it would have been rather like
being inside a tunnel. The lighting was poor, not unlike that
of the aisles today, but the interior would have been full of
candles and bright tapestries. There were large, permanently lit chandeliers over the altar, which had been donated by the king, paintings on the walls, and the smell of
incense and straw.

The effect of raising the vaults in the sixteenth century
and trebling the height of the windows was to make the
building soar. The way the window and rib arches slide out
of the shafts without capitals emphasizes this. The building
of 1150 was concerned not with height or length but with
rhythm. It is at Nouvion that we can see the emergence of
the passion for height in the mid-1160s, just after Senlis
had been completed.

Every second pier is compound, with drums in between,
but you must ignore the changes made when the transepts
were inserted. As we move our eyes across the walls, the alternation makes us move along the nave in steps, pausing
at each pair of bays. The rhythm is slow and measured,
with a special pause at the east where the piers are like a
theatre proscenium, behind which lies the slender columns
of the apse. Indeed, the seventeenth century so understood this that they highlighted the drama by installing the
Baroque Virgin with her angels on the gallery over the
altar.

THE WESTERN DOORWAY (ca. 1160)

The tall western jamb figures are nineteenth-century copies
of originals carved some twenty years after the Saint-Denis
narthex and the Chartres Royal Portal.

This, with Souillac, may be the first intercessionary
porch. Senlis concentrates on the death of Mary and her as-

*Choir of Senlis
cathedral.*

sumption, in the first public notification of the greatest spiritual change that had yet occurred within Christianity. At
Chartres the sculpture presents the truths in the coolest
way possible: it celebrates not an event that happened only
once but, as with the Christ child on Mary's lap, a condition
or truth. At Senlis the sculpture began a process which led
over the centuries to the theatrical art of the Baroque. It is
drama, for the Virgin is being crowned, and in the lintels
underneath she is being entombed. These are events, specific in time and happening only once, not eternal truths as
at Chartres. Heaven had never been depicted this way before. The drama of a heavenly event occupies the central
role. This is Mary, not in her eternal role as Mother of God,
but on the specific occasion she was crowned so she could
sit on God's right hand. As it seems that the entire western
bay of the cathedral was paid for by the king, he may have
had some influence on the subject matter. At that time the
kings of France were constantly seeking ways to reinforce
their authority, and the placement of a heavenly coronation
over the king's door could have been used to confer greater
sanctity on the royal coronation service.

There are also the labors of the months, with December
to May on the right and June to November on the left.
March is shown in spring, one month early, because the climate then was much hotter than it is today.

Projecting animals, western tower of Senlis cathedral.

THE SOUTH TRANSEPT (1504–1538)

As the Reformation took hold of Europe and people's religious perceptions changed, architecture changed too. Gothic was the style of an assured and universal Church. Three hundred years later the Gothic motifs still sufficed in the first years of the Reformation, more from habit than conviction. As the Counter-Reformation developed, the Church found a new style. It was not consciously dictated but grew out of the feeling that the old esthetics no longer sufficed. This may be why, around 1500, the masters began to fuse Gothic forms with Renaissance motifs.

The Senlis transepts show an early stage in this process. Examined in detail, nearly every architectural element is Gothic, if somewhat rounded and sharpened. There are few typical Renaissance moldings yet, and no acanthus leaves, but the figures in the central panel over the door and in the pinnacles of the flanking buttresses are completely Renaissance in their fullness, exuberance, and healthy certainty.

The rose window with ribbons of tracery is in full Flamboyant mood. There is lots of cheerfulness and gaiety. The doorway is surrounded by sculptured archivaults set into a pointed arch, producing complex shadows that are just lovely. The motifs and the elements are thoroughly Gothic, yet a new spirit has entered the work, as in the massive yet restless foliage just over the arches of the triforium and at the center of the rose.

The firm solidity of the adjacent western tower has been denied by using round buttresses and carving the flanking niches concave, thereby reducing the buttresses to small projections. Delicious curves weave behind and around the main forms as though the structure were dancing.

SENS, Cathedral of Saint-Étienne

Department of the Yonne, 119 km (74 miles) southeast of
Paris; Michelin map reference 61/14

1130s	Choir begun in transept chapels and finally vaulted by 1163. Work on the nave reached the western entry in the 1180s. Chapel on the first floor of the north tower dedicated in 1214. Around 1250 the clerestory windows in the choir enlarged upward, making the vault less domical.
1267	South tower collapsed and was rebuilt over the next 250 years. South portal sculpture carved shortly afterward.
1490–1520	Transepts constructed with their façades; the bell tower finished in 1534. The upper row of kings on the west was put up in 1848.

Sens is huge. The span is as wide as Chartres, the aisles
almost as high. Yet it was begun fifty years earlier, at about
the same time as Saint-Denis. Sens was the seat of the archbishop, the Canterbury of France. It may seem a little out-
of-the-way today, but it was once one of the most important
religious centers, hosting royal weddings and great convo-
cations such as the debate between Saint Bernard and Peter
Abelard in 1140 on the essence of the Trinity. With Senlis,
it is the earliest completed Gothic cathedral.

Originally there was no transept. Like Mantes, it had a
single vessel extending from the western doors to the apse.
The transepts were added just before 1500 by knocking out
the walls of one whole bay, demolishing half the six-part
vaults, and extending the space two bays in each direction.

The transepts give a center to the church, concentrating
the light and our attention in the middle rather than toward
the apse. It makes the space centrifugal, where it used to be
axial. To savor the difference, start at the western bay
where the transepts are not too noticeable, then quickly
walk to the crossing.

In the original building the feeling of size is awesome.
The bases and plinths are huge and are some four courses
above the floor. The alternation, by emphasizing every second pier, breaks the central space into square rather than
rectangular sections. One of the delights at Saint-Remi, for
example, is to stand at one end of the nave or aisle and appreciate the procession of four-part vaults as they sweep to
the far end of the building. But here the six-part vaults and
the double bays are more rhythmic, marching in measured
steps toward the altar.

The original eastern vaults were very domical, with

shorter windows than we see today, but with a boss at the same height. Consequently, the cells sloped steeply upward to the boss, as though it were a dome, separating each vault just as the alternating piers divided the plan. But around 1250 the authorities felt strongly that they wanted an integrated vault directing pilgrim toward the altar, and they pulled out the lateral cells, raised the windows fifty percent, and leveled off the crown of the vaults.

The master builder in charge of the vaults around 1160 was understandably concerned with the side thrusts from such an enormous span—the widest span yet vaulted. So he introduced here, possibly for the first time, flying buttresses. In earlier buildings arches had been built under the roof to stabilize the walls, but these arches were the first to be raised and exposed above the roofline. To begin with they were no more than a technical expedient, and they lacked the esthetic effect they were to acquire in the next generation. Although the walls and columns of Sens are thick, this invention paved the way for the lightweight architecture of Paris and Saint-Remi by transferring all responsibility for stability to the external walls.

The gallery is quite small, with two paired openings in each bay. Just as the double bay at aisle level is divided by a light pair of shafts, so the single bay in the next level is itself divided. This makes a sequence of openings which become smaller toward the vaults, for we must imagine the original clerestory windows being much shorter than they are now. Combined with the handling of the shafts, and their connections with the ribs, the interior shows the unified details and elements which were to characterize the classic Gothic style.

Some sense of the gargantuan qualities of this building

North door, west façade, Sens cathedral.

can be gauged by standing in the south aisle of the choir and looking into the fourteenth-century chapel of Notre-Dame next to the transept. Compare the delicacy of the chapel tracery with the simple aisle windows on the north side, and the small shafts and intricate arcading with the earlier massive columns and the heavy arcading on its enormous plinths nearby. Yet the aisle windows are enormous, wider in the ambulatory than those of Saint-Denis, and the aisle is taller than both the upper stories were before they raised the vaults. Perhaps this indicates what the Primate of France thought of his standing on earth.

SOISSONS, Cathedral of Saint-Gervais et Saint-Protais

Department of the Aisne, 98 km (61 miles) northeast of Paris; Michelin map reference 56/4

1176   South transept begun, completed around 1190. Simultaneously the tall adjacent nave aisle piers were put up as the first stage in rebuilding the rest of the cathedral.

1192   Choir begun, reached the top of the triforium in 1212, vaulted by 1225. Nave aisles almost completed, with the western doors. Façade finished at mid-century.

1250s   Western towers completed; north transept rebuilt in the mid-fourteenth century.

1918   Heavily damaged in the war, then restored.

THE SOUTH TRANSEPT (1176–1180s)

To appreciate this epitome of medieval confidence and delicacy, it is important that you move out of the central space and sit in the transept aisle, where you may be quiet and reflect on it.

The south transept is a delicate and intimate work. We can stand in the crossing and compare the differences in scale between the transept and the choir. Only one generation separates the two, yet light years separate the feelings they engender. The transept is close to us, domestic and unostentatious; here we feel content and in touch with the ever-peaceful present. It is small in scale and detailing, and we feel easy and relaxed inside it. The proportions are not superhuman, like those of the nave, and cannot be absorbed in a glance.

But the choir strives, soars, drags us out of the mundane to demand that we contemplate the eternal. It grips us and will not let go; it is not at rest, certain and grounded like the transept, but compels our commitment. The difference is not so much in the detailing or the elements as in their scale. It is a little like the change from Edwardian journal-

Choir, Soissons cathedral.

ism to our own, from the intimate to the stupendous and ambitious.

The transept, as at Braine and the cathedral at Laon nearby, represents the pinnacle of the medieval mystical viewpoint. At its core such a faith goes unnoticed, like Zen and the Dao. It is remarkable for its quiet, one might almost say its obscurity, yet it is just in these qualities that we should be looking for the soul of a period, not in the Baroque vigor or fiery energy of later work, the pyrotechnic structural skill of Rayonnant or the awesome safety of Jumièges, but in this delicate creation.

THE CHOIR (1192–1225)

The war damage in 1918 was considerable. Soissons was bombarded in the last months of the conflict and part of the nave was destroyed, as was the glass. Some of the masonry is still shrapnel-damaged. It is an open space, and the bare floor gives some idea of how commodious these buildings were in the Middle Ages, uncluttered by chairs or pews.

The choir was begun just before Chartres, and many of the same masters worked on it. Although much of what has been said about Chartres applies here, the tall cylindrical drums give Soissons a character of its own. The effect may seem a little meager, for the piers appear too thin to support what is above them. It may be that the chapter had originally intended, as at Longpont, to have a small triforium and a low clerestory, matching the south transept. The cathedral is well lit, and we can observe details as we cannot at Chartres. Notice particularly the delicately pointed aisle bosses, the flat-leafed capitals in the choir, the sharply projecting crockets in the nave, and above all the distinctive balance between the shafts that define the bays and the string courses that define the stories. These vertical and horizontal members seem to weave through one another like the strands of a Scholastic argument, knitting all views into one comprehensible whole.

The slender drum piers increase the verticality and give us the feeling of moving through a forest, directing us forward to the apse and upward into the vaults. Being slim, the piers do not hold our attention as the heavier *pilier cantonné* might or even as do the shorter drums in Paris. In one sense they seem not to be there at all.

The feeling that the piers here may be too thin for their function is alleviated by the enormously solid piers around the crossing and at the western end under the towers. As at Laon and Braine, a crossing tower had been planned, probably with a lantern, but as at Chartres, this idea was abandoned in the 1220s. Without the lantern, one can see how contained the space becomes. Where the lantern would suggest a world beyond the enclosure of the church shedding its light into us, the continuous vault forms a total boundary that is as impermeable as the walls. It feels more secure because our space is defined, but it is less illuminated in the spiritual sense. It does not imply the same trust or sense of adventure. Soissons is more passive and safer. We do not have to stand to be counted. The vaults place the same lid on spiritual ambition as does the tall roof and the elimination of the towers.

SOUILLAC, Abbey of Sainte-Marie

Department of the Lot, 66 km (41 miles) north of Cahors; Michelin map reference 75/18

1075   Choir begun, with the transepts. Work continued
       into the 1130s, with the sculpture from about
       1150. Nave probably finished about 1165.
1562   Damaged in the religious wars; secularized in
       1790; renovated in 1835.

THE ARCHITECTURE *(begun ca. 1075)*

Souillac is a pristine example of the domed churches of the twelfth century. In form it consists of cubes attached to a crossing with a cylindrical apse. There is almost no decoration and few capitals, as in Cistercian churches. The square nave bays are transformed into domes through triangular shapes in the corners called pendentives.

A dome has no corners that might allow us to define its form, so it looks as if there is nothing there. Domes were often painted blue, with stars to resemble the sky, or covered in gold leaf to symbolize the empyrean of heaven. Hence pilgrim under the dome feels he is the center of the universe.

Sit in one of the choir stalls and sense the space revolving around you. Sounds can reinforce this feeling; try the elemental sounds of "hu" and "ma," produced deep in your stomach, and see what happens. The effect can be powerful indeed, and if you dare, you will have these enormous spaces resonating within you as well as without, and you may glimpse how the monks felt every day.

In the apse the dome is separated only minimally from the walls and piers; they flow together so that our space and heaven's form a single undifferentiated universe. In the nave the dome is separated by a strongly projecting cornice, the sort of cornice with brackets that would normally be placed on the outside of the building just under the roof, with the open sky above. Placed on the inside, the cornice separates the dome-as-heaven from the walls-as-mundane-existence, so the empyrean is remoter from us than it is in the choir. As a result, we feel in the choir that heaven is all around, while the spaces of the nave are more tangible because the cornice has made heaven more remote.

We found a similar distinction at Nevers, where the choir actually was the mystical Paradise and the nave the mundane reality of the everyday—one for the church, one for the people. The choir represents the more immanental view coming into vogue during the twelfth century, while the nave represents the more traditional view that there was no mystic unity between spirit and earth, but an inviolate barrier.

THE SCULPTURE

Souillac is best known for its sculpture, and it is rare in a small church to find something so monumental on anything other than a judgment or a nativity.

The story of Theophilus was chosen to encourage the growing adoration of the Virgin as intercessor and, more mundanely, to help resolve some of the problems the Church was having with the local nobility and heretics. It was used to convert the latter by demonstrating that even the greatest sinner could find mercy through the Virgin, and it was used as an argument against those nobility who had sequestered tithes and church property in previous centuries.

At first one might be tempted to dismiss the panel as a crude and somewhat misshapen work, but it will repay study for what it demonstrates of the medieval mind. Every apparent distortion and misalignment contributes to the design; these were deliberate, not accidental or due to lack of skill. In a rather modern way, the message is present as much in the form as in the content.

The three key events have been arranged as though they were happening at the same time, even though they occurred in sequence. The sculptures connect meanings rather than events. The medieval viewer was quite comfortable with this, for his view of reality was more simultaneous than ours—what McLuhan called "mosaic vision." Nowadays we are conditioned by our scientific training to expect one cause to produce one effect, and in a similar way to that in which we read, we tend to define things one at a time rather than all in a heap. Compare this sculpture with our comic strips, where each event has a separate frame and the placement of the bubbles leads the reader through the sequence.

Theophilus was a deacon of the monastery of Adana in Cilicia. His abbot, misled by false reports, removed him from office, and Theophilus sold his soul to regain his office. In its popular form, the story presented the deacon as the victim of an iniquitous contract into which he is inveigled by the devil. This is not unlike the Church's views on the wrongful demands of the nobility. Theophilus finalizes the contract, as he would an act of feudal homage, by the clasping of hands. From this awful pledge only divine intervention can save him, and at the top the Virgin dives out of the sky, accompanied by a troop of angels, to rescue the wretched man from a situation of his own making. This is one of the earliest advertisements for the power of the Virgin. Because Theophilus prayed to her, he could reasonably hope for her aid. Normally the probability of his roasting in hell would have been astronomical, but suddenly justice can be tempered. She not only stands up for villains who have appealed to her—dare one call it the result of flattery?—but snatches them from the rightful mouths of the feudal lord/devil who held a legal contract over them. By showing that not all contracts were good and that evil ones could be broken, the story made it easier to justify the return to the Church of rights that the Church had had to relinquish earlier. It also appealed to all those hungry for salvation. It is interesting that Theophilus does not repent when he sees the full awfulness of the devil. No, he refuses to give up until he has received all the benefits of the agreement *and* regains his post. Only then does he repent—from a position of success.

The significance of this unedifying little story is that because Theophilus appeals to the Virgin, she arranges for the normal course of justice to be suspended. The moral is that, in a real world full of vice, you do not have to live a blameless life in order to be saved, you just have to perform the correct rituals in the right direction. Of course this message was presented within a package of faith and true repentance, but the essential issue of having used the devil and still being able to expunge the guilt was the most important one for the historical development of medieval society.

The jamb figure of Isaiah was carved for a doorway that was never built. His head, hands, hips, feet, and drapery twist, and the multiple angles produced by pushing the figure toward the edges of the stone block make it come alive. Among the Old Testament prophets, highest honors were reserved for Isaiah, who predicted the nuclear events of Christianity: the birth of the Virgin, the annunciation, the birth of Christ, and the day of judgment.

Next to it is the trumeau, or central door post. Here there are sharp-beaked creatures attacking others, little figures squashed under the lintel and hanging onto columns that bend under their loads; yet others lovingly clasp one another with gentle smiles. It is an abstract of both violence and tenderness.

STRASBOURG, Cathedral of Notre-Dame

Department of the Bas-Rhin, 488 km (303 miles) east of Paris; Michelin map reference 62/10

1015	Crypt built, enlarged in the twelfth century.
1176	Disastrous fire forced rebuilding of the apse, completed in the 1190s.
1220s	South transept begun, then work continued into the nave; west front begun in 1277. Western rose started about 1218; the front up to the towers completed by 1365. Octagonal spire completed in 1439, for a while the tallest in Europe at 433 feet (132 meters).
1332	Saint Catherine's chapel on the south begun, completed in 1349. Saint Lawrence chapel added onto the north in 1515.

Strasbourg was not part of France in the Middle Ages but was subject to the German emperors until the seventeenth century. The boundary between the French and German rulers lay to the west along the tops of the forested mountains between Strasbourg and Reims rather than down the centers of the great rivers as it does today.

Although Strasbourg has the appearance of a French Rayonnant church, it is Germanic in its detailing and proportions. Yet the western end would have been inconceivable without the extraordinary revolution that emerged from the Paris basin.

A traveler entering France from the east has the opportunity to examine in this building a host of concepts which are not brought together anywhere else. Each is discussed in its French context elsewhere in this guide, but it is worth showing what a Pandora's box of significance and meaning can be found in one place.

The apse is dark and inturned. The curved mosaics are

impenetrable, and they return us on ourselves. With little architectural decoration to hold it, the eye tends to flutter across the surface. The huge shafts and stupendously massive drum piers give a sense of eternity and changelessness that can be very secure. This is a fortress to faith, as at Saint-Benoît-sur-Loire or Jumièges.

Because the floor of the apse is raised above the nave, we look up to the altar and the celebrants. The highest places are usually associated with masculine aspects of the spiritual world, with upward strivings and authority. From the apse the clergy look down on pilgrim and, like God, are set apart from the worldly. This separation reflects the transcendental view that the spiritual world was totally separated from the earthly.

A dome over the crossing centralizes the space. The darkness, the small windows, and its steeply pointed shape suggest a blocked-off tunnel without an exit. It has the opposite effect of the bright lantern towers of Braine and Laon, which seem like skylights into heaven. Nor is it like the comfortable, broad, and humane enclosures to the west of France in Souillac or Cahors.

Under the choir is a cavelike crypt. Just as the mountain represents the male principle, the crypt represents the female, which remained hidden, present only by implication in the mandorla and the crypt, until the cult of the Virgin took Europe by storm during the 1130s. As in Saint-Denis, and unlike Mont-Saint-Michel, both the mountain and the cave are represented *inside* the building.

The bounded enclosure of the choir contrasts with the spaciousness of the nave. The west is in the Rayonnant style exported from the Paris Basin after the 1240s. It is a glowing extravaganza of huge stained glass windows occupying nearly the full width of the aisle walls, and in the upper zone the clerestory has been extended down behind the triforium. (See the descriptions of Beauvais and the Saint-Denis nave.)

The shafts seem to merge into the ribs of the vaults, making a smooth transition that articulates the surface. The structural members have been used to create a pattern that keeps our eye moving from side to side and from bay to bay, weaving backward and forward in ceaseless rhythms. In both senses of the word, the effect is superficial. We do not penetrate into the mass or into the structure, as we do at Chartres, but are kept at a distance. To the extent that the cathedral actually was the City, it has been removed from us.

Similarly on the west front, thin screens cover the tracery and hide the walls with the delicacy of fine spray, denying that any structure was needed. Even the sculpture is light, almost humorous, as if spirituality may have been a little too serious for these busy men.

The original drawings for the façade are in the local museum. One, the Riss A, is a Parisian design attributed to

Master Rudolph about 1265. Riss B was drawn by Master Erwin in 1277, but only the lower stage, with its three sculpted portals and pointed gables, was complete when work was halted by a fire in 1296. The octagonal spire is an incredible dare, little more than a collection of self-buttressing staircases; it was considered one of the wonders of the world.

Though the transepts were built after Chartres had been vaulted, they reflect little of what was happening in France. They are tall, but tallness could also be found at Cluny and Cahors. There is nothing of the light detailing of Paris, the gentle floating quality of Longpont, the balance of Chartres, or the luminosity of Laon.

The doomsday pillar in the south is superb, in part because the figures are closer to the floor than to the ceiling, in part because they are so individual. It shows little of the otherworldly qualities of the Chartres Royal Portal.

The transepts suggest that architects would probably have continued using most of the motifs for hundreds of years, were it not for the creative explosion that produced Gothic—an explosion fostered by what may have been a purely local combination of mysticism and hope. Indeed, we can see that it was not until Gothic had been fully defined that its concepts caught on and its style spread elsewhere.

The vaults over the two chapels on each side of the nave illustrate what happened to Export Gothic over the next three centuries. On the north the vault is like a net, stretched over our heads with brightly decorated intersections which distract from both the space and the ceremony. It is more like being inside a balloon inflated from below instead of being under an enclosure of stone. As in the nave, the surface is more important than the space it encloses.

The vaults in the southern chapel further deny the structure. These ribs do not rest on the shafts that would normally have carried them but are chopped off at the ends. The edges of the vault are set a little way from the walls, like a canvas canopy through which the shafts pass to support some other building. Has a screen been drawn between heaven and earth so that pilgrim may relax contentedly underneath without having to see beyond?

The two vaults illustrate how the structural and decorative unity of Braine and Orbais became motifs for a beautiful if meretricious art. Such cleverness and delight is appropriate to a palace or a town hall, but it sustains little of the mystic spiritualism of Chartres.

LE THORONET, Cistercian Abbey of Notre-Dame

Department of the Var, 64 km (40 miles) northeast of Toulouse; Michelin map reference 84/6

1150   Church begun at south side of the cloister; probably completed around 1190. Other monastic buildings finished after 1200.

1790   Became municipal property, neglected and threatened with demolition. Its remoteness and sound construction saved it. Restored in 1907.

This small Cistercian monastery in southwest France has been fortunate, for the drama of history and the wealth of later centuries has passed it by. Unchanged, it lies in unspoilt surroundings which help to recreate the quiet world of the monks.

It is austere, almost inhospitable; there is no welcoming portal sculpture or porch. It looks so old because no newer layers of style have been superimposed on it. Yet it is humane. A visitor stands in the apse and sings, the pure notes reverberating one after the other, tumbling along the vaults in poignant memory of centuries of chanting.

The austerity of the façade is carried throughout, yet it beautifully displays every element of medieval architecture in its simplest form, each stated as if it were a pure principle. The walls are as beautiful as any in France, with their precisely carved blocks, each squared and laid with a minimum of mortar in the manner called ashlar.

The wall is pierced with windows without frames or tracery and with unadorned splays inside and out which em-

Le Thoronet.

phasize the thickness and inherent stability of the walls. Their smallness makes the walls seem more protective.

The arches are both round and pointed, and like the walls, they are made from simply squared blocks. The piers are square, the shafts plain half-round with straightforward capitals and corbels. The latter appear to be suspended in a manner we discussed at Fontenay.

In the cloisters the paired openings could not be less ornate. Even the capitals are minimally shaped to fulfill their ancient function of transforming a circular shape into a square one.

The inner cloister arches are thinner than the outer encasing arch, so their relative importance is stated quite clearly. The inner arches are solely decorative infilling, for it is the outer arch that supports the wall and the vaults. The impost moldings which start each arch are obviously important in an otherwise unaccented design: they state that this is the junction between the vertical plane and the curved. They are like the extra space left between paragraphs to signal a new thought. These arches reflect the philosophy of the times: keep each concept explicit and distinct, do not muddy your thoughts or fudge your principles. Only such a clarified way of thinking could have produced both Scholasticism and Le Thoronet. But notice that the impost does not dominate the design. It is unostentatious, intended to expose functions and forms without distracting our attention from either.

Similarly, the light swelling or plinth at the base of the piers, which satisfies our need for a foundation, is too small to distract from the plainness of the wall.

There are both barrel and rib vaults in the cloister. The ribs and arches are finished square, everywhere in the best ashlar. Nothing is needless, and therefore the unexpected hits one with added force. Let us re-enter the church to examine some of these surprises.

The rose windows, which seem almost frivolous among all this austerity, were especially prized by the Cistercians. Another surprise is a curious eccentricity in the aisle vaults; they are pointed, with the ridge placed close to the arcade wall so that the vault seems to lean against it. The eccentricity helps to stabilize the side thrusts from the high vaults in the manner of Conques and Saint-Étienne in Caen. But what is so curious is that the ridge is just a foot or so from the wall. The minuscule section of vault showing on the nave side would seem to have hardly been worth the effort.

If you pace out the distance from the wall to the center of one of the aisle vaults, you will find it to be one-fifth of the width of the nave, while each of the three bays is two-fifths of the total width. Thus the whole nave, measured to the aisle ridges, forms the musical proportion of 5:6. The vaults were the most important factor in creating the superb acoustics of these buildings, as you yourself can judge by singing. It is therefore appropriate that this musical ratio is found in these vaults.

Cistercian churches are full of geometric ratios, as was every medieval building. Each bay, measured through the centers of the piers, forms the ratio of 9:10, but measured to the face of the walls, the area of the bay is square. Five of these squares makes the overall length from the western wall to the apse, while eight of the fifth divisions of the nave used to locate the ridge line will make the overall length of the transepts.

There are thus overlapping proportions. Measured to the centers of the piers, there is 1:2:1 in the aisle:nave:aisle widths. Measured to the face of the walls, each bay is square. And there are the fifths taken to the vaults. Each of these interwoven ratios expands into other parts of the building, forming a network of relationships that are woven like a great tapestry. And like a tapestry, each ratio tells a story which will often be relevant to the meanings of that part of the building.

Proportions are also used vertically. The square in each bay forms a cube to the string course. The cube is the "power" to the number, and just as we speak of "powers and principalities," so the cube represents the totality of all meaning attributed to the square. Similarly, the nine in the first ratio we mentioned is the power of the trinitarian three.

To these numbers of five, eight, nine, and ten should be added one for the apse, the two transept arms, three (for the number of bays in the nave), four (the chapels), six (the aisle bays), and seven (the bays with high vaults)—to have used every number from one to ten.

These arrangements were very meaningful in the Middle Ages, for if "God made the world in measure, number, and weight," as Saint Augustine wrote, then the proper use of the basic ten numbers would reflect His creation. It was therefore important to lay out His church according to the most sensitive symbolic measurements and ratios.

TOULOUSE, Basilica of Saint-Sernin
Once a Benedictine abbey

Department of the Haute-Garonne, 248 km (154 miles) southeast of Bordeaux; Michelin map reference 82/8

1060s	Work begun in choir, interrupted by the invasion from Moissac in 1081. Nave then begun, with consecration in 1096. West façade set out around 1150, completed in the seventeenth century. Octagonal crossing added with the top of the towers in the thirteenth century.
1500s	Upper parts of the western bays finished in the same style. Tradition was so strong that nothing

was altered; though the capitals are Renaissance, their forms remained twelfth century.

1860s   Heavily restored.

In the fourth century Saint Sernin was one of many martyrs who were dragged to their death by a bull. The main rival of the Christians at that time was the Mithraic creed devoted to bull worship, which was supported by the Roman soldiery. In a way it was a victory to have the opposition symbol kill your man, for he was then sanctified, proving that your side possessed the more powerful spirit. Bulls are, in a sense, still worshipped in the region today, though their sacrifice has been ritualized in the arena.

In an extraordinary escapade, the monks from Moissac stormed the church after work had begun on the choir in 1081. Their motive was commercial, for pilgrims traveling to Compostela brought enormous profits to churches with famous relics, especially those which were on one of the pilgrimage routes to Spain. Most of these monasteries owed some allegiance to Cluny, except for a number of key shrines that included Conques and Saint-Sernin, which remained independent. Conques was able to stay outside the order because of the fame of the relics of Saint Foy. Saint-Sernin did it by claiming they possessed the bodies of no fewer than six apostles, including the greater part of Saint James himself. This infuriated the Cluniacs, who

Use of brick and stone in the apse of Saint-Sernin, Toulouse.

were trying to maintain exclusive control over the lucrative trade.

The chapter appealed at once to the pope, who excommunicated the monks of Moissac, its abbot, and the count of Toulouse who had tacitly approved the takeover. The count promptly withdrew his support and wrote the pope an urgent letter promising to restore the canons. Much of the funds for building the nave may have come from his capitulation, and he and many of his family were buried by the south door, which is now blocked. The canons of Toulouse also learned a lesson, and they demoted some of their relics to reduce the competition with Santiago de Compostela.

The church is similar to Conques but on a grander scale, with double aisles. The interior elevation is very tall. It reflects pilgrim's desire to be lifted up and saved, raising him just off the ground and increasing his ecstasy. Like Paray-le-Monial, it throws us upward, and though the church is full of those spectacular riches the pilgrims so loved, it is simpler than the great Burgundian abbeys.

The pilgrims came in crowds, organized like modern tourists into groups and brought through the church in procession. The large pilgrimage churches were designed around a one-way passage that allowed pilgrim to pass in front of each altar in turn. Each could be adored and worshipped, while allowing time for pilgrim to be amazed at the richness of the place and the hope for salvation that each jewel-encrusted object gave.

The plan is not clear on entry, and one keeps discovering things. On passing through the nave, we are surprised to come across the huge spaces of the transepts. They are quite unexpected, and they enlarge our senses. The ambulatory itself, somewhat hidden, comes as a further surprise, as does the crypt off it. Indeed, each part of the building appears like one more unannounced mystery adding to the wonder at the immensity of it all.

The ambulatory passage and the chapels radiating from it like the spokes of a wheel created the most characteristic form of the Romanesque church. They were first employed in the tenth century at Tours on the Loire, and the form was rapidly adopted as the most appropriate for most pilgrimage churches from Conques and Chartres to Cluny and Paray-le-Monial. In theory this arrangement was supposed to allow services to continue in the choir without interruption from the visiting pilgrims. But all the popular sites seem to have had their veins clogged with too many people, as Abbot Suger's writings attest.

The builders tried to help people get closer to the major relics by building a narrow access from the ambulatory into the crypt, for they appreciated traffic flow as we do and planned sensibly to cope with it.

Unlike a parish church, the pilgrimage church is an embodiment of pilgrim himself: he sets out from the security of what he knows and his birthplace (the nave) to travel with the limited knowledge life has given him (the ambulatory) to the boundless potential offered by penance (the altars and relics). At home the daily round and the tradition of work turns even the strongest religious force into habit. But on the journey the traveler, as we know well today, becomes another person, sensitive to others and open to himself. The pilgrimage churches reflect this reality.

Saint-Sernin and Conques break with the past in the organization of the space. The *sequence* of bays blends into one unified field. The arches in the barrel vaults have no structural function but visually consolidate the interior. One experiences both the totality and the sequence. The piers are like a wall, massive, thick, and identical; their sharp corners define their limits. The spaces are right-angled and cubic, and so they tend to flow less than those spaces with more curvilinear boundaries. One is consistently aware that the building, inside and out, is the sum of all these units, even in the ambulatory.

TOURNUS, Church of Saint-Philibert
Once a Benedictine abbey

Department of the Saône-et-Loire, 100 km (62 miles) north of Lyon; Michelin map reference 69/20

1008	Narthex perhaps begun in the ninth century along with lower walls of the nave. Fire caused a rebuilding, possibly of the narthex, which was consecrated in 1019. Chapel of Saint-Valérian refurbished as a crypt.
1070	Ambulatory begun. Nave may have been vaulted, with the chapel of Saint-Michel over the narthex. In the next generation the rest of the choir; the crossing lantern about 1120; later the upper stages of the towers.
1300s	Chapel added on the north; others on the south in the next century.

The nave shows how inventive the masons were at this time, trying out all manner of vaulting and spatial solutions. One of the saddest consequences of the success of the Gothic mode was that it closed the door to further major experimentation. There were regional innovations, but the overall form and structure of the church was to change little after 1240.

There is a real feeling of ecstasy at Tournus, and it seems to come from the light and the particularly warm colors of the stonework.

The high vaults are the most logical and economical vaulting system devised, yet they are unique. The main arches over the nave are stabilized by the aisle vaults. Over them are laid a series of transverse barrel vaults. As the

Nave vaults, Tournus.

spans are small, they do not have to be heavy in construction and, most ingeniously, the side thrusts from one vault are absorbed by its neighbor. Thus they form a series of interstabilizing units, each balancing the other, and as long as the crossing and the westwork are massive enough, the vaults will never move.

No expensive flying buttresses were needed, no heavy lateral walls, and only minimal formwork. Most provoking of all, this system would have enabled the builders to eliminate all masonry between the piers of the side walls and to replace it with glass. Of all the vaulting types developed during this period, that of Tournus was the most economical and structurally secure. The reason it remained a unique experiment that failed to attract other architects may tell us a great deal about the meaning of these vaults.

A strong pattern of alternating colors on the arches seems to press down on us, as does the similar patterning at Vézelay. Vézelay does not disturb us, for its arches merge into groin vaults that tend to diminish the impact of the arches, while here the arches seem to isolate us from the vaults. One reason is that the walls over them are red in color; another is the cornice above that.

Symbolically, the arches rise out of the piers and thus are part of our world, whereas the barrels have been separated from us by texture, color, and the cornice. If the vault was paradise, then separation was not acceptable. In contrast, because the rib vault joined the ceiling to the wall shafts, the vault-as-empyrean could be integrated with our world.

Although the vaults are interesting and efficient, it is no wonder that these ideas were not taken further. Tournus demonstrates the truism that in the best art, the way it feels will often be more important than its cost or efficiency.

There is a superb little crypt, with an "ambulatory" that is roughly hewn, as out of rock. The little columns and intricate capitals form a delightful inner temple, which is quite unusual for the period. It is an early example of the temple/reliquary inside the mountain/cave. At the rear is a well that links the cave to the underground stream and the hidden needs of the unconscious.

TROYES, Church of Saint-Urbain

Department of the Aube, 158 km (98 miles) southeast of Paris; Michelin map reference 61/16, 17

1262   Choir begun with the lower courses of the western wall; the transepts followed, then the first part of the nave. In the next decades the lateral porches added, and the rest of the nave to the aisle vaulting capitals.
1286   Work temporarily roofed and abandoned. Consecration in 1389, though almost nothing had been added for a century.
1839   Nave aisles completed, then the rest of the nave and major repairs to 1905.

Saint-Urbain is one of the few churches whose history is well documented. It was started by Pope Urbain IV on the site of his father's cobbling shop. In May 1262 he wrote to the abbess of Notre-Dame-aux-Nonnains, the owner of his father's house, asking to purchase the site, and he engaged two men from the town, a canon and a burgher, to negotiate for him. On September 12, 1264, the pope sent these men 10,000 marks to finance the project. In October the pope was dead, perhaps poisoned.

His successor, Pope Clement IV, encouraged the work, and a consecration was planned for May 22, 1266, the feast day of Saint Urbain. The ceremony had to be canceled because vandals ransacked the construction site, having been hired by the abbess, who was violently opposed to the independence given to the new church in what had once been her territory.

Doors were smashed and the high altar destroyed. In the workshop, carts were overturned, leveling lines torn down, scaffolds wrecked, and tools scattered. When the canons had new doors built, the abbess had them broken down again. In October 1266 Clement IV issued a papal bull condemning the violence, and on November 8 the abbess and her assistants were summoned before the papal legate for a stern warning.

The second catastrophe was fire—or was it arson? The scaffolding and the choir roof burned down and the masonry was damaged. Expensive repairs depleted the building fund. The chapter tried to raise money by selling off some articles from the treasury. Cardinal Ancher donated 500 livres for the transepts, and on January 9, 1267, Pope Clement asked for donations from the faithful of the town.

But there was more trouble to come: Jean Langlois, who may have been the administrator, ran off with 2500 livres. When he was caught, the money was gone and he was packed off on a pilgrimage to atone for the crime. Between them, these events ruined the building and depleted the funds.

Hostilities continued after the fire; the nuns and their armed men blocked the papal legates from consecrating the church's cemetery. The rioting led to the excommunication of the nuns in 1269.

The church was still unfinished in 1286, the nave and west end having risen not far above their foundations. A "temporary" wooden roof covered the church until restoration was started in the nineteenth century.

THE ARCHITECTURE

Saint-Urbain is a special exercise in uncertainty.

Some claim that the pinnacle of Gothic was achieved at Chartres and Reims, that the radical elimination of the wall at the Sainte-Chapelle and Saint-Urbain was merely the beginning of a tragic disintegration, even decadence; others see these buildings as the natural evolution of Gothic from the premises established around 1200. Measured by its own standards, Gothic only fulfilled its own inner logic when the wall was virtually eliminated and the stone reduced to a magnificent glass cage.

In 1200 everybody *knew* that a real building was made from stone and mortar and that the stained glass of the windows merely replaced one part of the wall with glass. Understanding this, we can appreciate some of the contemporary sense of wonder at this precious little church, for illusion and uncertainty are more perfectly expressed here than in any other building.

From the outside of the choir the windows are not on the same plane as the wall, for there is another plane in front of them that spans the buttresses and supports the gables. These gables resemble tracery, with arches and little roses, that look as if they are still waiting for glass that has not yet been installed.

The structure has been pared away from the wall, with a narrow slit separating the buttress-as-support from the wall. The narrowness adds to the fragility because it is so unexpected, and it looks narrower because the sky can be seen

*West front of
Saint-Urbain,
Troyes, at night.*

through the slot. One asks oneself, If there is to be a space, why not make it a decent one and leave enough room for the buttress to act like a flyer? Or if it has to be so small, why put it here at all?

The outer tracery is detached from the inner as though one or the other were unreal. The buttress has been detached from the wall by a mere nothing. Both suggest that the real building inside these theatrical elements is also unreal.

The flying buttresses have almost no stonework at all over the arch. The air passes through them as if they were no more than leafless trees. This essential structural element, invented only a century before and so crucial to the stability of the building, has been reduced to nothingness. The fine roll molds and sharp corners along the edges desiccate the arch further.

The support for the inner end of the arch is hardly even a pier. The masonry is more like a mullion than a column that could support the vaults and the roof. Where the flyer arch meets this "pier" there is a thin arch which bends downward so that the flyer no longer seems to be supporting a weight from inside the building and is merely a decorative arch, pretending to carry loads but admitting there are none to be taken.

The inevitable question creates a tension in our minds: are we looking at a real structure or at a fantasy? Weightless, detached, and unreal, the structure floats without substance between gossamer members that do no more than decorate a void. There is no weight for the flyer to support, no glass for the tracery, no wall for the buttress—it is a church of soap bubbles and fairy floss.

When you look westward down the street you see in the distance the Flamboyant gables of the Church of Saint-Jean. The motifs are not unlike those of Saint-Urbain. Not much was to change in French architecture over the next two centuries.

It is hard to feel at ease here, as we do in Chartres, yet it is one of the most beautiful examples of theatrical illusion ever conceived, and it laid down a pattern for future architects to follow.

VÉZELAY, Basilica of Sainte-Madeleine
Once a Cluniac abbey

Department of the Yonne, 51 km (32 miles) south of Auxerre; Michelin map reference 65/15

1096	Nave begun, part of it consecrated in 1104. A fire in 1120 followed by restoration of the narthex sculpture, then the nave completed in the 1140s. Consecration in 1132.
1170s	The choir begun over the tenth-century crypt; completed around 1215.
1537	Abbey secularized; pillaged by the Huguenots in 1569; external sculpture mutilated during the Revolution. Major restoration after 1840, especially on the west front.

The abbey of Vézelay was founded in 864 by Gérard and destroyed by the Huns nine years later. Then Vézelay came under Cluniac control, and shortly afterward it was announced that the abbey possessed the remains of Mary Magdalen. It became a major pilgrimage center.

The taxes exacted from the local people to pay for the building works brought rebellion and bloodshed, as at Laon, Reims, and Chartres. Through half a century the citizens opposed and at times fought with the abbots, seeking freedom from taxes and fines.

The initial outbreak of violence occurred just after work on the basilica began. Pope Pascal II had authenticated the relics of Mary Magdalen, and pilgrims began to flock there in droves. In order to pay for the construction of a new church to hold the crowds, the abbot imposed heavy taxes on the townsfolk. The situation reached a climax when the people broke into the abbey and assassinated the abbot.

A long feud followed. In 1119 the townsfolk and the duke vandalized the sanctuary and damaged the relics. King Louis the Fat was called in to arbitrate. New disturbances arose in 1120, when many of the monastic buildings were

*Narthex entry to
Vézelay choir.*

burnt down, including the old basilica—with hundreds of
people in it. There were further conflicts in 1137 and after
the Crusades, when the abbot was forced to flee. In this in-
stance the king stepped in, nullified the count, sided with
the abbot, and dealt brutally with the town. Unrest continued until the town was placed under a papal interdict in
1154 and many of the leading citizens were condemned to
death.

THE NAVE AND NARTHEX (1096–1140s)

Vézelay was the first large church in France to be built with
the nave and aisles covered by groin vaults. Beautiful as the
nave is, it is the sculpture that attracts us. Much of it is the
work of one carver, Gislebertus, whose work at Autun bears
the signature "Gislebertus hoc fecit," or Gilbert made me.
The Latin suggests he may have had some knowledge of the
Church's language. His intellectual and artistic inventiveness is apparent in his work on the central tympanum and
at least fifty capitals inside.

The main tympanum has an overwhelming sense of authority. Christ is severe, centrally placed, immobile—in
contrast to the angular, energetic figures around Him. He
is commissioning the apostles to spread the Gospel, ruling
over heaven and earth, the sick wanting to be cured, and

the people from the edges of the world waiting to be converted. He sits directly over the central trumeau, supported on the axis of the world as the elemental tree.

Around the tympanum are a number of circular medallions in the archivaults. Below the lintel, on each side of the door, there are one and one-half circles, making three altogether. At the very top, just over Christ, there are another three and one-half circles. Ranged on either side are twelve more. The total is thirty and one-half, which multiplied by the twelve months (or the twelve apostles) will give the solar year.

Using the upper three and one-half twice reminds us of many ancient uses of this number. It represents the ratio of 7:2—seven, the number of all earthly cycles, and two, the first duality or the first breath from which all things were derived. The breakdown of the cycle into its dualistic nature is related to the end of time, when all things will return to their original substance. For this reason the figures inside these medallions represent the exit to the gate of hell. The dog is Cerberus, the guardian of Hades; the acrobat provides the balance needed for survival when passing through these dreadful gates, and the siren is for the tempter. In the half-medallion is a crane with bent neck, since ancient times the symbol for the summer solstice.

The winter solstice is represented in Capricorn in the lowest medallions. Besides summer and winter, there are the two times in the year when the length of the day is the same as the night. They are the equinoxes, and their signs are Aries and Scorpio, which appear at the center of each of the archivaults. Thus the four signs frame the figure of Christ as though He were the sun. This reinforces the axial location of the mandorla supported by the trumeau and makes Christ a *sol invictus,* radiant in glory, centralized as the apex of the universe.

The intellectual beauty of this arrangement is only one aspect of it. There is also a less positive message in the staring Christ, the pent-up energy, and the violence. None of the figures look at us; like Christ, they gaze over our heads to imply that they are beyond our mortal world. They do not ask to be loved, for the tension turns them into actors in some far-off drama. Just compare this to Chartres to feel their unconcern with our affairs.

This was consistent with the contemporary fear that, when faced with the final judgment, most people would be damned, and there was little they could do about it. It may be that the contradiction between thwarted hope and the fear of damnation fueled the violence we find in the sculpture. And there is a lot of violence, not only in the figures, which are turbulent and restless, but in the subject matter. It is as if the clergy has hunted the scriptures for scenes of violence which are also found at Moissac, but rarely seen after 1150. Judas is shown hanging himself. Samson shorn of his hair struggles with the desperation of the damned, and Jacob twice strives with the angels. Moses is depicted killing the Egyptian who abused a Jew in one scene, and brandishing a club against the man sacrificing to the golden calf in the other. Abraham, normally shown only raising his sword against his son, has shoved the sharp edge against his son's throat at Vézelay.

Yet there is hope in the right doorway. In this tympanum we find the Virgin as intercessor amid the weighing of souls, a little like her position at Cahors among the apostles. Where the Chartres tympanum is cool and calm, the Vézelay figures are energized and emotional.

THE CHOIR (1170–1215)

The choir is one of the finest Gothic designs outside the Paris Basin. The lower walls of the chapels up to the string course are recognizably Gothic; above that there was a change in masters, and the upper half of the walls between the chapels was left open, making the area as spacious as a double ambulatory. The lower walls up to the sills, with the dado arcade, were built by a team from Laon and the Soissonnais to the north. The rest of the aisles, with the curious openings, were designed by another master from nearby Burgundy.

It is amusing to observe the detailing and the carving of the capitals closely and to see just where the masters came from. There is a liberal sprinkling of men from the north who brought the new style with them, while most of the work was done by local people adapting themselves to unfamiliar ideas. This may account for the slightly bizarre feeling about the proportions and spaces.

Tragedy came to the abbey in 1280 when it was decided that the real relics of Mary Magdalen had never been moved from Saint-Maximin. The stream of pilgrims quickly diminished, and Vézelay's days of prosperity were over.

VIC (VICQ), Church of Saint-Martin-de-Tours

Department of the Indre, 66 km (41 miles) southwest of Bourges; Michelin map reference 68/19

1100	Church constructed; painted sometime before 1150; painted over perhaps in the sixteenth century.
1700s	Turned into a barn; in 1849 the paintings discovered under a layer of whitewash and preserved, largely through the efforts of Georges Sand.

The church has no architectural decoration. The design is simply a cubic sanctuary and half-round apse lit by small windows, though the window in the apse has been enlarged. The outside is as simple as Germigny-des-Prés, presenting plain walls to the few families of the village and the hot sun. But inside, once one's eyes have become accustomed to the darkness, one finds a new and wondrous world. The plain surfaces are covered by frescoes that were painted just after 1100.

Imagine more color, with intense blues and stronger greens and whites, to recreate the original rich effect. Most Romanesque buildings would have been painted in this way up to the time that stained glass became fashionable. Walls and ceilings were covered, also under the arches, in the window reveals, and across the roof beams—just like the mosaics of San Marco in Venice.

With candles and the flickering light from oil lamps, these figures would have come alive. The staring eyes and heavy brows, the dramatic clothes and definite gestures would be exaggerated, and pilgrim would be gazing into eternity.

The Christ in Majesty surrounded by the mandorla and the four evangelists in the apse recalls the great tympana of Chartres or Bourges. Most of the other panels depict the Easter cycle, with curious additional scenes of the expulsion and the martyrdom of Saint Peter. Two armored knights guard the entrance into the sanctuary and Ezekiel's angels flank Christ in Majesty, announcing His second coming.

A number of scenes concern Mary, especially on the wall facing the nave. As at Chartres, and unlike Moissac, her importance in ritual and dogma was increasing at this time.

GLOSSARY

Aisle	The side passage which surrounds the main vessel of the church.
Ambulatory	The extension of the aisles around the apse.
Apse	The eastern complex of the church, with all the parts within the curved section, including ambulatory, chapels, and rondpoint. Also called a chevet.
Arcade	The range of arches supported on piers which separates the aisle from the main space. Also a smaller range, as in the triforium.
Archivault	Voussoir with figures carved on it, as found over the tympanum of many entries.
Arris	A sharp edge formed by the meeting of two planes.
Ashlar	Masonry of squared, hewn stone, laid in courses.
Axis	The imaginary straight line around which the work or its elements are arranged symmetrically.
Axis mundi	The vertical axis of the universe.
Baldachin	The carved projection over a statue which protects it from the rain, usually embellished with windows and towers.
Barrel vault	A longitudinal vault with a semicylindrical form. See Vault.
Bay	A spatial division down the length of the building which divides it into sections from the floor to the roof. The pier marks the division between each bay. See Span.
Boss	The keystone of the vault where the ribs intersect, at times sculpted and pierced with a round hole.
Buttress	The projection on the outside wall to absorb the side thrusts from ribs or arches.
Capital	The carved stone which caps a column or pier, and which forms the transition between the shape of the column and the arches over it.
Cell	The curved infill between the ribs and the vault.
Centering	The temporary framework on which arches and ribs are supported while they are being put together.
Chevet	See Apse.
Choir	The eastern end of the church from crossing to apse.
Ciborium	A canopy over the high altar.

Clerestory	The uppermost story and the windows in it, above the aisles, gallery, and triforium.
Colonnette	Thin column, serving a secondary nonstructural purpose.
Compound pier	A vertical structural support made from many shafts attached to a masonry core.
Corbel	A projection out of a wall to support a lintel, a column, or a vault.
Cornice	Projecting decorated molding that runs horizontally around the outside of the building, designed to throw the rainwater clear of the face of the wall underneath. *See* Drip.
Crossing	The bay where the nave, choir, and transepts meet.
Crypt	The vaulted passage and chapels beneath the main floor.
Dado arcade	A decorative range of arches and piers set into the lower part of the wall.
Dome	A hemispherical vault, often supported on pendentives.
Drip	The small molding which runs across a buttress or over a window to throw the rain clear.
Drum	Vertical, cylindrical structural support. *Compare* Pier, Shaft, and Colonnette.
Embrasure	The angled side walls to the doorways, where the wall figures are placed.
En délit	Shafts erected in long lengths so that each piece rises past many courses of masonry. They are fixed into the wall with iron pegs or projecting stones. From the French term meaning "against the direction of the quarry bed."
Flying buttress	Where the high vaults meet the wall of the clerestory, the side thrust is carried to the outside buttresses by an arch or group of arches that span the aisle roof.
Footing	The lowest stonework of the building, which rests on the earth and transfers the loads of the building to the foundation below.
Formeret	The arch over a wall to carry the vault cell. *See* Respond.
Formwork	The temporary framework on which horizontal or inclined stonework is supported, such as the cells. Ribs and arches are supported on centering. *See* Scaffolding.
Gallery	Spacious middle story, usually vaulted, extending above the entire width of the aisle. Also called a tribune.
Gematria	Words translated into numbers for their symbolic meaning.
Going	In a staircase, the horizontal component as opposed to the riser, or vertical component. *See* Riser and Tread.
Gnosis	Sacred knowledge.
Griffe	The carving, usually of leaves, which covers the corner of the base where it projects beyond the torus molding.
Grisaille	Slightly mottled gray glass used in later Gothic churches in place of colored glass to improve the illumination.

Groin	The crease formed by the intersecting curves of a vault where not supported by a rib. *See* Boss, Cell, Rib.
High Gothic	The classical phase of development, epitomized by the cathedrals of Chartres and Reims.
Iconography	The subject matter of religious works.
Immanence	Religious belief which saw God as present in everything on earth, in each rock, seed, and living being.
Impost	The thin block of masonry between the carved part of the capital and the start of the arch overhead.
Jamb	The side frames to a door (the head is the lintel).
Key	The topmost stone of an arch.
Labyrinth	The canonic arrangement of paths representing the Way, and often including the names of the masters.
Lancet	A slender window with a round or pointed arch.
Lantern	The continuation of the crossing as a tower, illuminated by windows set above the level of the roof.
Ley lines	Large-scale connections between sacred sites.
Light	Window.
Lintel	The stone which forms the head or top of a door.
Misericord	A shelf set under the hinged seat of a choir stall which, when turned up, gave support to anyone standing in the stall.
Mullion	The upright shaft which divides a window into a number of lights.
Narthex	A vestibule placed to the west of the nave.
Nave	The central vessel of the church, between the aisles and under the high vaults; also the western half of the building.
Ogee	An arch with a convex curve in its upper section and a concave curve below.
Paris Basin	The limestone region between Chartres and Reims within which Gothic architecture was invented.
Pendentive	Curved infill transforming the square chamber into a circle for the support of a dome.
Pier	Compound columns supporting the arcades down each side of the main vessel, which may comprise groups of individual shafts or a *pilier cantonné*.
Pilier cantonné	Compound pier comprising a drum with four attached shafts.
Plinth	The lowest course under a pier or column, below the torus.
Porch	The covered projecting structure in front of the doorway.
Radiating chapels	Chapels which project out from the ambulatory along the line of its radius.
Respond	The shaft attached to the wall which supports a vault rib or arch. *See* Formeret.
Reveal	The vertical sides of a window or door opening,

	between the frame for the glass and the arris or corner of the wall plane.
Rib	The arch used to support the vault set diagonally to the bay, where the arch which is square to the bay is called the transverse arch.
Riser	The vertical face of a step, as opposed to the tread.
Roll mold	The round molding like a tube which forms part of the profile of an arch or frame.
Rondpoint	The innermost part of a circular apse.
Rose window	A round window, sometimes with tracery set into it.
Sanctuary	The straight eastern section of the church, consisting of the bays to the east of the crossing.
Scaffolding	The temporary platform that supports the workmen and materials during construction. *See* Formwork and Centering.
Scotia	Hollow space between two torus molds on a column base. *See* Torus.
Shaft	The attached column supporting a vault, including those around the piers and responds.
Sill	The stone which frames the underside of a window, to throw the water clear of the wall.
Span	The spatial division across the building which separates one arcade from another. It is perpendicular to the bay.
Spandrel	The triangular space between the outer curve of an arch and the rectangular frame enclosing it.
Splay	A chamfered edge to a door, a window, or a plinth.
Springing	The level from which the arch begins to curve inward from its support above the stilting.
Stilting	Vertical part of an arch, above the capital and below the voussoirs.
String course	A horizontal molding, like an internal drip.
Template	Full-size silhouette prepared by the master for the masons to use in shaping stones.
Torus	A roll mold, usually placed at the base of a column above the plinth. *See* Scotia.
Tracery	A pattern of stonework set within a window.
Transcendence	Religious belief that God and His world lie beyond an impenetrable barrier separating us from Him.
Transept	The lateral arms of the church, facing north and south.
Tread	The horizontal member of the staircase, where the riser is the vertical.
Tribune	*See* Gallery.
Triforium	The middle story, between the aisles and the clerestory, designed as a passage that is screened from the nave with an arcade of columns.
True	Perpendicular or square to a line or plane.
Trumeau	The central post of a doorway.
Tympanum	The space between the lintel and the arch that rises over it, often carved.
Vault	Arched masonry ceilings where the different parts of the curved stonework lean against each

other for support. *See* Barrel, Boss, Cell, and Rib.

Voussoir The wedge-shaped stones used to build an arch, with each bed joint on the radius of the curve of the arch. Where the underside is carved, it is called an archivault.

Wall figures The tall sculpted figures attached to columns in the doorway embrasures.

FURTHER READING

Adams, Henry. *Mont Saint Michel and Chartres*. New York: Viking Penguin, 1986.

Bony, Jean. *French Gothic Architecture of the 12th and 13th Centuries*. Berkeley: University of California Press, 1983.

Branner, Robert. *Gothic Architecture*. New York: Braziller, 1961.

Champeaux, Gerard de, and Sterckx, Dom Sebastien. *Introduction au monde des symboles*. Paris, 1966.

Chenu, M. D. *Toward Understanding Saint Thomas*. Translated by A. M. Landry and D. Hughes. Chicago: University of Chicago Press, 1963.

Cowdrey, H. E. J. *The Cluniacs and the Gregorian Reform*. Oxford: Oxford University Press, 1970.

Davy, Marie-Madeleine. *Initiation à la symbolique romane*. Paris, 1964.

Duby, Georges. *The Age of the Cathedrals*. Translated by Eleanor Levieux and Barbara Thompson. London: Croom Helm; Chicago: University of Chicago Press, 1981.

Fautier, Robert. *The Capetian Kings of France*. Translated by Lionel Butler and R. J. Adams. London: Macmillan, 1960.

Fitchen, John. *The Construction of Gothic Cathedrals*. Chicago: University of Chicago Press, 1977.

Focillon, Henri. *The Art of the West in the Middle Ages*. Oxford: Phaidon Press, 1963; Ithaca: Cornell University Press, 1980.

Geary, Patrick J. *Furta Sacra: Thefts of Relics in the Central Middle Ages*. Princeton: Princeton University Press, 1978.

Gimpel, Jean. *The Medieval Machine*. New York: Penguin, 1977.

Haskins, Charles H. *The Renaissance of the Twelfth Century*. Cambridge: Harvard University Press, 1971.

Hearn, M. F. *Romanesque Sculpture*. Ithaca, N.Y.: Cornell University Press, 1981.

Henderson, George. *Gothic*. Harmondsworth and New York: Penguin, 1967.

Huizinga, J. *The Waning of the Middle Ages*. New York: St. Martin's, 1984.

James, John. *The Contractors of Chartres*. Wyong, Australia: 1979–81; London: Croom Helm, 1980–82.

————. *Chartres: The Masons Who Built a Legend*. London: Routledge & Kegan Paul, 1982.

Katzenellenbogen, Adolf. *The Sculptural Programs of Chartres Cathedral*. New York: Norton, 1964.

Kraus, Henry. *The Living Theater of Medieval Art*. Philadelphia: University of Pennsylvania Press, 1972.

Lopez, Robert S. *The Commercial Revolution of the Middle Ages, 950–1350*. Cambridge: Cambridge University Press, 1976.

Mâle, Emile. *The Gothic Image: Religious Art in France of the Thirteenth Century*. Translated by Dora Nussey. New York: Harper & Row, 1972.

Panofsky, Erwin. *Gothic Architecture and Scholasticism*. New York: New American Library, 1974.

————. *Abbot Suger on the Abbey Church of Saint-Denis and Its Art Treasures*. Princeton: Princeton University Press, 1979.

Peters, Edward. *Christian Society and the Crusades*. Philadelphia: University of Pennsylvania Press, 1971.

Runciman, Steven. *A History of the Crusades*. Harmondsworth: Penguin; New York: Cambridge University Press, 1965.

Russell, J. C. *Population in Europe, 500–1500*. London, 1969.

Schapiro, Meyer. "The Romanesque Sculpture of Moissac." *Art Bulletin* 13 (1931): 464 ff.

Stoddard, Whitney. *Art and Architecture in Medieval France*. New York: Harper & Row, 1972.

Sumption, Jonathan. *The Albigensian Crusade*. London: Faber & Faber, 1978.

————. *Pilgrimage: An Image of Mediaeval Religion*. London: Faber & Faber, 1975.

Toynbee, Arnold J. *Religion and the Rise of Capitalism*. Harmondsworth: Penguin; New York: Oxford University Press, 1948.

Von Simson, Otto. *The Gothic Cathedral*. New York: Bollingen Foundation, 1973.

Ziegler, Philip. *The Black Death*. New York: Harper & Row, 1971.

INDEX